FROM THE PRINCE'S PULPIT
Volume I

FROM THE PRINCE'S PULPIT
Volume 1

Sermons on Grace

INCLUDING

A Defense of Calvinism

CHARLES HADDON SPURGEON

Edited by

CALEB POSTON

Copyright © 2020. **McGahan Publishing House**

All rights reserved. This publication may not be reproduced, stored, or transmitted in any form or by any means, electronic, mechanical, photocopying, recording, scanning, or otherwise without written permission from the publisher. It is illegal to copy this book, post it to a website, or distribute it by any other means without permission.

The text of the sermons themselves, as well as the treatise used as the preface, are in the public domain and, therefore, may be quoted, reproduced, stored, or transmitted freely. The foreword, footnotes, and arrangement of the material and this publication itself are under copyright.

978-1-951252-03-8 (Hardcover)

978-1-951252-04-5 (Paperback)

RELIGION/Sermons/Christian
RELIGION/Christian Theology/Soteriology
RELIGION/Christianity/Calvinist

McGahan Publishing House

www.mphbooks.com

"Between here and heaven, every minute that the Christian lives will be a minute of grace."

Charles Haddon Spurgeon

Contents

Foreword   iii
Preface: A Defense of Calvinism   vii

I   Total Depravity

HUMAN INABILITY   3
HUMAN DEPRAVITY AND DIVINE MERCY   19

II   Unconditional Election

UNCONDITIONAL ELECTION   37
PARTICULAR ELECTION   58

III   Limited Atonement

PARTICULAR REDEMPTION   77

IV   Irresistable Grace

EFFECTUAL CALLING   95

V   Perseverance of the Saints

FINAL PERSEVERANCE   111
THE FINAL PERSEVERANCE OF THE SAINTS   128

VI   The Doctrines of Grace in the Christian Life

SOVEREIGN GRACE AND MAN'S RESPONSIBILITY   147
HUMAN RESPONSIBILITY   164
THE DOCTRINES OF GRACE DO NOT LEAD TO SIN   181

Foreword

Charles Haddon Spurgeon (1834–1892)

Legendary Baptist pastor, Calvinist hero, *Prince of Preachers* — the imprint Charles Haddon Spurgeon has stamped upon the hearts of Christians is profound, and his influence today is likely stronger than it was within even his own congregation, the historic Metropolitan Tabernacle in London. Spurgeon is the most prolific Christian writer in history, authoring over 140 books, publishing a monthly magazine titled *The Sword and the Trowel*, writing over 500 personal letters each week, and transcribing what would end up being thousands of powerful sermons that have a timeless relevance for all Christian doctrinal traditions.

From the Prince's Pulpit is a collection of sermons and other writings of this legendary preacher, with each volume focusing on a specific topic, including prayer, Heaven, daily life, and other topics. This first volume, *Sermons on Grace*, focuses on the most important doctrine to Spurgeon: Calvinism, one of the two primary systems of soteriology.[1] In this volume, Spurgeon's thoughts on the five points of Calvinism and how they impact the Christian life are expounded upon through 11 sermons and one treatise. These sermons reveal Spurgeon's deep love for the doctrines of Calvinism, but, more importantly, they reveal Spurgeon's deep love for Christ and his great appreciation for the grace that God freely bestowed upon his undeserving life.

One cannot discuss Calvinism without also discussing Arminianism, the second primary soteriological system and rival to Calvinism. Though both systems speak highly of God's grace and the undeserving nature of humanity, they differ in the application of that grace. Calvinism, as is explored thoroughly by Spurgeon in this volume, focuses entirely on the grace of God and how humans are unable, in any way, to achieve any level of worthiness to attain that grace. Arminianism, on the other hand, places more responsibility on the shoulders of humans, teaching that, though unworthy of God's grace and unable to attain it on their own, humans *must*, by their own free will, come to belief in the Gospel — and often including other requirements — in order to receive God's grace. Therefore, humans share in the grace-giving process of God. In the sermons and treatise contained within this volume,

---

[1] The study of the doctrine of salvation

Spurgeon often brings up Arminianism and his belief that, though containing many faithful and legitimate brethren in Christ, it is not a biblically-correct conclusion regarding the grace of God and how it relates to humanity. However, Spurgeon does so with *grace*, fittingly: his strokes may paint a picture of Calvinism vs. Arminianism, but never Calvinist vs. Arminian.

The preface of this volume is from the pen of Spurgeon through one of his most famous treatises: *A Defense of Calvinism*. Upon reading this treatise, one will have a solid foundation on which to stand regarding the doctrines of grace when reading his sermons on the matter. In the treatise Spurgeon introduces the tenets of Calvinism, prominent Calvinists in history, and the opposing system of Arminianism, as well as prominent leaders within the system, including John Wesley. He also, as implied in its title, gives a defense of Calvinism in the treatise. After the preface are six parts, five of which correspond with the five letters of the Calvinist acronym, TULIP: **T**otal Depravity, **U**nconditional Election, **L**imited Atonement, **I**rresistible Grace, and **P**erseverance of the Saints. *T* has two sermons; *U* has two sermons, *L* and *I* both have one sermon, and *P* has two sermons. The final part contains three sermons about "The Doctrines of Grace in the Christian Life."

It is common for preachers to mention current events, political figures, and Christian leaders in their sermons. Indeed, Spurgeon was no different. Spurgeon preached and wrote in a time 130-150 years in our past. Therefore, he brings up figures, locations, and events that might not be recognized at first glance by many readers. Footnotes are included throughout the book to eliminate this potential barrier. These footnotes identify and give brief descriptions of names; they describe locations; they define theological systems that were prominent in Spurgeon's day but might not be today — and systems that are still well-known so a reader without such knowledge will learn. Some names and theological systems are repeated in different sermons, but the footnote is repeated each time so readers will always have that knowledge on hand.

Now, how is one supposed to read this book? What is the goal? Sermons are originally supposed to be heard, not read, so how can a Christian benefit from reading them? That depends on the approach of the reader: for the

Bible scholar and aspiring theologian, read it for information — learn about the doctrines of grace from one of the greatest Calvinists of all time; for the preacher, use this book to find material for your own sermons on grace — why reinvent the wheel? For the small-group leader or youth pastor, use Spurgeon's often elegant, yet simplified words to introduce your students to the doctrines of grace as taught within the Calvinist system; for the historian, use Spurgeon's sermons to learn about the perceptions of the competing theological systems and religions of the day, as well as societal issues that were relevant, including politics, slavery, and war. For the Christian just trying to live the most fruitful and humble life for Jesus Christ, apply Spurgeon's words to your own life. You may be unworthy of God's grace. Indeed, as Spurgeon taught, you are totally depraved. However, you are also totally *delivered* and a recipient of the unwavering grace and unending love of a God whose greatness extends beyond the scope of human understanding.

Blessings upon your reading,

Caleb Poston, Editor

Preface: A Defense of Calvinism

"The old truth that Calvin preached, that Augustine preached, that Paul preached, is the truth that I must preach today, or else be false to my conscience and my God. I cannot shape the truth; I know of no such thing as paring off the rough edges of a doctrine. John Knox's gospel is my gospel. That which thundered through Scotland must thunder through England again." — Charles Haddon Spurgeon

IT IS A GREAT THING to begin the Christian life by believing good solid doctrine. Some people have received twenty different "gospels" in as many years; how many more they will accept before they get to their journey's end, it would be difficult to predict. I thank God that He early taught me *the* gospel, and I have been so perfectly satisfied with it, that I do not want to know any other. Constant change of creed is sure loss. If a tree has to be taken up two or three times a year, you will not need to build a very large loft in which to store the apples. When people are always shifting their doctrinal principles, they are not likely to bring forth much fruit to the glory of God. It is good for young believers to begin with a firm hold upon those great fundamental doctrines which the Lord has taught in His Word. Why, if I believed what some preach about the temporary, trumpery salvation which only lasts for a time, I would scarcely be at all grateful for it; but when I know that those whom God saves He saves with an everlasting salvation, when I know that He gives to them an everlasting righteousness, when I know that He settles them on an everlasting foundation of everlasting love, and that He will bring them to His everlasting kingdom, oh, then I do wonder, and I am astonished that such a blessing as this should ever have been given to me!

"Pause, my soul! adore, and wonder!

Ask, 'Oh, why such love to me?'
Grace hath put me in the number
Of the Saviour's family:
Hallelujah!
Thanks, eternal thanks, to Thee!"

I suppose there are some persons whose minds naturally incline towards the doctrine of free-will. I can only say that mine inclines as naturally towards the doctrines of sovereign grace. Sometimes, when I see some of the worst characters in the street, I feel as if my heart must burst forth in tears of gratitude that God has never let me act as they have done! I have thought, if God had left me alone, and had not touched me by His grace, what a great sinner I should have been! I should have run to the utmost lengths of sin, dived into the very depths of evil, nor should I have stopped at any vice or folly, if God had not restrained me. I feel that I should have been a very king of sinners, if God had let me alone. I cannot understand the reason why I am saved, except upon the ground that God would have it so. I cannot, if I look ever so earnestly, discover any kind of reason in myself why I should be a partaker of Divine grace. If I am not at this moment without Christ, it is only because Christ Jesus would have His will with me, and that will was that I should be with Him where He is, and should share His glory. I can put the crown nowhere but upon the head of Him whose mighty grace has saved me from going down into the pit. Looking back on my past life, I can see that the dawning of it all was of God; of God effectively. I took no torch with which to light the sun, but the sun enlightened me. I did not commence my spiritual life—no, I rather kicked, and struggled against the things of the Spirit: when He drew me, for a time I did not run after Him: there was a natural hatred in my soul of everything holy and good. Wooings were lost upon me—warnings were cast to the wind—thunders were despised; and as for the whispers of His love, they were rejected as being less than nothing and vanity. But, sure I am, I can say now, speaking on behalf of myself, "He only is my salvation." It was He who turned my heart, and brought me down on my knees before

Him. I can in very deed, say with Doddridge[2] and Toplady[3]—

"Grace taught my soul to pray,
And made my eyes o'erflow;"
and coming to this moment, I can add—
"'Tis grace *has* kept me to this day,
And will not let me go."

Well can I remember the manner in which I learned the doctrines of grace in a single instant. Born, as all of us are by nature, an Arminian,[4] I still believed the old things I had heard continually from the pulpit, and did not see the grace of God. When I was coming to Christ, I thought I was doing it all myself, and though I sought the Lord earnestly, I had no idea the Lord was seeking me. I do not think the young convert is at first aware of this. I can recall the very day and hour when first I received those truths in my own soul—when they were, as John Bunyan[5] says, burnt into my heart as with a hot iron, and I can recollect how I felt that I had grown on a sudden from a babe into a man—that I had made progress in Scriptural knowledge, through having found, once for all, the clue to the truth of God. One week-night, when I was sitting in the house of God, I was not thinking much about the preacher's sermon, for I did not believe it. The thought struck me, *How did you come to be a Christian?* I sought the Lord. *But how did you come to seek the Lord?* The truth flashed across my mind in a moment—I should not have sought Him unless there had been some previous influence in my mind to *make me seek* Him. I prayed, thought I, but then I asked myself, *How came I to pray?* I was induced to pray by reading the Scriptures. *How came I to read the Scriptures?* I did read them, but what led me to do so? Then, in a moment, I saw that God was at the bottom of it all, and that He was the Author of my faith, and so

---

[2] Philip Doddridge, an eighteenth-century Congregationalist minister, educator, and hymnwriter

[3] Augustus Toplady, an eighteenth-century Anglican cleric and hymnwriter; a Calvinist opponent of John Wesley

[4] The belief that God's sovereignty and man's free will are compatible; the soteriological (study of salvation) rival to Calvinism

[5] Seventeenth-century English Puritan preacher and writer; author of *The Pilgrim's Progress*

the whole doctrine of grace opened up to me, and from that doctrine I have not departed to this day, and I desire to make this my constant confession, "I ascribe my change wholly to God."

I once attended a service where the text happened to be, *"He* shall choose our inheritance for us;" and the good man who occupied the pulpit was more than a little of an Arminian. Therefore, when he commenced, he said, "This passage refers entirely to our temporal inheritance, it has nothing whatever to do with our everlasting destiny, for," said he, "we do not want Christ to choose for us in the matter of Heaven or hell. It is so plain and easy, that every man who has a grain of common sense will choose Heaven, and any person would know better than to choose hell. We have no need of any superior intelligence, or any greater Being, to choose Heaven or hell for us. It is left to our own free-will, and we have enough wisdom given us, sufficiently correct means to judge for ourselves," and therefore, as he very logically inferred, there was no necessity for Jesus Christ, or anyone, to make a choice for us. We could choose the inheritance for ourselves without any assistance. "Ah!" I thought, "but, my good brother, it may be very true that we *could,* but I think we should want something more than common sense before we *should* choose aright."

First, let me ask, must we not all of us admit an over-ruling Providence, and the appointment of Jehovah's hand, as to the means whereby we came into this world? Those men who think that, afterwards, we are left to our own free-will to choose this one or the other to direct our steps, must admit that our entrance into the world was not of our own will, but that God had then to choose for us. What circumstances were those in our power which led us to elect certain persons to be our parents? Had we anything to do with it? Did not God Himself appoint our parents, native place, and friends? Could He not have caused me to be born with the skin of the Hottentot,[6] brought forth by a filthy mother who would nurse me in her "kraal," and teach me to bow down to Pagan gods, quite as easily as to have given me a pious mother, who would each morning and night bend her knee in prayer on my behalf?

---

[6] Racial term that refers to the Khoikhoi, the non-Bantu indigenous people of South Africa

Or, might He not, if He had pleased, have given me some profligate to have been my parent, from whose lips I might have early heard fearful, filthy, and obscene language? Might He not have placed me where I should have had a drunken father, who would have immured me in a very dungeon of ignorance, and brought me up in the chains of crime? Was it not God's Providence that I had so happy a lot, that both my parents were His children, and endeavoured to train me up in the fear of the Lord?

John Newton[7] used to tell a whimsical story, and laugh at it, too, of a good woman who said, in order to prove the doctrine of election, "Ah! sir, the Lord must have loved me before I was born, or else He would not have seen anything in me to love afterwards." I am sure it is true in my case; I believe the doctrine of election, because I am quite certain that, if God had not chosen me, I should never have chosen Him; and I am sure He chose me before I was born, or else He never would have chosen me afterwards; and He must have elected me for reasons unknown to me, for I never could find any reason in myself why He should have looked upon me with special love. So I am forced to accept that great Biblical doctrine. I recollect an Arminian brother telling me that he had read the Scriptures through a score or more times, and could never find the doctrine of election in them. He added that he was sure he would have done so if it had been there, for he read the Word on his knees. I said to him, "I think you read the Bible in a very uncomfortable posture, and if you had read it in your easy chair, you would have been more likely to understand it. Pray, by all means, and the more, the better, but it is a piece of superstition to think there is anything in the posture in which a man puts himself for reading: and as to reading through the Bible twenty times without having found anything about the doctrine of election, the wonder is that you found anything at all: you must have galloped through it at such a rate that you were not likely to have any intelligible idea of the meaning of the Scriptures."

If it would be marvelous to see one river leap up from the earth full-grown, what would it be to gaze upon a vast spring from which all the rivers of the

---

[7] An eighteenth-century English Anglican clergyman and abolitionist

earth should at once come bubbling up, a million of them born at a birth? What a vision would it be! Who can conceive it. And yet the love of God is that fountain, from which all the rivers of mercy, which have ever gladdened our race—all the rivers of grace in time, and of glory hereafter—take their rise. My soul, stand thou at that sacred fountain-head, and adore and magnify, for ever and ever, God, even our Father, who hath loved us! In the very beginning, when this great universe lay in the mind of God, like unborn forests in the acorn cup; long ere the echoes awoke the solitudes; before the mountains were brought forth; and long ere the light flashed through the sky, God loved His chosen creatures. Before there was any created being—when the ether was not fanned by an angel's wing, when space itself had not an existence, when there was nothing save God alone—even then, in that loneliness of Deity, and in that deep quiet and profundity, His bowels moved with love for His chosen. Their names were written on His heart, and then were they dear to His soul. Jesus loved His people before the foundation of the world—even from eternity! and when He called me by His grace, He said to me, "I have loved *thee* with an everlasting love: therefore with lovingkindness have I drawn thee."

Then, in the fulness of time, He purchased me with His blood; He let His heart run out in one deep gaping wound for me long ere I loved Him. Yea, when He first came to me, did I not spurn Him? When He knocked at the door, and asked for entrance, did I not drive Him away, and do despite to His grace? Ah, I can remember that I full often did so until, at last, by the power of His effectual grace, He said, "I must, I will come in;" and then He turned my heart, and made me love Him. But even till now I should have resisted Him, had it not been for His grace. Well, then since He purchased me when I was dead in sins, does it not follow, as a consequence necessary and logical, that He must have loved me first? Did my Saviour die for me because I believed on Him? No; I was not then in existence; I had then no being. Could the Saviour, therefore, have died because I had faith, when I myself was not yet born? Could that have been possible? Could that have been the origin of the Saviour's love towards me? Oh! no; my Saviour died for me long before I believed. "But," says someone, "He foresaw that you would have faith;

and, therefore, He loved you." What did He foresee about my faith? Did He foresee that I should get that faith myself, and that I should believe on Him of myself? No; Christ could not foresee that, because no Christian man will ever say that faith came of itself without the gift and without the working of the Holy Spirit. I have met with a great many believers, and talked with them about this matter; but I never knew one who could put his hand on his heart, and say, "I believed in Jesus without the assistance of the Holy Spirit."

I am bound to the doctrine of the depravity of the human heart, because I find myself depraved in heart, and have daily proofs that in my flesh there dwelleth no good thing. If God enters into covenant with unfallen man, man is so insignificant a creature that it must be an act of gracious condescension on the Lord's part; but if God enters into covenant with *sinful* man, he is then so offensive a creature that it must be, on God's part, an act of pure, free, rich, sovereign grace. When the Lord entered into covenant with me, I am sure that it was all of grace, nothing else but grace. When I remember what a den of unclean beasts and birds my heart was, and how strong was my unrenewed will, how obstinate and rebellious against the sovereignty of the Divine rule, I always feel inclined to take the very lowest room in my Father's house, and when I enter Heaven, it will be to go among the less than the least of all saints, and with the chief of sinners.

The late lamented Mr. Denham[8] has put, at the foot of his portrait, a most admirable text, "Salvation is of the Lord." That is just an epitome of Calvinism; it is the sum and substance of it. If anyone should ask me what I mean by a Calvinist, I should reply, "He is one who says, *Salvation is of the Lord.*" I cannot find in Scripture any other doctrine than this. It is the essence of the Bible. "He *only* is my rock and my salvation." Tell me anything contrary to this truth, and it will be a heresy; tell me a heresy, and I shall find its essence here, that it has departed from this great, this fundamental, this rock-truth, "God is my rock and my salvation." What is the heresy of Rome, but the addition of something to the perfect merits of Jesus Christ—the

---

[8] Joseph Denham Smith, a nineteenth-century Congregationalist pastor, evangelist, writer, and hymnwriter

bringing in of the works of the flesh, to assist in our justification? And what is the heresy of Arminianism but the addition of something to the work of the Redeemer? Every heresy, if brought to the touchstone, will discover itself here. I have my own private opinion that there is no such thing as preaching Christ and Him crucified, unless we preach what nowadays is called Calvinism. It is a nickname to call it Calvinism; Calvinism is the gospel, and nothing else. I do not believe we can preach the gospel, if we do not preach justification by faith, without works; nor unless we preach the sovereignty of God in His dispensation of grace; nor unless we exalt the electing, unchangeable, eternal, immutable, conquering love of Jehovah; nor do I think we can preach the gospel, unless we base it upon the special and particular redemption of His elect and chosen people which Christ wrought out upon the cross; nor can I comprehend a gospel which lets saints fall away after they are called, and suffers the children of God to be burned in the fires of damnation after having once believed in Jesus. Such a gospel I abhor.

"If ever it should come to pass,
That sheep of Christ might fall away,
My fickle, feeble soul, alas!
Would fall a thousand times a day."

If one dear saint of God had perished, so might all; if one of the covenant ones be lost, so may all be; and then there is no gospel promise true, but the Bible is a lie, and there is nothing in it worth my acceptance. I will be an infidel at once when I can believe that a saint of God can ever fall finally. If God hath loved me once, then He will love me for ever. God has a master-mind; He arranged everything in His gigantic intellect long before He did it; and once having settled it, He never alters it, "This shall be done," saith He, and the iron hand of destiny marks it down, and it is brought to pass. "This is My purpose," and it stands, nor can earth or hell alter it. "This is My decree," saith He, "promulgate it, ye holy angels; rend it down from the gate of Heaven, ye devils, if ye can; but ye cannot alter the decree, it shall stand for ever." God altereth not His plans; why should He? He is Almighty, and therefore can perform His pleasure. Why should He? He is the All-wise, and therefore cannot have planned wrongly. Why should He? He is the everlasting God, and therefore cannot die before His plan is accomplished. Why should He change? Ye worthless atoms of earth, ephemera of a day, ye creeping insects upon this bay-leaf of existence, ye may change *your* plans, but He shall never, never change *His*. Has He told me that His plan is to save me? If so, I am for ever safe.

"My name from the palms of His hands
Eternity will not erase;
Impress'd on His heart it remains,
In marks of indelible grace."

I do not know how some people, who believe that a Christian can fall from grace, manage to be happy. It must be a very commendable thing in them to be able to get through a day without despair. If I did not believe the doctrine of the final perseverance of the saints, I think I should be of all men the most miserable, because I should lack any ground of comfort. I could not say, whatever state of heart I came into, that I should be like a well-spring of water, whose stream fails not; I should rather have to take the comparison of an intermittent spring, that might stop on a sudden, or a reservoir, which I had no reason to expect would always be full. I believe that the happiest of Christians and the truest of Christians are those who never dare to doubt God, but who take His Word simply as it stands, and believe it, and ask no questions, just feeling assured that if God has said it, it will be so. I bear my willing testimony that I have no reason, nor even the shadow of a reason, to doubt my Lord, and I challenge Heaven, and earth, and hell, to bring any proof that God is untrue. From the depths of hell I call the fiends, and from this earth I call the tried and afflicted believers, and to Heaven I appeal, and challenge the long experience of the blood-washed host, and there is not to be found in the three realms a single person who can bear witness to one fact which can disprove the faithfulness of God, or weaken His claim to be trusted by His servants. There are many things that may or may not happen, but this I know *shall* happen—

"He *shall* present my soul,
Unblemish'd and complete,
Before the glory of His face,

With joys divinely great."

All the purposes of man have been defeated, but not the purposes of God. The promises of man may be broken—many of them are made to be broken—but the promises of God shall all be fulfilled. He is a promise-maker, but He never was a promise-breaker; He is a promise-keeping God, and every one of His people shall prove it to be so. This is my grateful, personal confidence, "The Lord *will* perfect that which concerneth *me*"—unworthy *me*, lost and ruined *me*. He will yet save me; and—

"I, among the blood-wash'd throng,
Shall wave the palm, and wear the crown,
And shout loud victory."

I go to a land which the plough of earth hath never upturned, where it is greener than earth's best pastures, and richer than her most abundant harvests ever saw. I go to a building of more gorgeous architecture than man hath ever builded; it is not of mortal design; it is "a building of God, a house not made with hands, eternal in the Heavens." All I shall know and enjoy in Heaven, will be given to me by the Lord, and I shall say, when at last I appear before Him—

"Grace all the work shall crown
Through everlasting days;
It lays in Heaven the topmost stone,
And well deserves the praise."

I know there are some who think it necessary to their system of theology to limit the merit of the blood of Jesus: if my theological system needed such a limitation, I would cast it to the winds. I cannot, I dare not allow the thought to find a lodging in my mind, it seems so near akin to blasphemy. In Christ's finished work I see an ocean of merit; my plummet finds no bottom, my eye discovers no shore. There must be sufficient efficacy in the blood of Christ, if God had so willed it, to have saved not only all in this world, but all in ten thousand worlds, had they transgressed their Maker's law. Once admit infinity into the matter, and limit is out of the question. Having a Divine Person for an offering, it is not consistent to conceive of limited value; bound and measure are terms inapplicable to the Divine sacrifice. The intent of the Divine purpose fixes the *application* of the infinite offering, but does not change it into a finite work. Think of the numbers upon whom God has bestowed His grace already. Think of the countless hosts in Heaven: if thou wert introduced there to-day, thou wouldst find it as easy to tell the stars, or the sands of the sea, as to count the multitudes that are before the throne even now. They have come from the East, and from the West, from the North, and from the South, and they are sitting down with Abraham, and with Isaac, and with Jacob in the Kingdom of God; and beside those in Heaven, think of the saved ones on earth. Blessed be God, His elect on earth are to be counted by millions, I believe, and the days are coming, brighter days than these, when there shall be multitudes upon multitudes brought to know the Saviour, and to rejoice in Him. The Father's love is not for a few only, but for an exceeding great company. "A great multitude, which no man could number," will be found in Heaven. A man can reckon up to very high figures; set to work your Newtons, your mightiest calculators, and they can count great numbers, but God and God alone can tell the multitude of His redeemed. I believe there will be more in Heaven than in hell. If anyone asks me why I think so, I answer, because Christ, in everything, is to "have the pre-eminence," and I cannot conceive how He could have the pre-eminence if there are to be more in the dominions of Satan than in Paradise. Moreover, I have never read that there is to be in hell a great multitude, which no man could number. I rejoice to know that the souls of all infants, as soon as they die, speed their way to Paradise. Think what a multitude there is of them! Then there are already in Heaven unnumbered myriads of the spirits of just men made perfect—the redeemed of all nations, and kindreds, and people, and tongues up till now; and there are better times coming, when the religion of Christ shall be universal; when—

"He shall reign from pole to pole,
With illimitable sway;"

when whole kingdoms shall bow down before Him, and nations shall be born in a day, and in the thousand years of the great millennial state there will be enough saved to make up all the deficiencies of the thousands of years that have gone before. Christ shall be Master everywhere, and His praise shall be sounded in every land. Christ shall have the pre-eminence at last; His train shall be far larger than that which shall attend the chariot of the grim monarch of hell.

Some persons love the doctrine of universal atonement because they say, "It is so beautiful. It is a lovely idea that Christ should have died for all men; it commends itself," they say, "to the instincts of humanity; there is something in it full of joy and beauty." I admit there is, but beauty may be often associated with falsehood. There is much which I might admire in the theory of universal redemption, but I will just show what the supposition necessarily involves. If Christ on His cross intended to save every man, then He intended to save those who were lost before He died. If the doctrine be true, that He died for all men, then He died for some who were in hell before He came into this world, for doubtless there were even then myriads there who had been cast away because of their sins. Once again, if it was Christ's intention to save all men, how deplorably has He been disappointed, for we have His own testimony that there is a lake which burneth with fire and brimstone, and into that pit of woe have been cast some of the very persons who, according to the theory of universal redemption, were bought with His blood. That seems to me a conception a thousand times more repulsive than any of those consequences which are said to be associated with the Calvinistic and Christian doctrine of special and particular redemption. To think that my Saviour died for men who were or are in hell, seems a supposition too horrible for me to entertain. To imagine for a moment that He was the Substitute for all the sons of men, and that God, having first punished the Substitute, afterwards punished the sinners themselves, seems to conflict with all my ideas of Divine justice. That Christ should offer an atonement and satisfaction for the sins of all men, and that afterwards some of those very men should be punished for the sins for which Christ had already atoned, appears to me to be the most monstrous iniquity that could ever have been imputed to Saturn, to Janus, to the goddess of the Thugs, or to the most diabolical heathen deities. God forbid that we should ever think thus of Jehovah, the just and wise and good!

There is no soul living who holds more firmly to the doctrines of grace than I do, and if any man asks me whether I am ashamed to be called a Calvinist, I answer—I wish to be called nothing but a Christian; but if you ask me, do I hold the doctrinal views which were held by John Calvin, I reply, I do in the main hold them, and rejoice to avow it. But far be it from me even to imagine that Zion contains none but Calvinistic Christians within her walls, or that there are none saved who do not hold our views. Most atrocious things have been spoken about the character and spiritual condition of John Wesley,[9] the modern prince of Arminians. I can only say concerning him that, while I detest many of the doctrines which he preached, yet for the man himself I have a reverence second to no Wesleyan; and if there were wanted two apostles to be added to the number of the twelve, I do not believe that there could be found two men more fit to be so added than George Whitefield[10] and John Wesley. The character of John Wesley stands beyond all imputation for self-sacrifice, zeal, holiness, and communion with God; he lived far above the ordinary level of common Christians, and was one "of whom the world was not worthy." I believe there are multitudes of men who cannot see these truths, or, at least, cannot see them in the way in which we put them, who nevertheless have received Christ as their Saviour, and are as dear to the heart of the God of grace as the soundest Calvinist in or out of Heaven.

I do not think I differ from any of my Hyper-Calvinistic[11] brethren in what I do believe, but I differ from them in what they do not believe. I do not hold any less than they do, but I hold a little more, and, I think, a little more of the truth revealed in the Scriptures. Not only are there a few cardinal doctrines, by which we can steer our ship North, South, East, or West, but as we study the Word, we shall begin to learn something about the North-west and North-east, and all else that lies between the four cardinal points. The system of truth revealed in the Scriptures is not simply one straight line, but two; and no man will ever get a right view of the gospel until he knows how to look at

---

[9] Eighteenth-century English Anglican cleric, evangelist, and theologian; founder of Methodism; one of the most prominent Arminians in church history

[10] Eighteenth-century English Anglican cleric and evangelist; one of the founders of Methodism; unlike his Arminian associate, John Wesley, Whitefield was a Calvinist

[11] An extreme branch of Calvinism that denies the requirement of belief in the Gospel for salvation

the two lines at once. For instance, I read in one Book of the Bible, "The Spirit and the bride say, Come. And let him that heareth say, Come. And let him that is athirst come. And whosoever will, let him take the water of life freely." Yet I am taught, in another part of the same inspired Word, that "it is not of him that willeth, nor of him that runneth, but of God that sheweth mercy." I see, in one place, God in providence presiding over all, and yet I see, and I cannot help seeing, that man acts as he pleases, and that God has left his actions, in a great measure, to his own free-will. Now, if I were to declare that man was so free to act that there was no control of God over his actions, I should be driven very near to atheism; and if, on the other hand, I should declare that God so over-rules all things that man is not free enough to be responsible, I should be driven at once into Antinomianism[12] or fatalism.[13] That God predestines, and yet that man is responsible, are two facts that few can see clearly. They are believed to be inconsistent and contradictory to each other. If, then, I find taught in one part of the Bible that everything is fore-ordained, *that is true*; and if I find, in another Scripture, that man is responsible for all his actions, *that is true*; and it is only my folly that leads me to imagine that these two truths can ever contradict each other. I do not believe they can ever be welded into one upon any earthly anvil, but they certainly shall be one in eternity. They are two lines that are so nearly parallel, that the human mind which pursues them farthest will never discover that they converge, but they do converge, and they will meet somewhere in eternity, close to the throne of God, whence all truth doth spring.

It is often said that the doctrines we believe have a tendency to lead us to sin. I have heard it asserted most positively, that those high doctrines which we love, and which we find in the Scriptures, are licentious ones. I do not know who will have the hardihood to make that assertion, when they consider that the holiest of men have been believers in them. I ask the man who dares to say that Calvinism is a licentious religion, what he thinks of the character of Augustine, or Calvin, or Whitefield, who in successive ages were

---

[12] The belief that those saved are not required to follow moral laws; rejects all forms of legalism

[13] The belief in destiny as the driving force for all actions and events

the great exponents of the system of grace; or what will he say of the Puritans, whose works are full of them? Had a man been an Arminian in those days, he would have been accounted the vilest heretic breathing, but now *we* are looked upon as the heretics, and they as the orthodox. *We* have gone back to the old school; *we* can trace our descent from the apostles. It is that vein of free-grace, running through the sermonizing of Baptists, which has saved us as a denomination. Were it not for that, we should not stand where we are today. We can run a golden line up to Jesus Christ Himself, through a holy succession of mighty fathers, who all held these glorious truths; and we can ask concerning them, "Where will you find holier and better men in the world?" No doctrine is so calculated to preserve a man from sin as the doctrine of the grace of God. Those who have called it "a licentious doctrine" did not know anything at all about it. Poor ignorant things, they little knew that their own vile stuff was the most licentious doctrine under Heaven. If they knew the grace of God in truth, they would soon see that there was no preservative from lying like a knowledge that we are elect of God from the foundation of the world. There is nothing like a belief in my eternal perseverance, and the immutability of my Father's affection, which can keep me near to Him from a motive of simple gratitude. Nothing makes a man so virtuous as belief of the truth. A lying doctrine will soon beget a lying practice. A man cannot have an erroneous belief without by-and-by having an erroneous life. I believe the one thing naturally begets the other. Of all men, those have the most disinterested piety, the sublimest reverence, the most ardent devotion, who believe that they are saved by grace, without works, through faith, and that not of themselves, it is the gift of God. Christians should take heed, and see that it always is so, lest by any means Christ should be crucified afresh, and put to an open shame.

I

Total Depravity

HUMAN INABILITY

March 7, 1858, at the Music Hall, Royal Surrey Gardens

"No man can come to me, except the Father which hath sent me draw him."
John 6:44

"COMING to Christ" is a very common phrase in Holy Scripture. It is used to express those acts of the soul wherein, leaving at once our self-righteousness, and our sins, we fly unto the Lord Jesus Christ, and receive his righteousness to be our covering, and his blood to be our atonement. Coming to Christ, then, embraces in it repentance, self-negation, and faith in the Lord Jesus Christ, and it sums within itself all those things which are the necessary attendants of these great states of heart, such as the belief of the truth, earnestness of prayer to God, the submission of the soul to the precepts of God's gospel, and all those things which accompany the dawn of salvation in the soul. Coming to Christ is just the one essential thing for a sinner's salvation. He that cometh not to Christ, do what he may, or think what he may, is yet in "the gall of bitterness and in the bonds of iniquity." Coming to Christ is the very first effect of regeneration. No sooner is the soul quickened than it at once discovers its lost estate, is horrified thereat, looks out for a refuge, and believing Christ to be a suitable one, flies to him and reposes in him. Where there is not this coming to Christ, it is certain that there is as yet no quickening; where there is no quickening, the soul is dead in trespasses and sins, and being dead it cannot enter into the kingdom of heaven. We have before us now an announcement very startling, some say very obnoxious.

Coming to Christ, though described by some people as being the very easiest thing in all the world, is in our text declared to be a thing utterly and entirely impossible to any man, unless the Father shall draw him to Christ. It shall be our business, then, to enlarge upon this declaration. We doubt not that it will always be offensive to carnal nature, but, nevertheless, the offending of human nature is sometimes the first step towards bringing it to bow itself before God. And if this be the effect of a painful process, we can forget the pain and rejoice in the glorious consequences.

I shall endeavour this morning, first of all, to notice man's inability, wherein it consists. Secondly, the Father's drawings—what these are, and how they are exerted upon the soul. And then I shall conclude by noticing a sweet consolation which may be derived from this seemingly barren and terrible text.

I. First, then, MAN'S INABILITY. The text says, "No man can come to me, except the Father which hath sent me draw him." Wherein does this inability lie?

First, it does not lie in any physical defect. If in coming to Christ, moving the body or walking with the feet should be of any assistance, certainly man has all physical power to come to Christ in that sense. I remember to have heard a very foolish Antinomian[14] declare, that he did not believe any man had the power to walk to the house of God unless the Father drew him. Now the man was plainly foolish, because he must have seen that as long as a man was alive and had legs, it was as easy for him to walk to the house of God as to the house of Satan. If coming to Christ includes the utterance of a prayer, man has no physical defect in that respect, if he be not dumb, he can say a prayer as easily as he can utter blasphemy. It is as easy for a man to sing one of the songs of Zion as to sing a profane and libidinous song. There is no lack of physical power in coming to Christ. All that can be wanted with regard to the bodily strength man most assuredly has, and any part of salvation which consists in that is totally and entirely in the power of man without any assistance from the Spirit of God. Nor, again, does this inability lie in any

---

[14] The belief that those saved are not required to follow moral laws; rejects all forms of legalism

mental lack. I can believe this Bible to be true just as easily as I can believe any other book to be true. So far as believing on Christ is an act of the mind, I am just as able to believe on Christ as I am able to believe on anybody else. Let his statement be but true, it is idle to tell me I cannot believe it. I can believe the statement that Christ makes as well as I can believe the statement of any other person. There is no deficiency of faculty in the mind: it is as capable of appreciating as a mere mental act the guilt of sin, as it is of appreciating the guilt of assassination. It is just as possible for me to exercise the mental idea of seeking God, as it is to exercise the thought of ambition. I have all the mental strength and power that can possibly be needed, so far as mental power is needed in salvation at all. Nay, there is not any man so ignorant that he can plead a lack of intellect as an excuse for rejecting the gospel. The defect, then, does not lie either in the body, or, what we are bound to call, speaking theologically, the mind. It is not any lack or deficiency there, although it is the vitiation of the mind, the corruption or the ruin of it, which, after all, is the very essence of man's inability.

Permit me to show you wherein this inability of man really does lie. It lies deep in his nature. Through the fall, and through our own sin, the nature of man has become so debased, and depraved, and corrupt, that it is impossible for him to come to Christ without the assistance of God the Holy Spirit. Now, in trying to exhibit how the nature of man thus renders him unable to come to Christ, you must allow me just to take this figure. You see a sheep; how willingly it feeds upon the herbage! You never knew a sheep sigh after carrion; it could not live on lion's food. Now bring me a wolf; and you ask me whether a wolf cannot eat grass, whether it cannot be just as docile and as domesticated as the sheep. I answer, no; because its nature is contrary thereunto. You say, "Well, it has ears and legs; can it not hear the shepherd's voice, and follow him whithersoever he leadeth it?" I answer, certainly; there is no physical cause why it cannot do so, but its nature forbids, and therefore I say it cannot do so. Can it not be tamed? cannot its ferocity be removed? Probably it may so far be subdued that it may become apparently tame; but there will always be a marked distinction between it and the sheep, because there is a distinction in nature. Now, the reason why man cannot come to Christ, is not because he cannot come, so far as his body or his mere power of mind is concerned, but because his nature is so corrupt that he has neither the will nor the power to come to Christ unless drawn by the Spirit. But let me give you a better illustration. You see a mother with her babe in her arms. You put a knife into her hand, and tell her to stab that babe to the heart. She replies, and very truthfully, "I cannot." Now, so far as her bodily power is concerned, she can, if she pleases; there is the knife, and there is the child. The child cannot resist, and she has quite sufficient strength in her hand immediately to stab it to its heart. But she is quite correct when she says she cannot do it. As a mere act of the mind, it is quite possible she might think of such a thing as killing the child, and yet she says she cannot think of such a thing; and she does not say falsely, for her nature as a mother forbids her doing a thing from which her soul revolts. Simply because she is that child's parent she feels she cannot kill it. It is even so with a sinner. Coming to Christ is so obnoxious to human nature that, although, so far as physical and mental forces are concerned, (and these have but a very narrow sphere in salvation) men could come if they would: it is strictly correct to say that they cannot and will not unless the Father who hath sent Christ doth draw them. Let us enter a little more deeply into the subject, and try to show you wherein this inability of man consists, in its more minute particulars.

I. First, it lies in the obstinacy of the human will. "Oh!" saith the Arminian,[15] "men may be saved if they will." We reply, "My dear sir, we all believe that; but it is just the if they will that is the difficulty. We assert that no man will come to Christ unless he be drawn; nay, we do not assert it, but Christ himself declares it—"Ye will not come unto me that ye might have life;' and as long as that "ye will not come' stands on record in Holy Scripture, we shall not be brought to believe in any doctrine of the freedom of the human will." It is strange how people, when talking about free-will, talk of things which they do not at all understand. "Now," says one, "I believe men can be saved if they will." My dear sir, that is not the question at all. The question is,

---

[15] The belief that God's sovereignty and man's free will are compatible; the soteriological (study of salvation) rival to Calvinism

are men ever found naturally willing to submit to the humbling terms of the gospel of Christ? We declare, upon Scriptural authority, that the human will is so desperately set on mischief, so depraved, and so inclined to everything that is evil, and so disinclined to everything that is good, that without the powerful. supernatural, irresistible influence of the Holy Spirit, no human will ever be constrained towards Christ. You reply, that men sometimes are willing, without the help of the Holy Spirit. I answer—Did you ever meet with any person who was? Scores and hundreds, nay, thousands of Christians have I conversed with, of different opinions, young and old, but it has never been my lot to meet with one who could affirm that he came to Christ of himself, without being drawn. The universal confession of all true believers is this—"I know that unless Jesus Christ had sought me when a stranger wandering from the fold of God, I would to this very hour have been wandering far from him, at a distance from him, and loving that distance well." With common consent, all believers affirm the truth, that men will not come to Christ till the Father who hath sent Christ doth draw them.

2. Again, not only is the will obstinate, but the understanding is darkened. Of that we have abundant Scriptural proof. I am not now making mere assertions, but stating doctrines authoritatively taught in the Holy Scriptures, and known in the conscience of every Christian man—that the understanding of man is so dark, that he cannot by any means understand the things of God until his understanding has been opened. Man is by nature blind within. The cross of Christ, so laden with glories, and glittering with attractions, never attracts him, because he is blind and cannot see its beauties. Talk to him of the wonders of the creation, show to him the many-coloured arch that spans the sky, let him behold the glories of a landscape, he is well able to see all these things; but talk to him of the wonders of the covenant of grace, speak to him of the security of the believer in Christ, tell him of the beauties of the person of the Redeemer, he is quite deaf to all your description; you are as one that playeth a goodly tune, it is true; but he regards not, he is deaf, he has no comprehension. Or, to return to the verse which we so specially marked in our reading, "The natural man receiveth not the things of the Spirit of God, for they are foolishness unto him: neither can he know them because

they are spiritually discerned;" and inasmuch as he is a natural man, it is not in his power to discern the things of God. "Well," says one, "I think I have arrived at a very tolerable judgment in matters of theology; I think I understand almost every point." True, that you may do in the letter of it; but in the spirit of it, in the true reception thereof into the soul, and in the actual understanding of it, it is impossible for you to have attained, unless you have been drawn by the Spirit. For as long as that Scripture stands true, that carnal men cannot receive spiritual things, it must be true that you have not received them, unless you have been renewed and made a spiritual man in Christ Jesus. The will, then, and the understanding, are two great doors, both blocked up against our coming to Christ, and until these are opened by the sweet influences of the Divine Spirit, they must be for ever closed to anything like coming to Christ.

3. Again, the affections, which constitute a very great part of man, are depraved. Man, as he is, before he receives the grace of God, loves anything and everything above spiritual things. If ye want proof of this, look around you. There needs no monument to the depravity of the human affections. Cast your eyes everywhere—there is not a street, nor a house, nay, nor a heart, which doth not bear upon it sad evidence of this dreadful truth. Why is it that men are not found on the Sabbath Day universally flocking to the house of God? Why are we not more constantly found reading our Bibles? How is it that prayer is a duty almost universally neglected? Why is it that Christ Jesus is so little beloved? Why are even his professed followers so cold in their affections to him? Whence arise these things? Assuredly, dear brethren, we can trace them to no other source than this, the corruption and vitiation of the affections. We love that which we ought to hate, and we hate that which we ought to love. It is but human nature, fallen human nature, that man should love this present life better than the life to come. It is but the effect of the fall, that man should love sin better than righteousness, and the ways of this world better than the ways of God. And again, we repeat it, until these affections be renewed, and turned into a fresh channel by the gracious drawings of the Father, it is not possible for any man to love the Lord Jesus Christ.

4. Yet once more—conscience, too, has been overpowered by the fall. I believe there is no more egregious mistake made by divines, than when they tell people that conscience is the vicegerent of God within the soul, and that it is one of those powers which retains its ancient dignity, and stands erect amidst the fall of its compeers. My brethren, when man fell in the garden, manhood fell entirely; there was not one single pillar in the temple of manhood that stood erect. It is true, conscience was not destroyed. The pillar was not shattered; it fell, and it fell in one piece, and there it lies along, the mightiest remnant of God's once perfect work in man. But that conscience is fallen, I am sure. Look at men. Who among them is the possessor of a "good conscience toward God," but the regenerated man? Do you imagine that if men's consciences always spoke loudly and clearly to them, they would live in the daily commission of acts, which are as opposed to the right as darkness to light? No, beloved; conscience can tell me that I am a sinner, but conscience cannot make me feel that I am one. Conscience may tell me that such-and-such a thing is wrong, but how wrong it is conscience itself does not know. Did any man s conscience, unenlightened by the Spirit, ever tell him that his sins deserved damnation? Or if conscience did do that, did it ever lead any man to feel an abhorrence of sin as sin? In fact, did conscience ever bring a man to such a self-renunciation, that he did totally abhor himself and all his works and come to Christ? No, conscience, although it is not dead, is ruined, its power is impaired, it hath not that clearness of eye and that strength of hand, and that thunder of voice, which it had before the fall; but hath ceased to a great degree, to exert its supremacy in the town of Mansoul. Then, beloved, it becomes necessary for this very reason, because conscience is depraved, that the Holy Spirit should step in, to show us our need of a Saviour, and draw us to the Lord Jesus Christ.

"Still," says one, "as far as you have hitherto gone, it appears to me that you consider that the reason why men do not come to Christ is that they will not, rather than they cannot." True, most true. I believe the greatest reason of man's inability is the obstinacy of his will. That once overcome, I think the great stone is rolled away from the sepulchre, and the hardest part of the battle is already won. But allow me to go a little further. My text does not say, "No man will come," but it says, "No man can come." Now, many interpreters believe that the can here, is but a strong expression conveying no more meaning than the word will. I feel assured that this is not correct. There is in man, not only unwillingness to be saved, but there is a spiritual powerlessness to come to Christ; and this I will prove to every Christian at any rate. Beloved, I speak to you who have already been quickened by the divine grace, does not your experience teach you that there are times when you have a will to serve God, and yet have not the power? Have you not sometimes been obliged to say that you have wished to believe. but you have had to pray, Lord, help mine unbelief?" Because, although willing enough to receive God's testimony, your own carnal nature was too strong for you, and you felt you needed supernatural help. Are you able to go into your room at any hour you choose, and to fall upon your knees and say, "Now, it is my will that I should be very earnest in prayer, and that I should draw near unto God?" I ask, do you find your power equal to your will? You could say, even at the bar of God himself, that you are sure you are not mistaken in your willingness; you are willing to be wrapt up in devotion, it is your will that your soul should not wander from a pure contemplation of the Lord Jesus Christ, but you find that you cannot do that, even when you are willing, without the help of the Spirit. Now, if the quickened child of God finds a spiritual inability, how much more the sinner who is dead in trespasses and sin? If even the advanced Christian, after thirty or forty years, finds himself sometimes willing and yet powerless—if such be his experience,—does it not seem more than likely that the poor sinner who has not yet believed, should find a need of strength as well as a want of will?

But, again, there is another argument. If the sinner has strength to come to Christ, I should like to know how we are to understand those continual descriptions of the sinner's state which we meet with in God's holy Word? Now, a sinner is said to be dead in trespasses and sins. Will you affirm that death implies nothing more than the absence of a will? Surely a corpse is quite as unable as unwilling. Or again, do not all men see that there is a distinction between will and power: might not that corpse be sufficiently quickened to get a will, and yet be so powerless that it could not lift as much as its hand or foot? Have we never seen cases in which persons have been just sufficiently re-animated to give evidence of life, and have yet been so near death that they could not have performed the slightest action? Is there not a clear difference between the giving or the will and the giving of power? It is quite certain, however, that where the will is given, the power will follow. Make a man willing, and he shall be made powerful; for when God gives the will, he does not tantalize man by giving him to wish for that which he is unable to do; nevertheless he makes such a division between the will and the power, that it shall be seen that both things are quite distinct gifts of the Lord God.

Then I must ask one more question: if all that were needed to make a man willing, do you not at once degrade the Holy Spirit? Are we not in the habit of giving all the glory of salvation wrought in us to God the Spirit? But now, if all that God the Spirit does for me is to make me willing to do these things for myself, am I not in a great measure a sharer with the Holy Spirit in the glory? and may I not boldly stand up and say, "It is true the Spirit gave me the will to do it, but still I did it myself, and therein will I glory; for if I did these things myself without assistance from on high, I will not cast my crown at his feet; it is my own crown, I earned it, and I will keep it." Inasmuch as the Holy Spirit is evermore in Scripture set forth as the person who worketh in us to will and to do of his own good pleasure, we hold it to be a legitimate inference that he must do something more for us than the mere making of us willing, and that therefore there must be another thing besides want of will in a sinner—there must be absolute and actual want of power.

Now, before I leave this statement, let me address myself to you for a moment. I am often charged with preaching doctrines that may do a great deal of hurt. Well, I shall not deny the charge, for I am not careful to answer in this matter. I have my witnesses here present to prove that the things which I have preached have done a great deal of hurt, but they have not done hurt either to morality or to God's Church; the hurt has been on the side of Satan. There are not ones or twos but many hundreds who this morning rejoice that they have been brought near to God; from having been profane Sabbath-breakers, drunkards, or worldly persons, they have been brought to know and love the Lord Jesus Christ; and if this be any hurt may God of his infinite mercy send us a thousand times as much. But further, what truth is there in the world which will not hurt a man who chooses to make hurt of it? You who preach general redemption, are very fond of proclaiming the great truth of God's mercy to the last moment. But how dare you preach that? Many people make hurt of it by putting off the day of grace, and thinking that the last hour may do as well as the first. Why, if we never preached anything which man could misuse, and abuse, we must hold our tongues for ever. Still says one, "Well then, if I cannot save myself, and cannot come to Christ, I must sit still and do nothing." If men do say so, on their own heads shall be their doom. We have very plainly told you that there are many things you can do. To be found continually in the house of God is in your power; to study the Word of God with diligence is in your power; to renounce your outward sin, to forsake the vices in which you indulge, to make your life honest, sober, and righteous, is in your power. For this you need no help from the Holy Spirit; all this you can do yourself; but to come to Christ truly is not in your power, until you are renewed by the Holy Ghost. But mark you, your want of power is no excuse, seeing that you have no desire to come, and are living in wilful rebellion against God. Your want of power lies mainly in the obstinacy of nature. Suppose a liar says that it is not in his power to speak the truth, that he has been a liar so long, that he cannot leave it off; is that an excuse for him? Suppose a man who has long indulged in lust should tell you that he finds his lusts have so girt about him like a great iron net that he cannot get rid of them, would you take that as an excuse? Truly it is none at all. If a drunkard has become so foully a drunkard, that he finds it impossible to pass a public—house without stepping in, do you therefore excuse him? No, because his inability to reform, lies in his nature, which he has no desire to restrain or conquer.

    The thing that is done, and the thing that causes the thing that is done, being both from the root of sin, are two evils which cannot excuse each other, What though the Ethiopian cannot change his skin, nor the leopard his spots? It is because you have learned to do evil that you cannot now learn to do well; and instead, therefore, of letting you sit down to excuse yourselves, let me put a thunderbolt beneath the seat of your sloth, that you may be startled by it and aroused. Remember, that to sit still is to be damned to all eternity. Oh! that God the Holy Spirit might make use of this truth in a very different manner! Before I have done I trust I shall be enabled to show you how it is that this truth, which apparently condemns men and shuts them out, is, after all, the great truth, which has been blessed to the conversion of men.

II. Our second point is THE FATHER'S DRAWINGS. "No man can come to me, except the Father which hath sent me draw him." How then does the Father draw men? Arminian divines generally say that God draws men by the preaching of the gospel. Very true; the preaching of the gospel is the instrument of drawing men, but there must be some thing more than this. Let me ask to whom did Christ address these words? Why, to the people of Capernaum, where he had often preached, where he had uttered mournfully and plaintively the woes of the law and the invitations of the gospel. In that city he had done many mighty works and worked many miracles. In fact, such teaching and such miraculous attestation had he given to them, that he declared that Tyre and Sidon would have repented long ago in sack-cloth and ashes, if they had been blessed with such privileges. Now, if the preaching of Christ himself did not avail to the enabling these men to come to Christ, it cannot be possible that all that was intended by the drawing of the Father was simply preaching. No, brethren, you must note again, he does not say no man can come except the minister draw him, but except the Father draw him. Now there is such a thing as being drawn by the gospel, and drawn by the minister, without being drawn by God. Clearly, it is a divine drawing that is meant, a drawing by the Most High God—the First Person of the most glorious Trinity sending out the Third Person, the Holy Spirit, to induce men to come to Christ. Another person turns round and says with a sneer, "Then do you think that Christ drags men to himself, seeing that they are unwilling!" I remember meeting once with a man who said to me, "Sir, you preach that Christ takes people by the hair of their heads and drags them to himself." I asked him whether he could refer to the date of the sermon wherein I preached that extraordinary doctrine, for if he could, I should be very much obliged. However, he could not. But said I, while Christ does not drag people to himself by the hair of their heads, I believe that, he draws them by the heart quite as powerfully as your caricature would suggest. Mark that in the Father's drawing there is no compulsion whatever; Christ never compelled any man to come to him against his will. If a man be unwilling to be saved, Christ does not save him against his will. How, then, does the Holy Spirit draw him? Why, by making him willing. It is true he does not use "moral suasion;" he knows a nearer method of reaching the heart. He goes to the secret fountain of the heart, and he knows how, by some mysterious operation, to turn the will in an opposite direction, so that, as Ralph Erskine[16] paradoxically puts it, the man is saved "with full consent against his will;" that is, against his old will he is saved. But he is saved with full consent, for he is made willing in the day of God's power. Do not imagine that any man will go to heaven kicking and struggling all the way against the hand that draws him. Do not conceive that any man will be plunged in the bath of a Saviour's blood while he is striving to run away from the Saviour. Oh, no. It is quite true that first of all man is unwilling to be saved. When the Holy Spirit hath put his influence into the heart, the text is fulfilled—"draw me and I will run after thee." We follow on while he draws us, glad to obey the voice which once we had despised. But the gist of the matter lies in the turning of the will. How that is done no flesh knoweth; it is one of those mysteries that is clearly perceived as a fact, but the cause of which no tongue can tell, and no heart can guess. The apparent way, however, in which the Holy Spirit operates, we can tell you. The first thing the Holy Spirit does when he comes into a man's heart is this: he finds him with a very good opinion of himself: and there is nothing which prevents a man coming to Christ like a good opinion of himself. Why, says man, "I don't want to come to Christ. I have as good a righteousness as anybody can desire. I feel I can walk into heaven on my own rights." The Holy Spirit lays bare his heart, lets him see the loathsome cancer that is there eating away his life, uncovers to him all the blackness and defilement of that sink of hell, the human heart, and then the man stands aghast. "I never thought I was like this. Oh! those sins I thought were little, have swelled out to an immense stature. What I thought was a mole-hill has grown into a mountain; it was but the hyssop

---

[16] Eighteenth-century Scottish churchman, minister, and poet

on the wall before, but now it has become a cedar of Lebanon. Oh," saith the man within himself, "I will try and reform; I will do good deeds enough to wash these black deeds out." Then comes the Holy Spirit and shows him that he cannot do this, takes away all his fancied power and strength, so that the man falls down on his knees in agony, and cries, "Oh! once I thought I could save myself by my good works, but now I find that

"Could my tears for ever flow,

Could my zeal no respite know,

All for sin could not atone,

Thou must save and thou alone.'"

Then the heart sinks, and the man is ready to despair. And saith he, "I never can be saved. Nothing can save me." Then, comes the Holy Spirit and shows the sinner the cross of Christ, gives him eyes anointed with heavenly eye-salve, and says, "Look to yonder cross. that Man died to save sinners; you feel that you are a sinner; he died to save you." And he enables the heart to believe, and to come to Christ. And when it comes to Christ, by this sweet drawing of the Spirit, it finds "a peace with God which passeth all understanding, which keeps his heart and mind through Jesus Christ our Lord." Now, you will plainly perceive that all this may be done without any compulsion. Man is as much drawn willingly, as if he were not drawn at all; and he comes to Christ with full consent, with as full a consent as if no secret influence had ever been exercised in his heart. But that influence must be exercised, or else there never has been and there never will be, any man who either can or will come to the Lord Jesus Christ.

III. And, now, we gather up our ends, and conclude by trying to make a practical application of the doctrine; and we trust a comfortable one. "Well," says one, "if what this man preaches be true, what is to become of my religion? for do you know I have been a long while trying, and I do not like to hear you say a man cannot save himself. I believe he can, and I mean to persevere; but if I am to believe what you say, I must give it all up and begin again." My dear friends, it will be a very happy thing if you do. Do not think that I shall be at all alarmed if you do so. Remember, what you are doing is building your house upon the sand, and it is but an act of charity if I can shake it a little for you. Let me assure you, in God's name, if your religion has no better foundation than your own strength, it will not stand you at the bar of God. Nothing will last to eternity, but that which came from eternity. Unless the everlasting God has done a good work in your heart, all you may have done must be unravelled at the last day of account. It is all in vain for you to be a church-goer or chapel-goer, a good keeper of the Sabbath, an observer of your prayers: it is all in vain for you to be honest to your neighbours and reputable in your conversation; if you hope to be saved by these things, it is all in vain for you to trust in them. Go on; be as honest as you like, keep the Sabbath perpetually, be as holy as you can. I would not dissuade you from these things. God forbid; grow in them, but oh, do not trust in them, for if you rely upon these things you will find they will fail you when most you need them. And if there be anything else that you have found yourself able to do unassisted by divine grace, the sooner you can get rid of the hope that has been engendered by it the better for you, for it is a foul delusion to rely upon anything that flesh can do. A spiritual heaven must be inhabited by spiritual men, and preparation for it must be wrought by the Spirit of God. "Well," cries another, "I have been sitting under a ministry where I have been told that I could, at my own option, repent and believe, and the consequence is that I have been putting it off from day to day. I thought I could come one day as well as another; that I had only to say, "Lord, have mercy upon me,' and believe, and then I should be saved. Now you have taken all this hope away for me, sir; I feel amazement and horror taking hold upon me." Again, I say, "My dear friend, I am very glad of it. This was the effect which I hoped to produce. I pray that you may feel this a great deal more. When you have no hope of saving yourself, I shall have hope that God has begun to save you. As soon as you say "Oh, I cannot come to Christ. Lord, draw me, help me,' I shall rejoice over you. He who has got a will, though he has not power, has grace begun in his heart, and God will not leave him until the work is finished." But, careless sinner, learn that thy salvation now hangs in God's hand. Oh, remember thou art entirely in the hand of God. Thou hast sinned against him, and if he wills to damn thee, damned thou art. Thou canst not resist his will nor thwart his purpose. Thou hast deserved his wrath, and if he chooses to pour the full shower of that wrath upon thy head, thou canst do nothing to avert it. If, on the other hand, he chooses to save thee, he is able to save thee to the very uttermost. But thou liest as much in his hand as the summer's moth beneath thine own finger. He is the God whom thou art grieving every day. Doth it not make thee tremble to think that thy eternal destiny now hangs upon the will of him whom thou hast angered and incensed? Dost not this make thy knees knock together, and thy blood curdle? If it does so I rejoice, inasmuch as this may be the first effect of the Spirit's drawing in thy soul. Oh, tremble to think that the God whom thou hast angered, is the God upon whom thy salvation or thy condemnation entirely depends. Tremble and "kiss the Son lest he be angry and ye perish from the way while his wrath is kindled but a little,"

Now, the comfortable reflection is this:—Some of you this morning are conscious that you are coming to Christ. Have you not begun to weep the penitential tear? Did not your closet witness your prayerful preparation for the hearing of the Word of God? And during the service of this morning, has not your heart said within you, "Lord, save me, or I perish, for save myself I cannot?" And could you not now stand up in your seat, and sing,

"Oh, sovereign grace my heart subdue;
I would be led in triumph, too,
A willing captive of my Lord,
To sing the triumph of his Word"?

And have I not myself heard you say in your heart—"Jesus, Jesus, my whole trust Is in thee: I know that no righteousness of my own can save me, but only thou, O Christ—sink or swim, I cast myself on thee?" Oh, my brother, thou art drawn by the Father, for thou couldst not have come unless he had drawn thee. Sweet thought! And if he has drawn thee, dost thou know what is the delightful inference? Let me repeat one text, and may that comfort thee: "The Lord hath appeared of old unto me, saying, I have loved thee with an everlasting love: therefore with lovingkindness have I drawn thee." Yes, my poor weeping brother, inasmuch as thou art now coming to Christ, God has drawn thee; and inasmuch as he has drawn thee, it is a proof that he has loved thee from before the foundation of the world. Let thy heart leap within thee, thou art one of his. Thy name was written on the Saviour's hands when they were nailed to the accursed tree. Thy name glitters on the breast-plate of the great High Priest to-day; ay, and it was there before the day-star knew its place, or planets ran their round. Rejoice in the Lord ye that have come to Christ, and shout for joy all ye that have been drawn of the Father. For this is your proof, your solemn testimony, that you from among men have been chosen in eternal election, and that you shall be kept by the power of God, through faith, unto the salvation which is ready to be revealed.

HUMAN DEPRAVITY AND DIVINE MERCY

FEBRUARY 19, 1865, AT THE METROPOLITAN TABERNACLE, NEWINGTON

"And the Lord smelled a sweet savor. And the Lord said in His heart, I will not again curse the ground anymore for man's sake; for the imagination of man's heart is evil from his youth; neither will I again destroy anymore every thing living as I have done."
Genesis 8:21

PETER tells us that Noah's ark and Baptism are figures of salvation. He puts the two together as pictures of the way by which we are saved. Noah was not saved by the world's being gradually reformed and restored to its primitive innocence, but a sentence of condemnation was pronounced and death, burial and resurrection ensued. Noah must go into the ark and become dead to the world. The floods must descend from Heaven and rise upward from their secret fountains beneath the earth. The ark must be submerged with many waters—here was burial. And then after a time Noah and his family must come out into a totally new world of resurrection life.

It is the same in the figure of Baptism. The person baptized, if he is already dead with Christ, is buried—not purified and improved—but buried beneath the waves. And when he rises he professes that he enjoys newness of life. Baptism is setting forth just what Noah's ark set forth—that salvation is by death and burial. You must be dead to the world. The flesh must be dead with

Christ, buried with Christ—not improved, not made better, but utterly put aside as unimprovable, as worthless, dead—a thing to be buried and to be forgotten.

And we must come forth in resurrection life, feeling that above us there is a new Heaven and beneath us a new earth where righteousness dwells, seeing that we are new creatures in Christ Jesus. It would be very instructive to dwell upon each point of the resemblance between Noah's deliverance and the salvation of every elect soul. Noah enters into the ark—there is a time when we distinctly enter into Christ and become one with Him. Noah was shut in the ark so that he could never come out again till God should open the door. There is a time when every child of God is shut in—when faith and full assurance give him an evidence that he is indissolubly one with Christ Jesus. He is grasped in Christ's hand so that none can pluck him out. He is hidden in Christ's loins so that none can separate him from the love of God.

Then comes the flood—there is a season in the Christian's experience when he discovers his own depravity. He is saved. He is in the ark. He is, however, still a sinner, still the subject of inbred lusts. Suddenly all these corruptions break up! They beat upon his ark, they assail his faith, they endeavor, if possible, to drown his soul in sin. But he is not destroyed by them—for, by the grace of God, he is where other men are not—he is where he cannot be drowned by sin. He is in Christ Jesus! He mounts as the floods deepen. The more he feels the depth of his depravity, the more he admires the fullness of the atoning sacrifice! The more terrible the temptation, the more joyous is his consolation in Christ Jesus.

And so he rises in holy communion towards his God. Then comes the wind—typical of the breath of the sacred Spirit by which the floods of corruption are calmed and peace reigns within and the soul sings, "Therefore being justified by faith we have peace with God through our Lord Jesus Christ." Then the tops of the mountains appear—sanctification takes place upon a part of the man. There are some bright graces which glisten out of the general flood of corruption. There are some points of his new-born nature which delight him with their beauty. His ark has grounded and settled—he no longer floats, so to speak, tossed about with a struggling faith and contending unbelief—he feels that as Christ Jesus is forever seated firmly at the right hand of God, so he, in Christ Jesus, has entered into rest.

The ark grounded on the top of Ararat—so does the Believer's experience come to a settled condition. He is no more moved about with fears and questions, but rejoices in hope of the Glory of God. He sends forth his thoughts in search after evidence of his complete salvation, and probably he sends out some of his own ignorant carnal expectations, just as Noah sent out the raven. These ignorant imaginations of what the work of the Spirit is go forth and they never return earnest prayers go to and fro. By and by they come back with a token for good, some choice mercy from the hand of God—an olive branch of assured peace—and the Believer surely knows not only that he is in Christ, not only that he is grounded in Christ, but that all the waters are calmed, all sin is gone, all danger removed, all death destroyed!

Then occurs a period where God opens the door. Christ had been as a sort of prison to the Christian up till then. The Cross had been a burden. He did not rejoice in liberty. But God the Father now comes with the blessed Spirit and opens the door and the Believer is fully at liberty in the new world. The saved soul's first act is, like Noah, to build an altar unto God and, as a priest, to offer sacrifice, which, as it rises to Heaven, is accepted because it is a memorial of Christ. The Lord smells a sweat savor and though the believing man is still full of sin and from his youth up has an evil imagination, yet he hears the Covenant voice which says, "I will no more curse, I will no more destroy."

He hears the Covenant promise which confirms forever the faithfulness of God and he rejoices to inherit, like Noah, a new world where righteousness dwells. I do not lay any stress upon these interpretations, but I know the Apostle says concerning Hagar and Sarah, "which things are an allegory." I believe that the book of Genesis is a book of dispensational Truth and if it were rightly read, not by the eye of curiosity, but by the heart of the student who has been made wise to see the deep things of God, very much of Divine and holy teaching would be discoverable in it.

But now I come to the text itself. We have here, first, a very sad and painful fact, "the imagination of man's heart is evil from his youth." We have, secondly, God's most extraordinary reasoning, "I will not again curse the ground for man's sake, for the imagination of man's heart is evil." Then, thirdly, we have some inferences less extraordinary but practical to ourselves from the text.

To begin, then, with the text, we have here A MOST PAINFUL FACT that man's nature is incurable—"the imagination of man's heart is evil from his youth." You will remember, before the flood, in the fifth verse of the sixth chapter it is written, "God saw that the wickedness of man was great in the earth, and that every imagination of the thoughts of his heart was only continually evil." After the flood it is just the same. The description in the sixth chapter belonged to all the antediluvian[17] race.

You might have hoped that after so terrible a judgment, when only a few—a picked and peculiar few—that is, eight, were saved by water, that then, as man began anew with a better stock, the old branches that were sere and rotten being cut away—that now the nature of man would be improved. It is not one whit so. The same God who, looking at man, declared that his imagination was evil before the flood, pronounces the very same verdict upon them afterwards. Oh God! How hopeless is human nature! How impossible is it that the carnal mind should be reconciled to God! How needful is it that You should give us new hearts and right spirits, seeing that the old nature is so evil that even the floods of Your judgments cannot cure it of its evil imaginations!

I would have you studiously notice the words used in both these passages—the antediluvian and the postdiluvian verdict of God. Look at the fifth verse of the sixth chapter—God saw not only outward sin that was great and multiplied and cried to Him for vengeance—He saw sin in the sons of men, the descendants of Cain. Worse still, He saw treachery and departure from God in the sons of the chosen ones, the sons of Seth had gone astray, also. The sons of God saw the daughters of men, that they were fair and the two races became mingled so as to produce monsters of iniquity. But, worse than that, He saw that the thoughts of men's hearts were evil—man could not think without being evil.

No, more! The substratum which underlies actual thought—unformed,

---

[17] Those who lived before the biblical flood

unfashioned thought—the eggs, the embryos of thought, called here the imagination of the thought, the first conception, the infant motions of the soul—all these God found to be evil. But observe, He says they were, "only evil." Not one trace of good! No gold amidst the dross, no light amidst the darkness—they were "only evil." And then He adds that word "continually." What? Never any repentance? Never any yearning towards the right? No pure drops of holiness now and then? No, never!

"Every imagination"—notice that word. The whole verse is most clear, a broom that sweeps man clean of all boasted good. "Every imagination"—when he was at his best, when he stood at God's altar, when he tried to be right—even then his thoughts had evil in them! Dr. Dick[18] says, "All man's thoughts, all his desires, all his purposes are evil, expressly or by implication because the subject of them is avowedly sinful, or because they do not proceed from a holy principle and are not directed to a proper end. It is not occasionally that the human soul is thus under the influence of depravity. This is its habit and state. It seems impossible to construct a sentence which should more distinctly express its total corruption than this."

Look at this other passage which is our text. You will see it gives a different phase of the same evil, but it does not abate one jot or tittle of it. It is still, "the imagination of man's heart." It is still the inward character, the core, the pith, the marrow of mankind which God is dealing with. It is not the stream which comes from man that is foul but the fountain of man—the innermost source of the fountain! The imagination of his heart is evil—and we are told here what we are not told in the other text—that his thoughts are evil from his youth, that is to say, from his earliest childhood.

And it would not be evil from his childhood in every case if there were not certain seeds of evil sown before that and therefore we can go further and in the words of Holy Scripture we can confess with sorrowful truthfulness—"Behold I was shapen in iniquity, and in sin did my mother conceive me." From the very earliest imaginable period in which human nature exists it is a defiled, tainted thing and only worthy of God's utter abhorrence! And were it not that

---

[18] Dr. John Dick, a nineteenth-century Scottish minister and theological writer

He smells a sweet savor in the sacrifice of Christ, He would say, as He did say in the sixth chapter, "He repented that He had made man on the earth and it grieved Him at His heart. And the Lord said, I will destroy man whom I have created from the face of the earth."

I have thus brought out this painful fact distinctly, I hope, before you. It is true both before and after the flood. If you want any proof of its being true now turn to the scores of passages of Scripture which all prove it. I think, however, if our time were limited, as it is this morning, I should prefer to mention the third chapter of Paul's Epistle to the Romans. It is the most sweeping description of the universality of human depravity that could possibly have been penned. I will read from the ninth to the nineteenth verse – "What then? Are we better than they? No, in no wise: for we have before proved both Jews and Gentiles, that they are all under sin as it is written, There is none righteous, no, not one: there is none that understands, there is none that seeks after God.

"They are all gone out of the way, they are together become unprofitable. There is none that does good, no, not one. Their throat is an open sepulcher. With their tongues have they used deceit. The poison of asps is under their lips: whose mouth is full of cursing and bitterness: their feet are swift to shed blood: destruction and misery are in their ways: and the way of peace they have not known: there is no fear of God before their eyes. Now we know that what things so ever the Law says, it says to them who are under the Law: that every mouth may be stopped and all the world may become guilty before God."

Jonathan Edwards[19] says upon this passage, "If the words which the Apostle uses here (Rom. 3:10-19) do not most fully and determinately signify a universality, no words ever used in the Bible, or elsewhere, are sufficient to do it. I might challenge any man to produce any one paragraph in the Scripture, from the beginning to the end, where there is such a repetition and accumulation of terms so strongly and emphatically and carefully formulated

---

[19] Eighteenth-century American Congregationalist minister, philosopher, revivalist preacher, and theologian

to express the most perfect and absolutely universality, or any place to be compared to it. What instance is there in the Scripture, or indeed any other writing when the meaning is only the much greater part?

"Where this meaning is signified in such a manner by repeating such expressions, 'They are all,' 'they are all together,' 'every one,' 'all the world' joined to multiplied negative terms, to show the universality to be without exception? Saying, 'There is no flesh,' 'there is none, there is none, there is none, there is none,' four times over. Besides the addition of, 'no, not one,' 'no, not one,' once and again… So that if this matter [universal depravity] is not here set forth plainly, expressly and fully, it must be because no words can do it. And it is not in the power of language, or any manner of terms and phrases, however contrived and heaped one upon another, determinately to let us remember the confessions of God's people."

You never heard a saint on his knees yet tell the Lord that he had a good nature, that he did not need renewing. Saints, as they grow in Divine Grace, are made to feel more and more acutely the evil of their old nature. You will find that those who are most like Christ have the deepest knowledge of their own depravity and are most humble while they confess their sinfulness. Those men who know not their own hearts may be able to boast, but that is simple ignorance, for if you will take down the biographies of any persons esteemed among us for holiness and for knowledge in the things of God, you will find them frequently crying out under a sense of inward carnality and sin.

If I may return to Scripture I cannot help quoting David, "Behold I was born in sin and shapen in iniquity." It is a most villainous thing that some persons try to slander David's mother and to suppose that there was something irregular about his birth which made him speak as he has done! Whereas there cannot be the slightest imputation upon that admirable woman. David himself speaks of her with intense respect and says, "Save the son of Your handmaid" as though he felt it no discredit to be the son of such a woman.

She was, doubtless, one of the excellent of the earth and yet, excellent as she was, it could not but be otherwise that in sin her son was conceived. Let us not at all attempt to escape from the force of what David says. He is using no exaggerated expressions. There is no indication of hyperbole throughout the whole Psalm. He is a broken-hearted man on his knees. He is confessing his own sin with Bathsheba and is not likely either to bring any accusation against his own mother or to use exaggerated terms! Beloved it is so. We, all of us, the best of us still have to bear about with us the marks of the unclean thing from which we sprang.

Take Paul again—was there ever a man who knew more of what sanctity of nature means, or who was brought nearer to the image of Christ? Yet he cries out, "Oh, wretched man that I am! Who shall deliver me from the body of this death." He finds no joy until he can say, "I thank God through Jesus Christ our Lord." Still I think we have another proof, namely, our own observation. We have lived long enough to observe with our own eyes and by our reading that sin is the universal disease of manhood. Is it not certain, according to observation, that man's heart is evil? They used to tell pretty tales about the charming innocence of men dwelling in the wooded bowers of primeval forests, untainted by the vices of civilization, unpolluted by the inventions of commerce and art.

The woods of America were searched and no such sweet babes of grace were discovered. The ferocity and cruelty of the Indians justify my saying that they were hateful and hating one another. The blood-red tomahawk might have been emblazoned as the Redman's coat of arms and his eyes glaring with revenge might be taken as the true index of his character. Travelers have penetrated of late into the center of Africa where we may expect to see nature in its primitive excellence and what is the report that is brought back to us? Why, it is nature in its primitive devilry, that is all!

Let such abominable tyrants as Messrs. Grant and Speke[20] describe to us indicate to us what man is when he is left in his primeval state, untainted by civilization—he is simply a greater devil—he is naked and he is not ashamed! In this, only, is he like our unfallen parents. Again, try the mildest races. There is the mild Hindu. You look into his gentle face and you cannot suppose

---

[20] James Augustus Grant (English) and John Hanning Speke (Scottish), nineteenth century explorers to Africa and elsewhere

him capable of cruelty. Trust well that mild Hindu, subdued by British arms so speedily and so cheerfully bowing his neck to the yoke. But you may as well trust the sleek and cunning tiger from his jungle—let the story of the Sepoy rebellion of a few years ago show us the gentleness of the mild Hindu!

Live among the mild Hindu and if you dare read the first chapter of Paul's Epistle to the Romans, remember that it is a decent account of what, in ordinary life, is practiced among the Hindu but which could not be more clearly described, because the mouth of modesty would refuse to speak it and the ears of modesty would tingle at the hearing of it. The life of the most respectable Hindu is tainted with vices too vile to mention. "Yes, but still," says one, "we must look at children, because sin may enter into us through education—let us look at children."

Very well, I am willing to look at children and I am unwilling that anybody should say a word that is harsh or severe against children's nature. But I will say that any man who declares children to be born perfect never was a father! If he would only watch his own child—not merely when that child has its toys around it and is pleased and happy, but when its little temper is ruffled—he would soon perceive evil nestling there. Your child without evil? You without eyes, you mean!! If you will only look and listen you will soon discover, if no other fault, this one, "they go astray from the womb, speaking lies."

One of the earliest vices of children which needs to be corrected with most constant and wise rigor is the tendency towards falsehood. It is all very pretty for people to talk about the innocence of children. But I would like them to have to keep one of the nursery schools like those at Manchester, where the children are left while the mothers are at work in the mills! They would soon discover in their pulling one another's hair, and scratching at one another's eyes, and such like pretty little diversions and innocent freaks, that they are not altogether the sweet babes of innocence they are supposed to be!

"Well," says one, "still, human nature may have some spiritual good in it. Look at the men who make illustrious the page of history—look at Socrates, for instance—religion did nothing for Socrates, but yet what a fine character he was." Who told you that? I will venture to say that the philosopher's character would not bear description in a decent assembly. We know from undoubted authority that the purest philosophers at times indulged in bestiality and filth. Solon[21] and Socrates were no exceptions. When Infidels hold up these sages as being such patterns of what human nature might become, they have history dead against them. "The whole head is sick and the whole heart faint. There is no soundness in it."

And this, be it remembered, is without an exception in the long history of humanity, say six thousand years. There is not one that has escaped contamination, not one who has come into the world clean, not one who dares go before his Maker's bar and say, "Great God, I have never sinned, but have kept Your Law from my youth up."

II. Now I want you to notice, in the second place, a most extraordinary thing—when I noticed it yesterday I was surprised and overwhelmed with grateful admiration—that is, GOD'S EXTRAORDINARY REASONING. Good reasoning, but most extraordinary. He says, "I will not again curse the ground anymore for man's sake; for the imagination of man's heart is evil from his youth." Strange logic! In the sixth chapter He said man was evil and therefore He destroyed him. In the eighth chapter He says man is evil from his youth and therefore He will not destroy him!

Strange reasoning! Strange reasoning!—to be accounted for by the little circumstance in the beginning of the verse, "the Lord smelled a sweet savor." There was a sacrifice there—that makes all the difference! When God looks on sin apart from sacrifice, Justice says, "Destroy! Destroy! Smite! Curse! Destroy!" But when there is a sacrifice, God looks on sin with eyes of mercy and though Justice says, "Destroy," He says, "No, I have punished My dear Son. I have punished Him and will spare the sinner." Mercy looks to see if she cannot find some loophole, something that she can make into an excuse why she may spare mankind.

Is then, natural depravity, an excuse for sin? Does God use it as such? No, Beloved—that our heart is vile is rather an aggravation of the vileness of our action than any excuse for it. Yet there is this one thing—we are born sinners and God sees there, I will say, a sort of loophole. Rightly, upon the terms of

---

[21] Athenian lawmaker, poet, and statesman

Justice, there is no conceivable reason why He should have mercy upon us. But Divine Grace makes and invents a reason. O may I be helped, while I try to show you where I think the ground of mercy lies! Devils fell separately—we have every reason to believe that every fallen angel sinned on his own account and fell. And it is very likely that on this account there was no possibility, as we know of, of their restoration—every separate fallen spirit was given up forever to chains and darkness and flames of fire.

But men! Men did not fall separately and individually. Our case is a somewhat different one from that of fallen angels. We, all of us, fell without our own consent, without having, in fact, any finger in it, actually. We fell federally in our covenant head—it is in consequence of our falling in Adam that our heart becomes evil from our youth. Now it looks to me as if God's mercy caught that. He seemed to say, "These My creatures have, according to my arrangement of federation, fallen representatively. Then I can save them representatively. They perished in one, Adam. I will save them in Another. They fell not by their own overt act, though, indeed, their own overt acts have added to this and deserve My wrath, but their first fall was not through themselves. They are sinful from their very infancy. Therefore He says, "I will deliver them by Another as they fell by another."

I do not know whether I can make it clear. I do not think that this was any reason before the bar of Justice why God should save us, for I believe that He might justly have condemned the whole race of Adam on account of Adam's sin and their own guilt. But I do think that this was a blessed loophole through which His mercy could, as it were, come fairly to the sons of men. "There," He says, "I made them not distinct individuals but a race. They fell as a race, they shall rise as an elect race—'As in Adam all die, even so in Christ shall all be made alive.' 'As by the transgression of one many were made sinners, so by the righteousness of one shall many be made righteous.' "

I think you see the drift of it, then. Man's being sinful, is in the logic of justice, a reason for punishment. Man's being sinful from his youth by inheritance from his federal head becomes, through mercy, a reason why Sovereign Grace should light upon men while fallen angels are left to perish forever. Oh, I bless God that I did not fall first of all myself. I do bless the day, now, that I fell in Adam, for it may be if I had never fallen in Adam I should have fallen in myself and then I must have been, like fallen angels, shut out forever from the Presence of God and in the flames of Hell! One of the old Divines used to say of Adam's sin, "Beata culpa" – "Happy fault!"

I dare not say that, but in one sense I will say, blessed Fall that renders it possible for me to rise! Blessed way of ruin which renders it possible for the blessed way of salvation to be brought about – salvation by Substitution! Salvation by Sacrifice! Salvation by a new Covenant Head, who for us is offered up that God may smell a sweet savor and may deliver us! I hope nobody will misconstrue what I have said and make out that I teach that human depravity is an excuse for sin – God forbid! It is only in the eyes of Divine Grace that it becomes the door of mercy.

You know if your child has offended you, you do not want to chastise him and yet you feel he deserves it. How you do try, if you are a loving parent, to find some reason why you may let him go. There is no reason – you know that. If you deal with him in terms of justice, there is no reason why having sinned he should not smart for it. But you keep casting about for an excuse – perhaps it is his mother's birthday and you let him off for that. Or else there was some little circumstance which softened the offense for which you may have him excused.

I do not know whether the story is true, but it is said of Queen Victoria when she was just queen – just a girl – she was asked to sign a death warrant for a person who, by court martial, had been condemned to die. It is told that she said to the Duke, "Cannot you find any reason why this man should be pardoned?" The Duke said, "No, it was a very great offense, he ought to be punished." "But was he a good soldier?" The Duke said he was a shamefully bad soldier, had always been noted as a bad soldier. "Well, cannot you invent for me any reason?" "Well," he said, "I have every reason to believe from testimony that he was a good man as a man, although a bad soldier." "That will do," she said, and she wrote across the warrant, "pardoned" – not because the man deserved it – but because she wanted a reason for having mercy.

So my God seems to look upon man and after He has looked him through and through and cannot see anything, at last He says, "He is evil from his youth," and he writes "Pardoned." He smells the sweet savor first and His heart is turned towards the poor rebel. Then He turns to him with mercy and blesses him.

III. But now, thirdly, by your leave and patience, I shall have to lead you to a few inferences from the doctrine of the depravity of man. If the heart is so evil, then it is impossible for us to enter Heaven as we are. We cannot suppose that those holy gates shall enclose those whose imaginations and thoughts are evil, and evil continually. No, if that is the place into which nothing shall enter that defiles, then no man being what he was in his first birth can ever stand there!

Another step. Then it is quite clear that if I am to enter Heaven no outward reform will ever do, for if I wash my face, that does not change my heart. And if I give up all my outward sins and become outwardly what I ought to be, yet still, if it is true that my heart is the villainous thing which Scripture says it is, then my outward reformation cannot touch that and I am still shut out of Heaven. If inside that cup and platter there is all this filthiness, I may cleanse the outside, but I have not touched that which will shut me out of Heaven.

I go, then, a little farther and I observe that I must have a new nature—not new practice only, but a new nature—not new thoughts or new words, but a new nature so as to become a totally new man. And when I draw the inference, I have Scripture to back me at once, for what does Jesus say to Nicodemus? "You must be born again." But what is to be born again? To my first birth, I owe all I am by nature. I must get a second birth to which I am to owe all I am as I enter Heaven. Multitudes of persons have been saying, "What is Regeneration?" Here they have been writing hundreds of pamphlets and no two of them agree upon what Regeneration is except that they say that a man may be regenerated and not converted.

Here is an extraordinary thing! An unconverted man who is regenerated? One who is an enemy to God and yet he has in himself a new nature? He has been born again and yet is not converted to God? What? A Regeneration that does not convert? A Regeneration, in fact, that leaves men just where they were before? But to every babe in Christ the word, "regenerate," is as plain as possible—he wants no definition, no description. "To be born again? Why," he says, "I comprehend that it is to be made over again, a new creature in Christ Jesus! My first birth makes me a creature—my second birth makes me a new creature and I become what I never was before."

I must remember that what is needed in me is not to bring out and develop what is good in me, for, according to God's Word in the sixth of Genesis, there is nothing good, it is only evil. Grace does not enter to educate the germs of holiness within me, for there is no germ of good in man at all—he is "evil continually"— and every imagination is "only evil." I must, then, die to sin! My old nature must be slain, it cannot be mended! It is too bad, too rotten to be patched up—that must die. By the death of Jesus it must be destroyed. It must be buried with Christ and I must rise in resurrection life to conformity with my Lord Jesus.

Well then, advancing one step further—It is clear if I must be this before I can enter Heaven that I cannot give myself a new nature. A crab tree cannot transform itself into an apple tree! If I am a wolf I cannot make myself a sheep. Water can rise to its own proper level, but it cannot go beyond it without pressure. I must have, then, something worked in me more than I can work in myself and this, indeed, is good Scriptural doctrine. "That which is born of the flesh"—what is it? When the flesh has done its very best what is it?—"That which is born of the flesh is flesh"—it is filthy to begin with and filth comes of it—only "that which is born of the Spirit is spirit: marvel not that I said unto you you must be born again."

My soul must come under the hand of the Spirit. Just as a piece of clay is on the potter's wheel and is made to revolve and is touched by the fingers of the potter and molded into what he wishes it to be, so must I lie passively in the hands of the Spirit of God and He must work in me to will and to do of His own good pleasure. And then I shall begin to work out my own salvation with fear and trembling, but never, never till then. I must have more than nature can give me, more than my mother gave me, more than my father gave me, more than flesh and blood can produce under the most favorable circumstances. I must have the Spirit of God from Heaven.

Then comes this inquiry, "Have I received it? What is the best evidence of it?" The best evidence of it is this—Am I resting upon Christ Jesus, alone, for salvation? You generally find on potters' vessels that there is a certain mark so that you can know who made them. I want to know whether I am a vessel fit for the Master's use, molded by His hands and fashioned by His Spirit. Now, every single vessel that comes out of God's hands has a Cross on it. Have you the Cross on you? Are you resting upon Christ's bloody Atonement made on Calvary? Is He to your soul your one rock of refuge—your one only hope? Can you say this morning—

"Nothing in my hands I bring,
Simply to Your Cross I cling—
Naked, come to You for dress;
Helpless, look to You for Grace.
Black, I to the fountain fly,
Wash me, Savior, or I die!"?

Then, my Brothers and Sisters, you have a new heart and a right spirit! You are a new creature in Christ Jesus, for simple faith in Christ is what the old Adam never could attain! A simple faith in Jesus is the great, sure mark of a work of the Holy Spirit in your soul by which you are made to be a partaker of the inheritance of the saints in light. "Whoever believes that Jesus is the Christ is born of God." Do you believe that Jesus is the Christ? Do you take Him to be God's Anointed to you? Do you trust yourself to Him to plead for you, to work for you, to fulfill the Law for you, to offer Atonement for you?

If so, if Jesus is the Christ to you—you are born of God. The Spirit which is in you now will drive out the old nature, slay it utterly, cut it up root and branch and you shall one day bear the image of the heavenly, even as you have till now borne the image of the earthly. May God bless these words of mine to your souls' good.

"Eternal Spirit, we confess
And sing the wonders of Your Grace!
Your power conveys our blessings down
From God the Father and the Son.
Enlightened by Your heavenly ray,
Our shades and darkness turn to day.
Your inward teachings make us know

FROM THE PRINCE'S PULPIT

Our danger and our refuge, too.
Your power and glory works within,
And breaks the chains of reigning sin,
Does our imperious lusts subdue,
And forms our wretched hearts anew.
The troubled conscience knows Your voice,
Your cheering Words awake our joys;
Your Words allay the stormy wind,
And calm the surges of the mind."

II

Unconditional Election

UNCONDITIONAL ELECTION

SEPTEMBER 2, 1855, AT NEW PARK STREET CHAPEL, SOUTHWARK

"because God has from the beginning chosen you to salvation through sanctification of the Spirit and belief of the truth: Whereunto He called you by our Gospel, to the obtaining of the glory of our Lord Jesus Christ."
2 Thessalonians 2:13, 14

IF there were no other text in the Sacred Word except this one I think we should all be bound to receive and acknowledge the truthfulness of the great and glorious doctrine of God's ancient choice of His family. But there seems to be an inveterate prejudice in the human mind against this doctrine—and although most other doctrines will be received by professing Christians, some with caution, others with pleasure—this one seems to be most frequently disregarded and discarded. In many of our pulpits it would be reckoned a high sin and treason to preach a sermon upon election because they could not make it what they call a "practical" discourse.

I believe they have erred from the truth. Whatever God has revealed He has revealed for a purpose. There is nothing in Scripture which may not, under the influence of God's Spirit, be turned into a practical discourse—"for all Scripture is given by inspiration of God and is profitable" for some purpose of spiritual usefulness. It is true, it may not be turned into a free will discourse—that we know right well—but it can be turned into a practical free grace discourse. And free grace practice is the best practice when the true doctrines of God's immutable love are brought to bear upon the hearts of saints and sinners. Now, I trust this morning some of you who are startled at the very sound of this word will say, "I will give it a fair hearing. I will lay aside my prejudices, I will just hear what this man has to say."

Do not shut your ears and say at once, "It is high doctrine." Who has authorized you to call it high or low? Why should you oppose yourself to God's doctrine? Remember what became of the children who found fault with God's Prophet and exclaimed, "Go up, you bald-head; go up, you bald-head." Say nothing against God's doctrines, lest haply some evil beast should come out of the forest and devour you, also. There are other woes beside the open judgment of Heaven—take heed that these fall not on your head. Lay aside your prejudices—listen calmly, listen dispassionately—hear what Scripture says.

And when you receive the truth, if God should be pleased to reveal and manifest it to your souls, do not be ashamed to confess it. To confess you were wrong yesterday is only to acknowledge that you are a little wiser today. Instead of being a reflection on yourself, it is an honor to your judgment and shows that you are improving in the knowledge of the Truth of God. Do not be ashamed to learn and to cast aside your old doctrines and views. But take up that which you may more plainly see to be in the Word of God. And if you do not see it to be here in the Bible—whatever I may say, or whatever authorities I may plead—I beseech you, as you love your souls, reject it. And if from this pulpit you ever hear things contrary to this Sacred Word, remember that the Bible must be first and God's minister must lie underneath it.

We must not stand on the Bible to preach—we must preach with the Bible above our heads. After all we have preached, we are well aware that the mountain of truth is higher than our eyes can discern—clouds and darkness are round about its summit and we cannot discern its topmost pinnacle. Yet we will try to preach it as well as we can. But since we are mortal and liable to err, exercise your judgment—"Try the spirits, whether they are of God"—and if on mature reflection on your bended knees you are led to disregard election—a thing which I consider to be utterly impossible—then forsake it. Do not hear it preached, but believe and confess whatever you see to be God's Word. I can say no more than that by way of introduction.

Now, first. I shall speak a little concerning the truthfulness of this doctrine—"God has from the beginning chosen you to salvation." Secondly, I shall try to prove that this election is absolute—"He has from the beginning chosen you to salvation," not for sanctification, but "through sanctification of the Spirit and belief of the truth." Thirdly, this election is eternal because the text says, "God has from the beginning chosen you." Fourthly, it is personal—"He has chosen you."

Then we will look at the effects of the doctrine—see what it does. And lastly, as God may enable us, we will try and look at its tendencies and see whether it is indeed a terrible and licentious doctrine. We will take the flower and like true bees, see whether there is any honey whatever in it—whether any good can come of it—or whether it is an unmixed, undiluted evil.

First, I must try and prove that the doctrine is TRUE. And let me begin with an argumentum ad hominen—I will speak to you according to your different positions and stations. There are some of you who belong to the Church of England and I am happy to see so many of you here. Though now and then I certainly say some very hard things about Church and State, yet I love the old Church, for she has in her communion many godly ministers and eminent saints. Now I know you are great Believers in what the Articles declare to be sound doctrine. I will give you a specimen of what they utter concerning election, so that if you believe them, you cannot avoid receiving election. I will read a portion of the 17th Article[22] upon Predestination and Election:

"Predestination to life is the everlasting purpose of God, whereby (before the foundations of the world were laid) He has continually decreed by His counsel secret to us, to deliver from curse and damnation those whom He has chosen in Christ out of mankind and to bring them by Christ to everlasting salvation, as vessels made to honor. Wherefore they which are endued with so excellent a benefit of God are called according to God's purpose by His Spirit working in due season: they through grace obey the calling: they are justified freely: they are made sons of God by adoption: they are made like the image of His only-begotten Son Jesus Christ: they walk religiously in good works

---

[22] From "The 39 Articles" of the Church of England (1571)

and at length, by God's mercy, they attain to everlasting felicity."

Now, I think any Churchman, if he is a sincere and honest believer in Mother Church, must be a thorough believer in election. True, if he turns to certain other portions of the Prayer Book, he will find things contrary to the doctrines of free grace and altogether apart from Scriptural teaching. But if he looks at the Articles, he must see that God has chosen His people unto eternal life. I am not so desperately enamored, however, of that book as you may be—and I have only used this Article to show you that if you belong to the Establishment of England you should at least offer no objection to this doctrine of predestination.

Another human authority whereby I would confirm the doctrine of election is the old Waldensian Creed. If you read the creed of the old Waldenses[23]—emanating from them in the midst of the burning heat of persecution—you will see that these renowned professors and confessors of the Christian faith did most firmly receive and embrace this doctrine as being a portion of the Truth of God. I have copied from an old book one of the Articles of their faith: "That God saves from corruption and damnation those whom He has chosen from the foundations of the world, not for any disposition, faith, or holiness that before saw in them, but of His mere mercy in Christ Jesus His Son, passing by all the rest according to the irreprehensible reason of His own free will and justice."

It is no novelty, then, that I am preaching no new doctrine. I love to proclaim these strong old doctrines which are called by nickname Calvinism but which are surely and verily the revealed Truth of God as it is in Christ Jesus. By this truth I make a pilgrimage into the past and as I go I see father after father, confessor after confessor, martyr after martyr, standing up to shake hands with me. Were I a Pelagian,[24] or a believer in the doctrine of free will, I should have to walk for centuries all alone. Here and there a heretic of no very honorable character might rise up and call me Brother. But taking these

---

[23] A twelfth-century ascetic movement within Christianity in France

[24] The belief that the fall of Adam did not taint man and that humans are still able, by their own free will, to choose good or evil without any divine intervention or assistance

things to be the standard of my faith, I see the land of the ancients peopled with my Brothers and Sisters—I behold multitudes who confess the same as I do and acknowledge that this is the religion of God's own Church.

I also give you an extract from the old Baptist Confession. We are Baptists in this congregation—the greater part of us at any rate—and we like to see what our own forefathers wrote. Some two hundred years ago the Baptists assembled together and published their articles of faith to put an end to certain reports against their orthodoxy which had gone forth to the world. I turn to this old book—which I have just published—Baptist Confession of Faith—and I find the following as the 3rd Article: "By the decree of God for the manifestation of His glory some men and angels are predestinated, or foreordained to eternal life through Jesus Christ to the praise of His glorious grace. Others being left to act in their sin to their just condemnation to the praise of His glorious justice. These angels and men thus predestinated and foreordained, are particularly and unchangeably designed and their number so certain and definite that it cannot be either increased or diminished. Those of mankind that are predestinated to life, God, before the foundation of the world was laid, according to His eternal and immutable purpose and the secret counsel and good pleasure of His will, has chosen in Christ unto everlasting glory out of His mere free grace and love, without any other thing in the creature as condition or cause moving Him hereunto."

As for these human authorities, I care not one rush for all three of them. I care not what they say, pro or con, as to this doctrine. I have only used them as a kind of confirmation to your faith, to show you that while I may be railed upon as a heretic and as a hyper-Calvinist,[25] after all I am backed up by antiquity. All the past stands by me. I do not care for the present. Give me the past and I will hope for the future. Let the present rise up in my teeth, I will not care. What though a host of the Churches of London may have forsaken the great cardinal doctrines of God, it matters not. If a handful of us stand alone in an unflinching maintenance of the sovereignty of our God, if we are

---

[25] An extreme branch of Calvinism that denies the requirement of belief in the Gospel for salvation

beset by enemies, yes, and even by our own Brothers and Sisters who ought to be our friends and helpers, it matters not—if we can but count upon the past—the noble army of martyrs, the glorious host of confessors. They are our friends. They are the witnesses of truth and they stand by us. With these for us, we will not say that we stand alone, but we may exclaim, "Lo, God has reserved unto Himself seven thousand that have not bowed the knee unto Baal." But the best of all is—God is with us!

The great Truth of God is always the Bible and the Bible alone. My Hearers, you do not believe in any other book than the Bible, do you? If I could prove this from all the books in Christendom—if I could fetch back the Alexandrian library and prove it there—you would not believe it any more. But you surely will believe what is in God's Word. I have selected a few texts to read to you. I love to give you a whole volley of texts when I am afraid you will distrust a truth so that you may be too astonished to doubt, if you do not in reality believe. Just let me run through a catalogue of passages where the people of God are called elect. Of course if the people are called elect, there must be election. If Jesus Christ and His Apostles were accustomed to call Believers by the title of elect, we must certainly believe that they were so, otherwise the term does not mean anything. Jesus Christ says, "Except that the Lord had shortened those days, no flesh should be saved; but for the elect's sake, whom He has chosen, He has shortened the days."

"False Christs and false prophets shall rise and shall show signs and wonders, to seduce, if it were possible, even the elect." "Then shall He send His angels and shall gather together His elect from the four winds, from the uttermost parts of the earth to the uttermost part of Heaven" (Mark 13:20, 22, 27). "Shall not God avenge His own elect who cry day and night unto Him, though He bear long with them" (Luke 18:7)? Together with many other passages which might be selected, wherein either the word "elect," or "chosen," or "foreordained," or "appointed," is mentioned—or the phrase "My sheep," or some similar designation, showing that Christ's people are distinguished from the rest of mankind.

But you have concordances and I will not trouble you with texts. Throughout the Epistles the saints are constantly called "the elect." In the Colossians we find Paul saying, "Put on therefore, as the elect of God, holy and beloved, bowels of mercies." When he writes to Titus, he calls himself, "Paul, a servant of God and an Apostle of Jesus Christ, according to the faith of God's elect." Peter says, "Elect according to the foreknowledge of God the Father." Then if you turn to John, you will find he is very fond of the word. He says, "The elder to the elect lady." And he speaks of our "elect sister." And we know where it is written, "The church that is at Babylon, elected together with you."

They were not ashamed of the word in those days. They were not afraid to talk about it. Nowadays the word has been dressed up with diversities of meaning and persons have mutilated and marred the doctrine so that they have made it a very doctrine of devils. I do confess that many who call themselves Believers have gone to rank Antinomianism.[26] But not withstanding this, why should I be ashamed of it, if men wrest it? We love God's Truth on the rack as well as when it is walking upright. If there were a martyr whom we loved before he came on the rack we should love him more still when he was stretched there.

When God's Truth is stretched on the rack, we do not call it falsehood. We love not to see it racked but we love it even when racked because we can discern what its proper proportions ought to have been if it had not been racked and tortured by the cruelty and inventions of men. If you will read many of the Epistles of the ancient fathers you will find them always writing to the people of God as the "elect." Indeed the common conversational term used among many of the Churches by the primitive Christians to one another was that of the "elect." They would often use the term to one another showing that it was generally believed that all God's people were manifestly "elect."

But now for the verses that will positively prove the doctrine. Open your Bibles and turn to John 15:16 and there you will see that Jesus Christ has chosen His people, for He says, "You have not chosen Me, but I have chosen you and ordained you, that you should go and bring forth fruit and that your fruit should remain: that whatsoever you shall ask of the Father in My name, He may give it you." Then in the 19th verse, "If you were of the world, the

---

[26] The belief that those saved are not required to follow moral laws; rejects all forms of legalism

world would love his own, but because you are not of the world, but I have chosen you out of the world, therefore the world hates you." Then in the 17th verses, "For I have given unto them the words which You gave Me; and they have received them and have known surely that I came out from You and they have believed that You did send Me. I pray for them: I pray not for the world, but for them which You have given Me for they are Yours."

Turn to Acts 13:48: "And when the Gentiles heard this, they were glad and glorified the Word of the Lord; and as many as were ordained to eternal life believed." They may try to split that passage into hairs if they like—but it says, "ordained to eternal life" in the original as plainly as it possibly can. And we do not care about all the different commentaries thereupon. You scarcely need to be reminded of Romans 8, because I trust you are all well-acquainted with that chapter and understand it by this time. In the 29th and following verses, it says, "For whom He did foreknow, He also did predestinate to be conformed to the image of His Son, that He might be the firstborn among many Brethren. Moreover, whom He did predestinate, them He also called: and whom He called, them He also justified and whom He justified, them He also glorified. What shall we then say to these things? If God is for us, who can be against us? He that spared not His own Son, but delivered Him up for us all, how shall He not with Him also freely give us all things? Who shall lay anything to the charge of God's elect?"

It would also be unnecessary to repeat the whole of the 9th chapter of Romans. As long as that remains in the Bible, no man shall be able to prove Arminianism.[27] So long as that is written there, not the most violent contortions of the passage will ever be able to exterminate the doctrine of election from the Scriptures. Let us read such verses as these—"For the children being not yet born, neither having done any good or evil, that the purpose of God according to election might stand, not of works, but of Him that calls; it was said unto her, The elder shall serve the younger." Then read the 22nd verse, "What if God, willing to show His wrath and to make His

---

[27] The belief that God's sovereignty and man's free will are compatible; the soteriological (study of salvation) rival to Calvinism

power known, endured with much longsuffering the vessels of wrath fitted to destruction? And that He might make known the riches of His glory on the vessels of mercy, which He had afore prepared unto glory?"

Then go on to Romans 11:7 – "What then? Israel has not obtained that which he seeks for; but the election has obtained it and the rest were blinded." In the 6th verse of the same chapter, we read – "Even so then at this present time also there is a remnant according to the election of grace." You, no doubt, all recollect the passage in 1 Corinthians 1:26 - 29: "For you see your calling, Brethren, how that not many wise men after the flesh, not many mighty, not many noble are called: but God has chosen the foolish things of the world to confound the wise; and God has chosen the weak things of the world to confound the things which are mighty; and base things of the world and things which are despised, has God chosen, yes and things which are not, to bring to nothing things which are: that no flesh should glory in His presence."

Again, remember the passage in 1 Thessalonians 5:9 – "God has not appointed us to wrath, but to obtain salvation by our Lord Jesus Christ," and then you have my text, which methinks would be quite enough. But, if you need any more, you can find them at your leisure if we have not quite removed your suspicions as to the doctrine not being true. Methinks, my Friends, that this overwhelming mass of Scripture testimony must stagger those who dare to laugh at this doctrine. What shall we say of those who have so often despised it and denied its Divinity? What shall we say to those who have railed at its justice and dared to defy God and call Him an Almighty tyrant, when they have heard of His having elected so many to eternal life? Can you, O Rejecter, cast it out of the Bible? Can you take the penknife of Jehudi and cut it out of the Word of God?

Would you be like the women at the feet of Solomon and have the child rent in halves that you might have your half? Is it not here in Scripture? And is it not your duty to bow before it and meekly acknowledge what you understand not – to receive it as the Truth even though you could not understand its meaning? I will not attempt to prove the justice of God in having thus elected some and left others. It is not for me to vindicate my Master. He will speak for Himself and He does so—"But, O man, who are you that replies against God? Shall the thing formed say to Him that formed it, Why have you made me thus? Has not the potter power over the clay of the same lump to make one vessel unto honor and another unto dishonor?" Who is he that shall say unto his father, "What have you begotten? ... or unto his mother, "What have you brought forth?" "I am the Lord—I form the light and create darkness. I, the Lord, do all these things. Who are you that replies against God? Tremble and kiss His rod; bow down and submit to His scepter; impugn not His justice and arraign not His acts before your bar, O man!"

But there are some who say, "It is hard for God to choose some and leave others." Now, I will ask you one question. Is there any of you here this morning who wishes to be holy, who wishes to be regenerate, to leave off sin and walk in holiness? "Yes, there is," says someone, "I do." Then God has elected you. But another says, "No. I don't want to be holy. I don't want to give up my lusts and my vices." Why should you grumble, then, that God has not elected you? For if you were elected you would not like it, according to your own confession. If God this morning had chosen you to holiness, you say you would not care for it. Do you not acknowledge that you prefer drunkenness to sobriety, dishonesty to honesty? You love this world's pleasures better than religion—then why should you grumble that God has not chosen you to religion?

If you love religion, He has chosen you to it. If you desire it, He has chosen you to it. If you do not, what right have you to say that God ought to have given you what you do not wish for? Supposing I had in my hand something which you do not value and I said I shall give it to such-and-such a person—you would have no right to grumble that I did not give it to you. You could not be so foolish as to grumble that the other has got what you do not care about. According to your own confession many of you do not want religion—do not want a new heart and a right spirit—do not want the forgiveness of sins. You do not want sanctification. You do not want to be elected to these things—then why should you grumble?

You count these things but as husks and why should you complain of God who has given them to those whom He has chosen? If you believe them to be good and desire them, they are there for you. God gives liberally to all those who desire—but first of all He makes them desire—otherwise they never would. If you love these things, He has elected you to them and you may have them. But if you do not, who are you that you should find fault with God when it is your own desperate will that keeps you from loving these things? Suppose a man in the street should say, "What a shame it is I cannot have a seat in the Chapel to hear what this man has to say." And suppose he says, "I hate the preacher—I can't bear his doctrine—but still it's a shame I have not a seat."

Would you expect a man to say so? No—you would at once say, "That man does not care for it. Why should he trouble himself about other people having what they value and he despises?" You do not like holiness, you do not like righteousness. If God has elected me to these things, has He hurt you by it? "Ah, but," say some, "I thought it meant that God elected some to Heaven and some to Hell." That is a very different matter from the Gospel doctrine. He has elected men to holiness and to righteousness and through that to Heaven. You must not say that He has elected these simply to Heaven and others only to Hell. He has elected you to holiness if you love holiness. If any of you love to be saved by Jesus Christ—Jesus Christ elected you to be saved. If any of you desire to have salvation you are elected to have it—if you desire it sincerely and earnestly. But, if you don't desire it, why on earth should you be so preposterously foolish as to grumble because God gives that, which you do not like, to other people?

II. Thus I have tried to say something with regard to the Truth of the doctrine of election. And now, briefly, let me say that election is absolute, that is, it does not depend upon what we are. The text says, "God has from the beginning chosen us unto salvation." But our opponents say that God chooses people because they are good—that He chooses them on account of sundry works which they have done. Now, we ask in reply to this, what works are those on account of which God elects His people? Are they what we commonly call "works of Law"?—works of obedience which the creature can render? If so, we reply to you—If men cannot be justified by the works of the Law, it seems to us pretty clear that they cannot be elected by the works of the Law. If they cannot be justified by their good deeds, they cannot be saved by them.

Then the decree of election could not have been formed upon good works. "But," say others, "God elected them on the foresight of their faith." Now God gives faith, therefore He could not have elected them on account of faith which He foresaw. There shall be twenty beggars in the street and I determine to give one of them a shilling. Will anyone say that I determined to give that one a shilling—that I elected him to have the shilling—because I foresaw that he would have it? That would be talking nonsense.

In like manner to say that God elected men because He foresaw they would have faith—which is salvation in the germ—would be too absurd for us to listen to for a moment. Faith is the gift of God. Every virtue comes from Him. Therefore it cannot have caused Him to elect men, because it is His gift. Election, we are sure, is absolute and altogether apart from the virtues which the saints have afterwards. What if a saint should be as holy and devout as Paul? What if he should be as bold as Peter, or as loving as John? Still he could claim nothing but what he received from his Maker.

I never knew a saint yet of any denomination who thought that God saved him because He foresaw that he would have these virtues and merits. Now, my Brethren, the best jewels that the saint ever wears, if they are jewels of our own fashioning, are not of the first water. There is something of earth mixed with them. The highest grace we ever possess has something of earthliness about it. We feel this when we are most refined, when we are most sanctified and our language must always be—

"I the chief of sinners am;

Jesus died for me."

Our only hope, our only plea, still hangs on grace as exhibited in the Person of Jesus Christ. And I am sure we must utterly reject and disregard all thought that our graces, which are gifts of our Lord, which are His right hand planting, could have ever caused His love. And we ever must sing—

"What was there in us that could merit esteem

Or give the Creator delight?

It was even so, Father, we ever must sing,

Because it seemed good in Your sight"

"He will have mercy on whom He will have mercy." He saves because He will save. And if you ask me why He saves me, I can only say because He would do it. Is there anything in me that should recommend me to God? No. I lay aside everything. I had nothing to recommend me. When God saved me I was the most abject, lost and ruined of the race. I lay before Him as an infant in my blood. Verily, I had no power to help myself. O how wretched did I feel and know myself to be! It you had something to recommend you to God, I never had. I will be content to be saved by grace, unalloyed, pure grace. I can boast of no merits. If you can do so, still I cannot. I must sing–

"Free grace alone from the first to the last
Has won my affection and held my soul fast."

III. Then, thirdly, this election is ETERNAL. "God has from the beginning chosen you unto eternal life." Can any man tell me when the beginning was? Years ago we thought the beginning of this world was when Adam came upon it. But we have discovered that thousands of years before that God was preparing chaotic matter to make it a fit abode for man, putting races of creatures upon it who might die and leave behind the marks of His handiwork and marvelous skill before He tried His hand on man. But that was not the beginning, for Revelation points us to a period long before this world was fashioned–to the days when the morning stars were begotten–when, like drops of dew, from the fingers of the morning stars and constellations fell trickling from the hand of God. When, by His own lips, He launched forth ponderous orbs. When with His own hand He sent comets, like thunderbolts, wandering through the sky to find one day their proper sphere.

We go back to years gone by, when worlds were made and systems fashioned, but we have not even approached the beginning yet. Until we go to the time when all the universe slept in the mind of God as yet unborn–until we enter the eternity where God the Creator lived alone, everything sleeping within Him, all creation resting in His mighty gigantic thought–we have not guessed the beginning. We may go back, back, back, ages upon ages. We may go back, if we might use such strange words, whole eternities and yet never arrive at the beginning. Our wings might be tired, our imagination would die away. Could it outstrip the lightnings flashing in majesty, power and rapidity, it would soon weary itself before it could get to the beginning.

But God from the beginning chose His people. When the unnavigated ether was yet unfanned by the wing of a single angel, when space was shoreless, or else unborn when universal silence reigned and not a voice or whisper shocked the solemnity of silence. When there was no being and no motion, no time and nothing but God Himself, alone in His eternity—when without the song of an angel, without the attendance of even the cherubim—long before the living creatures were born, or the wheels of the chariot of Jehovah were fashioned—even then, "in the beginning was the Word," and in the beginning God's people were one with the Word and "in the beginning He chose them into eternal life."

Our election, then, is eternal. I will not stop to prove it, I only just run over these thoughts for the benefit of young beginners that they may understand what we mean by eternal, absolute election.

IV. And, next, the election is PERSONAL. Here again, our opponents have tried to overthrow election by telling us that it is an election of nations—and not of people. But here the Apostle says, "God has from the beginning chosen you." It is the most miserable shift on earth to make out that God has not chosen persons but nations, because the very same objection that lies against the choice of persons lies against the choice of a nation. If it were not just to choose a person it would be far more unjust to choose a nation, since nations are but the union of multitudes of persons. To choose a nation seems to be a more gigantic crime—if election is a crime—than to choose one person.

Surely to choose ten thousand would be reckoned to be worse than choosing one—to distinguish a whole nation from the rest of mankind seems to be a greater extravaganza in the acts of Divine Sovereignty than the election of one poor mortal and leaving out another. But what are nations but men? What are whole peoples but combinations of different units? A nation is made up of that individual, and that, and that. And if you tell me that God chose the Jews, I say then, He chose that Jew and that Jew and that Jew. And if you say He chooses Britain, then I say He chooses that British man and that British man and that British man.

So that it is the same thing after all. Election then is personal—it must be so. Everyone who reads this text and others like it, will see that Scripture continually speaks of God's people one by one and speaks of them as having been the special subjects of election—

"Sons we are through God's election,
Who in Jesus Christ believe;
By eternal destination
Sovereign Grace we here receive."

We know it is personal election

The other thought is—for my time flies too swiftly to enable me to dwell at length upon these points—that election produces GOOD RESULTS. "He has from the beginning chosen you unto sanctification of the Spirit and belief of the Truth." How many men mistake the doctrine of election altogether! And how my soul burns and boils at the recollection of the terrible evils that have accrued from the spoiling and the wresting of that glorious portion of God's glorious Truth!

How many are there who have said to themselves, "I am elect," and have sat down in sloth and worse than that! They have said, "I am the elect of God," and with both hands they have done wickedness. They have swiftly run to every unclean thing because they have said, "I am the chosen child of God, irrespective of my works, therefore I may live as I like and do what I like." O, Beloved! Let me solemnly warn everyone of you not to carry the truth too far—or, rather not to turn the truth into error, for we cannot carry it too far. We may overstep the truth—we can make that which was meant to be sweet for our comfort a terrible mixture for our destruction.

I tell you there have been thousands of men who have been ruined by misunderstanding election—who have said, "God has elected me to Heaven and to eternal life"—but they have forgotten that it is written, God has elected them "through sanctification of the Spirit and belief of the Truth." This is God's election—election to sanctification and to faith. God chooses His people to be holy and to be Believers. How many of you here, then, are Believers? How many of my congregation can put their hands upon their hearts and say, "I trust in God that I am sanctified"? Is there one of you who says, "I am elect"?

One of you says, "I trust I am elect"—but I jog your memory about some vicious act that you committed during the last six days. Another of you says, "I am elect"—but I would look you in the face and say, "Elect? You are a most cursed hypocrite and that is all you are." Others would say, "I am elect"—but I would remind them that they neglect the mercy seat and do not pray. Oh, Beloved! Never think you are elect unless you are holy. You may come to Christ as a sinner but you may not come to Christ as an elect person until you can see your holiness. Do not misconstrue what I say—do not say, "I am elect," and yet think you can be living in sin.

That is impossible. The elect of God are holy. They are not pure, they are not perfect, they are not spotless—but conclude himself elect except in his holiness. He may be elect and yet lying in darkness but he has no right to believe it. No one can say it, if there is no evidence of it. The man may live one day but he is dead at present. If you are walking in the fear of God, trying to please Him and to obey His Commandments, doubt not that your name has been written in the Lamb's Book of Life from before the foundation of the world.

And, lest this should be too high for you, note the other mark of election, which is faith—belief of the Truth of God. Whoever believes God's Truth and believes on Jesus Christ is elect. I frequently meet with poor souls who are fretting and worrying themselves about this thought—"What if I should not be elect!" "Oh, Sir," they say, "I know I put my trust in Jesus. I know I believe in His name and trust in His blood. But what if I should not be elect?" Poor dear creature! You do not know much about the Gospel or you would never talk so, for he that believes is elect. Those who are elect, are elect unto sanctification and unto faith. If you have faith you are one of God's elect. You may know it and ought to know it for it is an absolute certainty.

If you, as a sinner, look to Jesus Christ this morning and say—

"Nothing in my hands I bring,

Simply to Your Cross I cling,"

you are elect. I am not afraid of election frightening poor saints or sinners. There are many divines who tell the enquirer, "election has nothing to do with you." That is very bad, because the poor soul is not to be silenced like that. If you could silence him so it might be well—but he will think of it, he can't help it. Say to him then, if you believe on the Lord Jesus Christ you are elect. If you will cast yourself on Jesus, you are elect. I tell you—the chief of sinners—this morning—I tell you in His name—if you will come to God without any works of your own, cast yourself on the blood and righteousness of Jesus Christ—if you will come now and trust in Him, you are elect—you were loved of God from before the foundation of the world, for you could not do that unless God had given you the power and had chosen you to do it.

Now you are safe and secure if you do but come and cast yourself on Jesus Christ and wish to be saved and to be loved by Him. But think not that any man will be saved without faith and without holiness. Do not conceive, my Hearers, that some decree, passed in the dark ages of eternity will save your souls, unless you believe in Christ. Do not sit down and fancy that you are to be saved without faith and holiness. That is a most abominable and accursed heresy and has ruined thousands.

Lay not election as a pillow for you to sleep on, or you may be ruined. God forbid that I should be sewing pillows under armholes that you may rest comfortably in your sins. Sinner! There is nothing in the Bible to palliate your sins. But if you are condemned, O Man! If you are lost, O Woman! You will not find in this Bible one drop to cool your tongue, or one doctrine to palliate your guilt. Your damnation will be entirely your own fault and your sin will richly merit it—because you believe not you are condemned. "You believe not because you are not of My sheep. You will not come to Me that you might have life."

Do not fancy that election excuses sin—do not dream of it—do not rock yourself in sweet complacency in the thought of your irresponsibility. You are responsible. We must give you both things. We must have Divine Sovereignty and we must have man's responsibility. We must have election, but we must ply your hearts—we must send God's Truth at you. We must speak to you and remind you of this, that while it is written, "In Me is your help," yet it is also written, "O Israel, you have destroyed yourself."

V. Now, lastly, what are the true and legitimate tendencies of right conceptions concerning the doctrine of election? First, I will tell you what the doctrine of election will make saints do under the blessing of God. And, secondly what it will do for sinners if God blesses it to them.

First, I think election, to a saint, is one of the most stripping doctrines in all the world—to take away all trust in the flesh or all reliance upon anything except Jesus Christ. How often do we wrap ourselves up in our own righteousness and array ourselves with the false pearls and gems of our own works and doings? We begin to say, "Now I shall be saved, because I have this and that evidence." Instead of that, it is naked faith that saves—that faith and that alone unites to the Lamb irrespective of works, although it is productive of them.

How often do we lean on some work other than that of our own Beloved Jesus and trust in some might, other than that which comes from on High? Now if we would have this might taken from us we must consider election. Pause, my Soul, and consider this. God loved you before you had a being. He loved you when you were dead in trespasses and sins and sent His Son to die for you. He purchased you with His precious blood before you could say His name. Can you then be proud?

I know nothing, nothing again, that is more humbling for us than this doctrine of election. I have sometimes fallen prostrate before it when endeavoring to understand it. I have stretched my wings and, eagle-like, I have soared towards the sun. Steady has been my eye and true my wing for a season. But, when I came near it and the one thought possessed me—"God has from the beginning chosen you unto salvation," I was lost in its lustre. I was staggered with the mighty thought—and from the dizzy elevation down came my soul, prostrate and broken, saying, "Lord, I am nothing, I am less than nothing. Why me? Why me?"

Friends, if you want to be humbled, study election, for it will make you humble under the influence of God's Spirit. He who is proud of his election is not elect—and he who is humbled under a sense of it may believe that he is. He has every reason to believe that he is, for it is one of the most blessed effects of election that it helps us to humble ourselves before God.

Once again—Election in the Christian should make him very fearless and very bold. No man will be so bold as he who believes that he is elect of God. What cares he for man if he is chosen of his Maker? What will he care for the pitiful chirpings of some tiny sparrows when he knows that he is an eagle of a royal race? Will he care when the beggar points at him—when the blood royal of heaven runs in his veins? Will he fear if all the world stand against him? If earth be all in arms abroad, he dwells in perfect peace—for he is in the secret place of the tabernacle of the Most High, in the great pavilion of the Almighty.

"I am God's," he says, "I am distinct from other men. They are of an inferior race. Am I not noble? Am I not one of the aristocrats of Heaven? Is not my name written in God's Book?" Does he care for the world? No—like the lion that cares not for the barking of the dog, he smiles at all his enemies—and when they come too near him, he moves himself and dashes them to pieces. What cares he for them? He walks about them like a colossus—while little men walk under him and understand him not.

His brow is made of iron, his heart is of flint—what does he care for man? No—if one universal hiss came up from the wide world, he would smile at it, for he would say—

"He that has made his refuge God,
Shall find a most secure abode."

I am one of His elect. I am chosen of God and precious—and though the world cast me out, I fear not. Ah, you timeserving professors, some of you will bend like the willows. There are few oaken-Christians nowadays that can stand the storm—and I will tell you the reason. It is because you do not believe yourselves to be elect. The man who knows he is elect will be too proud to sin—he will not humble himself to commit the acts of common people.

The believer in God's Truth will say, "I compromise my principles? I change my doctrines? I lay aside my views? I hide what I believe to be true? No! Since I know I am one of God's elect, in the very teeth of all men I shall speak God's Truth, whatever man may say." Nothing makes a man so truly bold as to feel that he is God's elect. He shall not quiver, he shall not shake—who knows that God has chosen him.

Moreover, election will make us holy. Nothing under the gracious influence of the Holy Spirit can make a Christian more holy than the thought that he is chosen. "Shall I sin," he says, "after God has chosen me? Shall I transgress after such love? Shall I go astray after so much loving kindness and tender mercy? No, my God, since You have chosen me, I will love You. I will live to You—

"Since You, the everlasting God,

My Father are become."

I will give myself to You to be Yours forever, by election and by redemption, casting myself on You and solemnly consecrating myself to Your service.

And now, lastly, to the ungodly. What says election to you? First, you ungodly ones, I will excuse you for a moment. There are many of you who do not like election and I cannot blame you for it, for I have heard those preach election who have sat down and said, "I have not one word to say to the sinner." Now, I say you ought to dislike such preaching as that and I do not blame you for it. But, I say, take courage, take hope, O you Sinner, that there is election!

So far from dispiriting and discouraging you, it is a very hopeful and joyous thing that there is an election. What if I hopelessness and say, "Then how can I be saved, since none are elect?" But, I say, there is a multitude of elect, beyond all counting—a host that no mortal can number. Therefore, take heart, poor Sinner! Cast away your despondency—may you not be elect as well as any other?—for there is a host innumerable chosen! There is joy and comfort for you!

Then, not only take heart, but go and try the Master. Remember, if you were not elect, you would lose nothing by it. What did the four lepers say? "Let us fall unto the host of the Syrians, for if we stay here we must die and if we go to them we can but die." O Sinner! Come to the Throne of electing mercy! You may die where you are. Go to God—and, even supposing He should spurn you, suppose His uplifted hand should drive you away—a thing impossible—yet you will not lose anything. You will not be more damned for that. Besides, supposing you are damned, you would have the satisfaction at least of being able to lift up your eyes in Hell and say, "God, I asked mercy of You and You would not grant it. I sought it, but You did refuse it."

That you shall never say, O Sinner! If you go to Him and ask Him, you shall receive—for He never has spurned one yet! Is not that hope for you? What though there is an allotted number, yet it is true that all who seek belong to that number. Go and seek—and if you should be the first one to go to Hell, tell the devils that you did perish thus—tell the demons that you are a castaway after having come as a guilty sinner to Jesus. I tell you it would disgrace the Eternal—with reverence to His name—and He would not allow such a thing. He is jealous of His honor and He could not allow a sinner to say that.

But ah, poor Soul! Do not think thus, that you can lose anything by coming. There is yet one more thought—do you love the thought of election this morning? Are you willing to admit its justice? Do you say, "I feel that I am lost. I deserve it and if my brother is saved I cannot murmur. If God destroys me, I deserve it, but if He saves the person sitting beside me, He has a right to do what He will with His own and I have lost nothing by it."

Can you say that honestly from your heart? If so, then the doctrine of election has had its right effect on your spirit and you are not far from the kingdom of Heaven. You are brought where you ought to be, where the Spirit wants you to be—and being so this morning, depart in peace! God has forgiven your sins. You would not feel that if you were not pardoned—you would not feel that if the Spirit of God were not working in you. Rejoice, then, in this! Let your hope rest on the Cross of Christ. Think not on election, but on Christ Jesus. Rest on Jesus—Jesus first, last and without end.

PARTICULAR ELECTION

MARCH 22, 1857, AT THE MUSIC HALL, ROYAL SURREY GARDENS

"Wherefore the rather, brethren, give diligence to make your calling and election sure: for if you do these things, you shall never fall: For so an entrance shall be ministered unto you abundantly into the everlasting kingdom of our Lord and Savior Jesus Christ."
2 Peter 1:10-11

IT is exceedingly desirable that in the hours of worship and in the house of prayer our minds should be as much as possible divested of every worldly thought. Although the business of the week will very naturally struggle with us to encroach upon the Sabbath, it is our business to guard the Sabbath from the intrusion of our worldly cares, as we would guard an oasis from the overwhelming irruption of the sand. I have felt, however, that today we should be surrounded with circumstances of peculiar difficulty in endeavoring to bring our minds to spiritual matters. For of all times perhaps the most unlikely for getting any good in the sanctuary, if that depends upon mental abstraction, election times are the worst.

So important in the minds of most men are political matters that very naturally after the hurry of the week, combined with the engrossing pursuit of elections, we are apt to bring the same thoughts and the same feelings into the house of prayer and speculate, perhaps, even in the place of worship, whether a conservative or a liberal shall be returned for our borough. Or whether for the City of London there shall be returned Lord John Russell,[28] Baron Rothschild[29] or Mr. Currie.[30]

I thought, this morning, Well, it is of no use my trying to stop this great train in its progress. People are just now going on at an express rate on these matters. I think I will be wise and instead of endeavoring to turn them off the line, I will turn the points, so that they may still continue their pursuits with the same swiftness as ever, but in a new direction. It shall be the same line. They shall still be traveling in earnest towards election but perhaps I may have some skill to turn the points so that they shall be enabled to consider election in a rather different manner.

When Mr. Whitfield[31] was once applied to use his influence at a general election, he returned answer to his lordship who requested him that he knew very little about general elections but that if his lordship took his advice he would make his own particular "calling and election sure," which was a very proper remark. I would not, however, say to any persons here present, despise the privilege which you have as citizens. Far be it from me to do it. When we become Christians we do not leave off being Englishmen. When we become professors of religion we do not cease to have the rights and privileges which citizenship has bestowed on us.

Let us, whenever we shall have the opportunity of using the right of voting, use it as in the sight of Almighty God, knowing that for everything we shall be brought into account and for that among the rest, seeing that we are entrusted with it. And let us remember that we are our own governors, to a great degree and that if at the next election we should choose wrong governors we shall have nobody to blame but ourselves, however wrongly they may afterwards act, unless we exercise all prudence and prayer to Almighty God to direct our

---

[28] Whig and Liberal politician who served two terms as the Prime Minister of Great Britain (1846-1852, 1865-1866).

[29] A title in the Peerage of the United Kingdom for members of the Rothschild banking family; likely a reference to Sir Anthony Nathan Rothschild of Tring Park, the first Baronet

[30] Likely a reference to Sir Frederick Currie, a British diplomat and Baronet

[31] Eighteenth-century English Anglican cleric and evangelist; one of the founders of Methodism; unlike his Arminian associate, John Wesley, Whitefield was a Calvinist

hearts to a right choice in this matter. May God so help us and may the result be for His glory, however unexpected that result may be to any of us!

Having said so much, let me, then, turn the points and draw you to a consideration of your own particular calling and election, bidding you in the words of the Apostle, "the rather, Brethren, give diligence to make your calling and election sure: for if you do these things, you shall never fall: for so an entrance shall be ministered unto you abundantly into the everlasting kingdom of our Lord and Savior Jesus Christ."

We have here, first of all, two fundamental points in religion—"calling and election." We have here, secondly, some good advice—"to make our calling and election sure," or, rather, to assure ourselves that we are called and elected. And then, in the third place, we have some reasons given us why we should use this diligence to be assured of our election—because, on the one hand, we shall so be kept from falling and on the other hand, we shall attain unto "an abundant entrance into the everlasting kingdom of our Lord and Savior Jesus Christ."

First of all, then, there are the TWO IMPORTANT MATTERS IN RELIGION—secrets, both of them, to the world—only to be understood by those who have been quickened by Divine Grace—"CALLING AND ELECTION."

By the word "calling" in Scripture, we understand two things—one, the general call, which in the preaching of the Gospel is given to every creature under Heaven. The second call (that which is here intended) is the special call—which we call the effectual call, whereby God secretly, in the use of means, by the irresistible power of His Holy Spirit, calls out of mankind a certain number, whom He Himself has before elected. He calls them from their sins to become righteous, from their death in trespasses and sins to become living spiritual men and from their worldly pursuits to become the lovers of Jesus Christ.

The two callings differ very much. As Bunyan puts it, very prettily, "By His common call He gives nothing. By His special call He always has something to give. He has also a brooding voice for them that are under His wing. And He has an outcry to give the alarm when He sees the enemy come." What we have to obtain as absolutely necessary to our salvation, is a special calling, made in us – not to our ears but to our hearts – not to our mere fleshly understanding but to the inner man, by the power of the Spirit. And then the other important thing is election. As without calling there is no salvation, so without election there is no calling.

Holy Scripture teaches us that God has from the beginning chosen us who are saved unto holiness through Jesus Christ. We are told that as many as are ordained unto eternal life believe and that their believing is the effect of their being ordained to eternal life from before all worlds. However much this may be disputed, as it frequently is, you must first deny the authenticity and full inspiration of the Holy Scripture before you can legitimately and truly deny it.

And since, without doubt, I have many here who are members of the Episcopal church, allow me to say to them what I have often said before, "You, of all men, are the most inconsistent in the world unless you believe the doctrine of election, for if it is not taught in Scripture there is this one thing for an absolute certainty, it is taught in your Articles." Nothing can be more forcibly expressed, nothing more definitely laid down than the doctrine of predestination in the Book of Common Prayer. Although we are told what we already know, that that doctrine is a high mystery and is only to be handled carefully by men who are enlightened.

However, without doubt, it is the doctrine of Scripture that those who are saved are saved because God chose them to be saved and are called as the effect of that first choice of God. If any of you dispute this, I stand upon the authority of Holy Scripture. Yes, and if it were necessary to appeal to tradition, which I am sure it is not and no Christian man would ever do it, yet I would take you upon that point. For I can trace this doctrine through the lips of a succession of holy men, from this present moment to the days of Calvin. From there to Augustine and from there on to Paul himself and even to the lips of the Lord Jesus Christ.

The doctrine is without doubt, taught in Scripture and were not men too proud to humble themselves to it, it would universally be believed and received as being no other than manifest Truth. Why, Sirs, do you not believe that God loves His children? And do you not know that God is unchangeable?

Therefore, if He loves them now He must always have loved them. Do you not believe that if men are saved God saves them? And if so, can you see any difficulty in admitting that because He saves them there must have been a purpose to save them—a purpose which existed before all worlds? Will you not grant me that? If you will not, I must leave you to the Scriptures themselves. And if they will not convince you on the point, then I must leave you unconvinced.

It will be asked however, why is calling here put before election seeing election is eternal and calling takes place in time? I reply, because calling is first to us. The first thing which you and I can know is our calling—we cannot tell whether we are elect until we feel that we are called. We must, first of all, prove our calling and then our election is most certainly sure. "Moreover, whom He did predestinate, them He also called—and whom He called, them He also justified—and whom He justified, them he also glorified." Calling comes first in our apprehension. We are by God's Spirit called from our evil estate, regenerated and made new creatures and then, looking backward, we behold ourselves as being most assuredly elect because we were called.

Here, then, I think I have explained the text. There are the two things which you and I are to prove to be sure to ourselves—whether we are called and whether we are elected. And oh, dear Friends, this is a matter about which you and I should be very anxious. For consider what an honorable thing it is to be elected. In this world it is thought a mighty thing to be elected to the House of Parliament. But how much more honorable to be elected to eternal life? To be elected to "the Church of the first born, whose names are written in Heaven." To be elected to be a compeer of angels, to be a favorite of the living God, to dwell with the Most High among the fairest of the sons of light, nearest the eternal Throne!

Election in this world is but a short-lived thing but God's election is eternal. Let a man be elected to a seat in the House—seven years must be the longest period that he can hold his election. But if you and I are elected according to the Divine purpose, we shall hold our seats when the day-star shall have ceased to burn. When the sun shall have grown dim with age and when the eternal hills shall have bowed themselves with weakness. If we are chosen of God and precious, then are we chosen forever, for God changes not in the objects of His election. Those whom He has ordained He has ordained to eternal life, "and they shall never perish, neither shall any man pluck them out of His hand."

It is worthwhile to know ourselves elect, for nothing in this world can make a man more happy or more valiant than the knowledge of his election. "Nevertheless," said Christ to His Apostles, "rejoice not in this but rather rejoice that your names are written in Heaven"—that being the sweetest comfort, the honeycomb that drops with the most precious drops of all, the knowledge of our being chosen by God. And this, too, Beloved, makes a man valiant. When a man by diligence has attained to the assurance of his election you cannot make him a coward. You can never make him cry quit even in the thickest battle. He holds the standard firm and cleaves his foes with the scimitar of Truth.

"Was not I ordained by God to be the standard bearer of this Truth? I must, I will stand by it, despite you all," he says to every enemy, "Am I not a chosen king? Can floods of water wash out the sacred unction from a king's bright brow? No, never! And if God has chosen me to be a king and a priest unto God forever and ever, come what may or come what will—the lion's teeth, the fiery furnace, the spear, the rack, the stake—all these things are less than nothing, seeing I am chosen of God unto salvation."

It has been said that the doctrine of election naturally makes men weak. It is a lie. It may seem so in theory but in practice it has always been found to be the reverse. The men who have believed in destiny and have held fast and firm by it, have always done the most valiant deeds. There is one point in which this is akin even with Mahomet's[32] faith. The deeds that were done by him were chiefly done from a firm confidence that God had ordained him to his work.

Never had Cromwell[33] driven his foes before him if it had not been in the

---

[32] Alternate spelling of Muhammad, the founder of Islam

[33] Oliver Cromwell, an English general and statesman; led the Parliament of England's armies against King Charles I in the English Civil War

stern strength of this almost omnipotent Truth. And there shall scarcely be found a man strong to do great and valiant deeds unless, confident in the God of Providence, he looks upon the accidents of life as being steered by God. He then gives himself up to God's firm predestination, to be borne along by the current of His will, contrary to all the wills and all the wishes of the world. "Wherefore the rather, Brethren, give diligence to make your calling and election sure."

II. Come, then, here is the second point—GOOD ADVICE. "Make your calling and election sure." Not towards God, for they are sure to Him—make them sure to yourself. Be quite certain of them. Be fully satisfied about them. In many of our dissenting places of worship very great encouragement is held out to doubting. A person comes before the pastor and says, "Oh, Sir, I am so afraid I am not converted. I tremble lest I should not be a child of God. Oh, I fear I am not one of the Lord's elect."

The pastor will put out his hands to him and say, "Dear Brother, you are all right so long as you can doubt." Now, I hold that is altogether wrong. Scripture never says, "He that doubts shall be saved," but "He that believes." It may be true that the man is in a good state. It may be true that he wants a little comfort. But his doubts are not good things, nor ought we to encourage him in his doubts. Our business is to encourage him out of his doubts and by the grace of God to urge him to "give all diligence to make his calling and election sure," not to doubt it but to be sure of it.

Ah, I have heard some hypocritical doubters say, "Oh, I have had such doubts whether I am the Lord's," and I have thought to myself, "And so have I very great doubts about you." I have heard some say they do tremble so because they are afraid they are not the Lord's people and the lazy fellows sit in their pews on Sunday and just listen to the sermon but they never think of giving diligence. They never do good, perhaps are inconsistent in their lives and then talk about doubting. It is quite right they should doubt—it is well they should and if they did not doubt we might begin to doubt for them.

Idle men have no right to assurance. The Scripture says, "Give diligence to make your calling and election sure." Full assurance is an excellent attainment. It is profitable for a man to be certain in this life and absolutely sure of his own calling and election. But how can he be sure? Now, many of our more ignorant hearers imagine that the only way they have of being assured of their election is by some revelation, some dream and some mystery. I have enjoyed very hearty laughs at the expense of some people who have trusted in their visions.

Really, if you had passed among so many shades of ignorant professing Christians as I have and had to resolve so many doubts and fears, you would be so infinitely sick of dreams and visions that you would say, as soon as a person began to speak about them, "Now, do just hold your tongue." "Sir," said a woman, "I saw blue lights in the front parlor when I was in prayer and I thought I saw the Savior in the corner and I said to myself I am safe."[34]

And yet there are tens of thousands of people in every part of the country and members, too, of Christian bodies, who have no better grounds for their belief that they are called and elected, than some vision equally ridiculous, or the equally absurd hearing of a voice. A young woman came to me some time ago. She wanted to join the Church and when I asked her how she knew herself to be converted she said she was down at the bottom of the garden and she thought she heard a voice and she thought she saw something up in the clouds that said to her so-and-so. "Well," I said to her, "that thing may have been the means of doing good to you but if you put any trust in it, it is all over with you."

A dream, yes, and a vision, may often bring men to Christ. I have known many who have been brought to Him by them, beyond a doubt, though it has been mysterious to me how it was. But when men bring these forward as a proof of their conversion, there is the mistake—because you may see fifty thousand dreams and fifty thousand visions and you may be a fool for all that and all the bigger sinner for having seen them. There is better evidence to be had than all this—"Give diligence to make your calling and election sure."

"How, then," says one, "am I to make my calling and election sure?" Why, thus—if you would get out of a doubting state—get out of an idle state. If you

---

[34] Spurgeon here narrated a remarkable story of a poor woman who was possessed with a singular delusion.

would get out of a trembling state, get out of an indifferent lukewarm state. For lukewarmness and doubting and laziness and trembling very naturally go hand in hand. If you would enjoy the eminent grace of the full assurance of faith under the blessed Spirit's influence and assistance, do what the Scripture tells you—"Give diligence to make your calling and election sure."

Wherein shall you be diligent? Note how the Scripture has given us a list. Be diligent in your faith. Take care that your faith is of the right kind—that it is not a creed but a credence—that it is not a mere belief of doctrine but a reception of doctrine into your heart and the practical light of the doctrine in your soul. Take care that your faith results from necessity—that you believe in Christ because you have nothing else to believe in. Take care it is simple faith, hanging alone on Christ, without any other dependence but Jesus Christ and Him crucified.

And when you have given diligence about that, give diligence next to your courage. Labor to get virtue. Plead with God that He would give you the face of a lion, that you may never be afraid of any enemy—however much he may jeer or threaten you but that you may with a consciousness of right, go on, boldly trusting in God. And having, by the help of the Holy Spirit, obtained that, study well the Scriptures and get knowledge. For a knowledge of doctrine will tend very much to confirm your faith. Try to understand God's Word. Get a sensible, spiritual idea of it.

Get, if you can, a system of divinity out of God's Bible. Put the doctrines together. Get real, theological knowledge, founded upon the infallible Word. Get a knowledge of that science which is most despised but which is the most necessary of all, the science of Christ and of Him crucified and of the great Doctrines of Grace. And when you have done this, "Add to your knowledge temperance." Take heed to your body—be temperate there. Take heed to your soul—be temperate there. Be not drunken with pride. Be not lifted up with self-confidence. Be temperate. Be not harsh towards your friends, nor bitter to your enemies. Get temperance of lip, temperance of life, temperance of heart, temperance of thought.

Be not passionate—be not carried away by every wind of doctrine. Get temperance and then add to it by God's Holy Spirit patience. Ask Him to give you that patience which endures affliction, which, when it is tried, shall come forth as gold. Array yourself with patience, that you may not murmur in your sicknesses. That you may not curse God in your losses, nor be depressed in your afflictions. Pray, without ceasing, until the Holy Spirit has nerved you with patience to endure unto the end.

And when you have that, get godliness. Godliness is something more than religion. The most religious men may be the most godless men and sometimes a godly man may seem to be irreligious. Let me just explain that seeming paradox. A real religious man is a man who sighs after sacraments, attends churches and chapels and is outwardly good but goes not farther. A godly man is a man who does not look so much to the dress as to the person—he looks not to the outward form but to the inward and spiritual grace. He is a godly man, as well as attentive to religion. Some men, however, are godly and to a great extent despise form. They may be godly, without some degree of religion.

But a man cannot be fully righteous without being godly in the true meaning of each of these words, though not in the general vulgar sense of them. Add to your patience an eye to God. Live in His sight, dwell close to Him. Seek for fellowship with Him and you have got godliness. And then to that add brotherly love. Be loving towards all the members of Christ's Church. Have a love to all the saints, of every denomination. And then add to that charity, which opens its arms to all men and loves them. And when you have got all these, then you will know your calling and election. And just in proportion as you practice these Heavenly rules of life, in this Heavenly manner, will you come to know that you are called and that you are elect.

But by no other means can you attain to a knowledge of that, except by the witness of the Spirit, bearing witness with your spirit that you are born of God and then witnessing in your conscience that you are not what you were but are a new man in Christ Jesus and are therefore called and therefore elected.

A man over there says he is elect. He gets drunk. Yes, you are elect by the devil, Sir. That is about your only election. Another man says, "Blessed be God, I don't care about evidences a bit. I am not so legal as you are!" No, I dare say you are not. But you have no great reason to bless God about it, for, my dear Friend, unless you have these evidences of a new birth take heed to yourself. "God is not mocked—whatsoever a man sows, that shall he also reap." "Well," says another, "but I think that doctrine of election a very licentious doctrine." Think on as long as you please but please to bear me witness that as I have preached it today there is nothing licentious about it. Very likely you are licentious and you would make the doctrine licentious, if you believed it.

But "to the pure all things are pure." He who receives God's Truth in his heart does not often pervert it and turn aside from it unto wicked ways. No man, let me repeat, no man has any right to believe himself elect of God unless he has been renewed by God. No man has any right to believe himself called unless his life is in the main consistent with his vocation and he walks worthy of that whereunto he is called. Out with an election that lets you live in sin! Away with it! Away with it! That was never the design of God's Word and it never was the doctrine of Calvinists either. Though we have been lied against and our teachings perverted, we have always stood by this—that good works, though they do not procure nor in any degree merit salvation, yet they are the necessary evidences of salvation.

And unless they are in men the soul is still dead, uncalled and unrenewed. The nearer you live to Christ the more you imitate Him. The more your life is conformed to Him and the more simply you hang upon Him by faith, the more certain you may be of your election in Christ and of your calling by His Holy Spirit. May the Holy One of Israel give you the sweet assurance of grace, by affording you "tokens for good" in the graces which He enables you to manifest.

III. And now I shall close up by giving you THE APOSTLE'S REASONS WHY YOU SHOULD MAKE YOUR CALLING AND ELECTION SURE.

I put in one of my own to begin with. It is because, as I have said, it will make you so happy. Men who doubt their calling and election cannot be full of joy. But the happiest saints are those who know and believe it. You know our friends say this is a howling wilderness and you know my reply to it is that they make all the howling themselves. There would not be much howling if they were to look up a little more and look down a little less. For by faith they would make it blossom like the rose and give to it the excellence and glory of Carmel and Sharon.

But why they howl so much is because they do not believe. Our happiness and our faith are to a great degree proportionate. They are Siamese twins to the Christian. They must flourish or decay together—

"When I can say my God is mine,
Then I can all my griefs resign;
Can tread the world beneath my feet,
And all that earth calls good or great"

But ah—

"When gloomy doubts prevail,
I fear to call Him mine;
The streams of comfort seem to fail,
And all my hopes decline"

Only faith can make a Christian lead a happy life.

But now for Peter's reasons. First, because "if you do these things you shall never fall." "Perhaps," says one, "in attention to election we may forget our daily walk and like the old philosopher who looked up to the stars we may walk on and tumble into the ditch!" "No, no," says Peter, "if you take care of your calling and election, you shall not trip but with your eyes up there, looking for your calling and election, God will take care of your feet and you shall never fall."

Is it not very notable, that in many churches and chapels, you do not often hear a sermon about today? It is always either about old eternity, or else about the millennium. Either about what God did before man was made, or else about what God will do when all are dead and buried. Pity they do not tell us something about what we are to do today, now, in our daily walk and conversation! Peter removes this difficulty. He says, "This point is a practical point. For you can only answer your election for yourself by taking care of your practice. And while you are so taking care of your practice and assuring yourself of your election, you are doing the best possible thing to keep you from falling."

And is it not desirable that a true Christian should be kept from falling?

Mark the difference between falling and falling away. The true Believer can never fall away and perish. But he may fall and injure himself. He shall not fall and break his neck. But a broken leg is bad enough, without a broken neck. "Though he fall he shall not be utterly cast down." But that is no reason why he should dash himself against a stone. His desire is that day by day he may grow more holy. That hour by hour he may be more thoroughly renewed, until conformed to the image of Christ, he may enter into bliss eternal. If, then, you take care of your calling and election, you are doing the best thing in the world to prevent you from falling, for in so doing you shall never fall.

And now, the other reason and then I shall have almost concluded. "For so an entrance shall be ministered unto you abundantly into the everlasting kingdom of our Lord and Savior Jesus Christ."

An "abundant entrance" has sometimes been illustrated in this way—You see yonder ship? After a long voyage, it has neared the haven but is much injured, the sails are rent to ribbons and it is in such a forlorn condition that it cannot come up to the harbor—a steam-tug is pulling it in with the greatest possible difficulty. That is like the righteous being "scarcely saved." But do you see that other ship? It has made a prosperous voyage and now, laden to the water's edge, with the sails all up and with the white canvass filled with the wind, it rides into the harbor joyously and nobly. That is an "abundant entrance."

And if you and I are helped by God's Spirit to add to our faith, virtue and so on, we shall have at the last "an abundant entrance into the kingdom of our Lord Jesus Christ." There is a man who is a Christian. But, alas, there are many inconsistencies in his life for which he has to mourn. He lies there, dying on his bed. The thought of his past life rushes upon him. He cries, "O Lord, have mercy upon me, a sinner," and the prayer is answered. His faith is in Christ and he shall be saved. But oh, what griefs he has upon his bed. "Oh if I had served my God better! And these children of mine—if I had but trained them up better, 'in the nurture and admonition of the Lord!'

"I am saved," says he, "but alas, alas! Though it is a great salvation, I cannot enjoy it yet. I am dying in gloom and clouds and darkness. I trust, I hope, I shall be gathered to my fathers but I have no works to follow me—or very few indeed, for though I am saved, I am but just saved—saved 'so as by fire.' " Here is another one. He, too, is dying. Ask him what his dependence is—he tells you, "I rest in none else but Jesus." But mark him as he looks back to his past life. "In such a place," says he, "I preached the Gospel and God helped me." And though with no pride about him—he will not congratulate himself upon what he has done—yet does he lift his hands to Heaven and he blesses God that throughout a long life he has been able to keep his garments white. That he has served his Master.

And now, like a shock of corn fully ripe, he is about to be gathered into his Master's garner. Listen to him! It is not the feeble lisp of the trembler. But with "victory, victory, victory!" for his dying shout. He shuts his eyes and dies like a warrior in his glory. That is the "abundant entrance." Now, the man that "gives diligence to make his calling and election sure," shall ensure for himself, "an abundant entrance into the kingdom of our Lord Jesus Christ."

What a terrible picture is hinted at in these words of the Apostle—"Saved so as by fire!" Let me try and present it to you. The man has come to the edge of Jordan, the time has arrived for him to die. He is a Believer—just a Believer. But his life has not been what he could wish. Not all that he now desires that it had been. And now stern death is at him and he has to take his first step into the Jordan. Judge of his horror, when the flames surround his foot. He treads upon the hot sand of the stream. He takes the next step. His hair is well near on end. Though his eyes are fixed on Heaven on the other side of the shore his face is yet marked with horror. He takes another step and he is all bathing in fire. Another step and he is up to his very loins in flames—"saved, so as by fire."

A strong hand has grasped him that drags him onward through the stream. But how dreadful must be the death even of the Christian when he is saved "so as by fire"! There on the river's brink, astonished, he looks back and sees the liquid flames through which he has been called to walk as a consequence of his indifference in this life. Saved he is—thanks to God. And his Heaven shall be great and his crown shall be golden and his harp shall be sweet and his hymns shall be eternal and his bliss unfading—but his dying moment, the last article of death, was blackened by sin. And he was saved "so as by fire!"

Mark the other man. He, too, has to die. He has often feared death. He dips the first foot in Jordan. As his body trembles, his pulse waxes faint and even his eyes are well near closed. His lips can scarcely speak but still he says, "Jesus, You are with me, You are with me, passing through the stream!" He takes another step and the waters now begin to refresh him. He dips his hand and tastes the stream and tells those who are watching him in tears, that to die is blessed. "The stream is sweet," he says, "it is not bitter—it is blessed to die." Then he takes another step and when he is well near submerged in the stream and lost to vision, he says—

"And when you hear my eye strings break,

How sweet my minutes roll –

A mortal paleness on my cheek

But glory in my soul!"

That is the "abundant entrance" of the man who has manfully served his God—who, by Divine Grace, has had a path unclouded and serene—who, by diligence, has "made his calling and election sure," and therefore, as a reward, not of debt but of grace, has entered Heaven with higher honors and with greater ease than others equally saved but not saved in so splendid a manner.

Just one thought more. It is said that the entrance is to be "ministered to us." That gives me a sweet hint that, I find, is dwelt upon by Doddridge.[35] Christ will open the gates of Heaven but the heavenly train of virtues—the works which follow us—will go up with us and minister an entrance to us. I sometimes think if God should enable me to live and die for the good of these congregations, so that many of them shall be saved, how sweet it will be to enter Heaven and when I shall come there, to have an entrance ministered to me not by Christ alone but by some of you for whom I have ministered.

One shall meet me at the gate and say, "Minister, you were the cause of my salvation!" And another and another and another shall all exclaim the same. When Whitfield entered Heaven—that highly honored servant of the Lord—I

---

[35] Philip Doddridge, an eighteenth-century Congregationalist minister, educator, and hymnwriter

think I can see the hosts rushing to the gate to meet him. There are thousands there that have been brought to God by him. Oh how they open wide the gates. And how they praise God that he has been the means of bringing them to Heaven. And how they do minister unto him an abundant entrance!

There will be some of you, perhaps, in Heaven, with starless crowns—for you never did good to your fellow creatures. You never were the means of saving souls—you are to have crowns without stars. But "they that turn many to righteousness"—"yours are the stars, forever and ever." And an entrance shall be abundantly ministered to them. I do want to get a heavy crown in Heaven—not to wear but to have all the more costly gift to give to Christ. And you ought to desire the same, that you may have all the more honors and so have the more to cast at His feet, with—"Not unto us but unto Your name, O Christ, be the glory!" "Rather, Brethren, give all diligence to make your calling and election sure."

And now, to conclude. There are some of you with whom this text has nothing to do. You cannot "make your calling and election sure," for you have not been called. And you have no right to believe that you are elected, if you have never been called. To such of you, let me say, do not ask whether you are elected first but ask whether you are called. And go to God's house and bend your knee in prayer. And may God, in His infinite mercy, call you! And mark this—If any of you can say—

"Nothing in my hands I bring,

Simply to Your Cross I cling."

If any of you, abjuring your self-righteousness, can now come to Christ and take Him to be your All in All—you are called, you are elect. "Make your calling and election sure," and go on your way rejoicing! May God bless you. And to Father, Son and Holy Spirit, be glory forever more! Amen.

III

Limited Atonement

PARTICULAR REDEMPTION

FEBRUARY 28, 1858, AT THE MUSIC HALL, ROYAL SURREY GARDENS

"Even as the Son of man came not to be ministered unto, but to minister, and to give his life a ransom for many."
Matthew 20:28

WHEN first it was my duty to occupy this pulpit and preach in this hall, my congregation assumed the appearance of an irregular mass of persons collected from all the streets of this city to listen to the Word. I was then simply an evangelist, preaching to many who had not heard the Gospel before. By the grace of God, the most blessed change has taken place and now, instead of having an irregular multitude gathered together, my congregation is as fixed as that of any minister in the whole city of London. I can from this pulpit observe the countenances of my friends who have occupied the same places, as nearly as possible, for these many months. And I have the privilege and the pleasure of knowing that a very large proportion, certainly three-fourths of the persons who meet together here are not persons who stray here from curiosity, but are my regular and constant hearers.

And observe that my character also has been changed. From being an evangelist, it is now my business to become your pastor. You were once a motley group assembled to listen to me but now we are bound together by the ties of love. Through association we have grown to love and respect each other and now you have become the sheep of my pasture and members of my flock. And I have now the privilege of assuming the position of a pastor in this place, as well as in the Chapel where I labor in the evening. I think, then, it will strike the judgment of every person that as both the congregation and the office have now changed, the teaching itself should in some measure suffer a difference.

It has been my desire to address you from the simple Truths of the Gospel. I have very seldom, in this place, attempted to dive into the deep things of God. A text which I have thought suitable for my congregation in the evening, I should not have made the subject of discussion in this place in the morning. There are many high and mysterious doctrines which I have often taken the opportunity of handling in my own place that I have not taken the liberty of introducing here, regarding you as a company of people casually gathered together to hear the Word.

But now, since the circumstances are changed, the teaching will be changed also. I shall not now simply confine myself to the doctrine of the faith, or the teaching of Believer's Baptism. I shall not stay upon the surface of matters, but shall venture, as God shall guide me, to enter into those things that lie at the basis of the religion that we hold so dear. I shall not blush to preach before you the doctrine of God's Divine Sovereignty. I shall not stagger to preach in the most unreserved and unguarded manner the doctrine of Election. I shall not be afraid to propound the great Truth of the Final perseverance of the Saints. I shall not withhold that undoubted Truth of Scripture the Effectual Calling of God's elect. I shall endeavor, as God shall help me to keep back nothing from you who have become my flock. Seeing that many of you have now "tasted that the Lord is gracious," we will endeavor to go through the whole system of the doctrines of grace—that saints may be edified and built up in their most holy faith.

I begin this morning with the doctrine of Redemption. "He gave His life a ransom for many." The doctrine of Redemption is one of the most important doctrines of the system of faith. A mistake on this point will inevitably lead to a mistake through the entire system of our belief.

Now, you are aware that there are different theories of Redemption. All Christians hold that Christ died to redeem, but all Christians do not teach the same redemption. We differ as to the nature of atonement and as to the design of redemption. For instance, the Arminian[36] holds that Christ, when He died, did not die with an intent to save any particular person. And they teach that Christ's death does not in itself secure, beyond doubt, the salvation of any man man who pleases may attain unto eternal life. Consequently, they are obliged to hold that if man's will would not give way and voluntarily surrender to grace, then Christ's atonement would be worthless.

They hold that there was no particularity and specialty in the death of Christ. Christ died, according to them, as much for Judas in Hell as for Peter who mounted to Heaven. They believe that for those who are consigned to eternal fire, there was as true and real a redemption made as for those who now stand before the Throne of the Most High. Now we believe no such thing. We hold that Christ, when He died, had an object in view and that object will most assuredly and beyond a doubt, be accomplished. We measure the design of Christ's death by the effect of it. If anyone asks us, "What did Christ design to do by His death?" We answer that question by asking him another—"What has Christ done, or what will Christ do by His death?"

For we declare that the measure of the effect of Christ's love is the measure of the design of it. We cannot so belie our reason as to think that the intention of Almighty God could be frustrated, or that the design of so great a thing as the atonement can by any way whatever, be missed of. We hold—we are not afraid to say what we believe—that Christ came into this world with the intention of saving "a multitude which no man can number." And we believe that as the result of this every person for whom He died must, beyond the shadow of a doubt, be cleansed from sin and stand, washed in His blood, before the Father's Throne. We do not believe that Christ made any effectual atonement for those who are forever damned. We dare not think that the blood of Christ was ever shed with the intention of saving those whom God foreknew never would be saved—and some of whom were even in Hell when Christ, according to some men's account, died to save them.

I have thus just stated our theory of redemption and hinted at the differ-

---

[36] The belief that God's sovereignty and man's free will are compatible; the soteriological (study of salvation) rival to Calvinism

ences which exist between two great parties in the professing Church. It shall be now my endeavor to show the greatness of the redemption of Christ Jesus. And by so doing I hope to be enabled by God's Spirit to bring out the whole of the great system of redemption so that it may be understood by us all, even if all of us cannot receive it. For you must bear this in mind that some of you, perhaps, may be ready to dispute things which I assert. But you will remember that this is nothing to me. I shall at all times teach those things which I hold to be true, without let or hindrance from any man breathing. You have the like liberty to do the same in your own places and to preach your own views in your own assemblies, as I claim the right to preach mine, fully, and without hesitation.

Christ Jesus "gave His life a ransom for many." And by that ransom He wrought out for us a great redemption. I shall endeavor to show the greatness of this redemption, measuring it in five ways. We shall note its greatness, first of all, from the heinousness of our own guilt, from which He has delivered us. Secondly, we shall measure His redemption by the sternness of Divine justice. Thirdly, we shall measure it by the price which He paid—the pangs which He endured. Then we shall endeavor to magnify it, by noting the deliverance which He actually worked out. And we shall close by noticing the vast number for whom this redemption is made, who in our text are described as "many."

First, then, we shall see that the redemption of Christ was no little thing, if we do but measure it, first, by our OWN SINS. My Brethren, for a moment look at the hole of the pit from where you were dug, and the quarry where you were hewn. You who have been washed, cleansed and sanctified, pause for a moment and look back at the former state of your ignorance. The sins in which you indulged, the crimes into which you were hurried, the continual rebellion against God in which it was your habit to live. One sin can ruin a soul forever. It is not in the power of the human mind to grasp the infinity of evil that slumbers in the heart of one solitary sin. There is a very infinity of guilt couched in one transgression against the majesty of Heaven. If, then, you and I had sinned but once, nothing but an atonement infinite in value could ever have washed away the sin and made satisfaction for it.

But has it been once that you and I have transgressed? No, my Brethren—our iniquities are more in number than the hairs of our head. They have mightily prevailed against us. We might as well attempt to number the sands upon the seashore—or count the drops which in their aggregate do make the ocean—as attempt to count the transgressions which have marked our lives. Let us go back to our childhood. How early we began to sin! How we disobeyed our parents and even then learned to make our mouth the house of lies! In our childhood how full of wantonness and waywardness we were! Headstrong and giddy, we preferred our own way and burst through all restraints which godly parents put upon us.

Nor did our youth sober us. Wildly we dashed, many of us, into the very midst of the dance of sin. We became leaders in iniquity. We not only sinned ourselves but we taught others to sin. And as for your manhood, you that have entered upon the prime of life—you may be more outwardly sober, you may be somewhat free from the dissipation of your youth—but how little has the man become bettered! Unless the sovereign grace of God has renewed us, we are now no better than we were when we began. And even if it has operated, we have still sins to repent of, for we all lay our mouths in the dust, and cast ashes on our head, and cry, "Unclean! Unclean!

And oh! you that lean wearily on your staff, the support of your old age, have you not sins still clinging to your garments? Are your lives as white as the snowy hairs that crown your head? Do you not still feel that transgression besmears the skirts of your robe and mars its spotlessness? How often are you now plunged into the ditch, till your own clothes do abhor you! Cast your eyes over the sixty, the seventy, the eighty years during which God has spared your lives. And can you for a moment think it possible that you can number up your innumerable transgressions, or compute the weight of the crimes which you have committed? O you stars of Heaven! The astronomer may measure your distance and tell your height, but O you sins of mankind! You surpass all thought! O you lofty mountains! The home of the tempest, the birthplace of the storm! Man may climb your summits and stand wonderingly upon your snows. But you hills of sin! You tower higher than our thoughts. You chasms of transgressions! You are deeper than our imagination dares to dive.

Do you accuse me of slandering human nature? It is because you know it not! If God had once manifested your heart to yourself, you would bear me witness that so far from exaggerating, my poor words fail to describe the desperateness of our evil. Oh, if we could each of us look into our hearts today—if our eyes could be turned within, so as to see the iniquity that is graven as with the point of the diamond upon our stony hearts—we should then say to the minister that however he may depict the desperateness of guilt, yet can he not by any means surpass it. How great then, Beloved, must be the ransom of Christ, when He saved us from all these sins!

The men for whom Jesus died, however great their sin, when they believe, are sanctified from all their transgressions. Though they may have indulged in every vice and every lust which Satan could suggest, and which human nature could perform—yet once believing, by God's grace, all their guilt is washed away. Year after year may have coated them with blackness, till their sin has become of double dye, but in one moment of faith, one triumphant moment of confidence in Christ, the great redemption takes away the guilt of numerous years. No, more. If it were possible for all the sins that men have done, in thought, or word, or deed since worlds were made, or time began—to meet on one poor head—the great redemption is all-sufficient to take all these sins away and wash the sinner whiter than the driven snow!

Oh, who shall measure the heights of the Savior's all-sufficiency? First, tell how high is sin and then, remember that as Noah's flood prevailed over the tops of earth's mountains, so the flood of Christ's redemption prevails over the tops of the mountains of our sins. In Heaven's courts there are today men that once were murderers and thieves and drunkards and whoremongers, and blasphemers and persecutors. But they have been washed—they have been sanctified. Ask them from where the brightness of their robes has come and where their purity has been achieved, and they, with united breath, will tell you that they have washed their robes and made them white in the blood of the Lamb. O you troubled consciences! O you weary and heavy-laden ones! O you that are groaning on account of sin! The great redemption now proclaimed to you is all-sufficient for your wants. And though your numerous sins exceed the stars that deck the sky, here is an atonement made for them all—a river which can overflow the whole of them, and carry them away from you forever.

This, then, is the first measure of the atonement—the greatness of our guilt.

II. Now, secondly, we must measure the great redemption BY THE STERNNESS OF DIVINE JUSTICE. "God is love," always loving, but my next proposition does not at all interfere with this assertion. God is sternly just, inflexibly severe in His dealings with mankind. The God of the Bible is not the God of some men's imagination, who thinks so little of sin that He passes it by without demanding any punishment for it. He is not the God of the men who imagine that our transgressions are such little things, such mere peccadilloes that the God of Heaven winks at them and suffers them to die forgotten.

No. Jehovah, Israel's God has declared concerning Himself, "The Lord your God is a jealous God." It is His own declaration, "I will by no means clear the guilty." "The soul that sins, it shall die." Learn, my Friends, to look upon God as being as severe in His justice as if He were not loving—and yet as loving as if He were not severe. His love does not diminish His justice nor does His justice, in the least degree, make warfare upon His love. The two things are sweetly linked together in the atonement of Christ. But, mark, we can never understand the fullness of the atonement till we have first grasped the Scriptural Truth of God's immense justice.

There was never an ill word spoken, nor an ill thought conceived, nor an evil deed done for which God will not have punishment from someone or another. He will either have satisfaction from you, or else from Christ. If you have no atonement to bring through Christ you must forever lie paying the debt which you never can pay, in eternal misery. For as surely as God is God, He will sooner lose His Godhead than suffer one sin to go unpunished, or one particle of rebellion not revenged. You may say that this character of God is cold, stern, and severe. I cannot help what you say of it. It is nevertheless true. Such is the God of the Bible. And though we repeat it is true that He is love, it is no more true that He is love than that He is full of justice—for every good thing meets in God and is carried to perfection—while love reaches to consummate loveliness, justice reaches to the sternness of inflexibility in Him.

He has no bend, no warp in His Character. No attribute so predominates as to cast a shadow upon the other. Love has its full sway and justice has no narrower limit than His love. Oh, then, Beloved, think how great must have been the substitution of Christ when it satisfied God for all the sins of His people. For man's sin God demands eternal punishment. And God has prepared a Hell into which He casts those who die impenitent. Oh, my Brothers and Sisters, can you think what must have been the greatness of the atonement which was the substitution for all this agony which God would have cast upon us, if He had not poured it upon Christ? Look! Look! Look with solemn eye through the shades that part us from the world of spirits and see that house of misery which men call Hell! You cannot endure the spectacle!

Remember that in that place there are spirits forever paying their debt to Divine Justice, but though some of them have been there these six thousand years sweltering in the flame, they are no nearer a discharge than when they began. And when ten thousand times ten thousand years shall have rolled away, they will no more have made satisfaction to God for their guilt than they have done up till now. And now can you grasp the thought of the greatness of your Savior's mediation when He paid your debt and paid it all at once so that there now remains not one farthing of debt owing from Christ's people to their God, except a debt of love? To Justice the Believer owes nothing. Though he owed originally so much that eternity would not have been long enough to suffice for the paying of it, yet in one moment Christ did pay it all. That the man who believes is entirely sanctified from all guilt and set free from all punishment through what Jesus has done. Think, then, how great His atonement if He has done all this.

I must just pause here and utter another sentence. There are times when God the Holy Spirit shows to men the sternness of Justice in their own consciences. There is a man here today who has just been cut to the heart with a sense of sin. He was once a free man, a libertine, in bondage to none. But now the arrow of the Lord sticks fast in his heart and he has come under a bondage worse than that of Egypt. I see him today—he tells me that his guilt haunts him everywhere. The Negro slave, guided by the pole star, may escape the cruelties of his master and reach another land where he may be free.[37] But this man feels that if he were to wander the whole world over he could not escape from guilt. He that has been bound by many irons can not find a file that can unbind him and set him at liberty. This man tells you that he has tried prayers and tears and good works, but cannot get the shackles from his wrists. He feels as a lost sinner still—and emancipation—do what he may, seems to him impossible.

The captive in the dungeon is sometimes free in thought, though not in body. Through his dungeon walls his spirit leaps and flies to the stars, free as the eagle that is no man's slave. But this man is a slave in his thoughts—he cannot think one bright, one happy thought. His soul is cast down within him. The iron has entered into his spirit and he is sorely afflicted. The captive sometimes forgets his slavery in sleep but this man cannot sleep. By night he dreams of Hell, by day he seems to feel it. He bears a burning furnace of flame within his heart and do what he may, he cannot quench it. He has been confirmed, he has been baptized, he takes the sacrament, he attends a Church or he frequents a Chapel. He regards every rubric and obeys every canon—but the fire burns still.

He gives his money to the poor, he is ready to give his body to be burned. He feeds the hungry, he visits the sick, he clothes the naked—but the fire burns still—do what he may he cannot quench it. O, you sons of weariness and woe! This that you feel is God's Justice in full pursuit of you—and happy are you that you feel this—for now to you I preach this glorious Gospel of the blessed God! You are the man for whom Jesus Christ has died. For you He has satisfied stern Justice. And now all you have to do to obtain peace and conscience, is just to say to your adversary who pursues you, "Look you there! Christ died for me. My good works would not stop you, my tears would not appease you. Look you there! There stands the Cross, there hangs the bleeding God! Hark to His death-shriek! See Him die! Are you not satisfied now?" And when you have done that, you shall have the peace of God which

---

[37] Spurgeon was a staunch opponent of American slavery and was often barred from speaking in the United States because of his abolitionist views.

passes all understanding, which shall keep your heart and mind through Jesus Christ your Lord—and then shall you know the greatness of His atonement.

III. In the third place, we may measure the greatness of Christ's Redemption by THE PRICE HE PAID. It is impossible for us to know how great were the pangs of our Savior but yet some glimpse of them will afford us a little idea of the greatness of the price which He paid for us. O Jesus, who shall describe Your agony?—

"Come, all you springs,
Dwell in my head and eyes. Come, clouds and rain!
My grief has need of all the watery things,
That nature has produced. Let every vein
Suck up a river to supply my eyes,
My weary weeping eyes—too dry for me,
Unless they get new conduits, new supplies
To bear them out and with my state agree."

O Jesus! You were a sufferer from Your birth, a man of sorrows and grief's acquaintance. Your sufferings tell on You in one perpetual shower, until the last dread hour of darkness. Then not in a shower, but in a cloud, a torrent, a cataract of grief Your agonies did dash upon You. See Him yonder! It is a night of frost and cold, but He is all abroad. It is night. He sleeps not—He is in prayer. Hark to His groans! Did ever man wrestle as He wrestles? Go and look in His face! Was ever such suffering depicted upon mortal countenance as you can there behold? Hear His own words? "My soul is exceeding sorrowful, even unto death." He rises. He is seized by traitors and is dragged away.

Let us step to the place where just now He was engaged in agony. O God! And what is this we see? What is this that stains the ground? It is blood! From where did it come? Had He some wound which oozed afresh through His dire struggle? Ah, no. "He sweat, as it were, great drops of blood, falling down to the ground." O agonies that surpass the word by which we name you! O sufferings that cannot be compassed in language! What could you be that thus could work upon the Savior's blessed frame and force a bloody sweat to fall from His entire body?

This is the beginning—this is the opening of the tragedy. Follow Him mournfully, you sorrowing Church, to witness the consummation of it. He is hurried through the streets. He is first to one bar and then to another. He is cast and condemned before the Sanhedrin. He is mocked by Herod, He is tried by Pilate. His sentence is pronounced—"Let Him be crucified!" And now the tragedy comes to its height. His back is bared. He is tied to the low Roman column. The bloody scourge plows furrows on His back. And with one stream of blood His back is red—a crimson robe that proclaims Him emperor of misery. He is taken into the guard room. His eyes are bound and then they buffet Him and say, "Prophesy, who it was that smote You?"

They spit into His face. They plait a crown of thorns and press His temples with it. They array Him in a purple robe. They bow their knees and mock Him. All silently He stands. He answers not a word. "When He was reviled, He reviled not again," but committed Himself unto Him whom He came to serve. And now they take Him and with many a jeer and jibe they drive Him from the place and hurry Him through the streets. Emaciated by continual fasting and depressed with agony of spirit He stumbles beneath His Cross."

Daughters of Jerusalem! He faints in your streets. They raise Him up. They put His Cross upon another's shoulders and they urge Him on, perhaps with many a spear-prick, till at last He reaches the mount of doom. Rough soldiers seize Him, and hurl Him on His back. The transverse wood is laid beneath Him, His arms are stretched to reach the necessary distance. The nails are grasped. Four hammers at one moment drive four nails through the most tender parts of His body. And there He lies upon His own place of execution dying on His Cross. It is not done yet. The Cross is lifted by the rough soldiers. There is the socket prepared for it. It is dashed into its place. They fill up the place with earth. And there it stands.

But see the Savior's limbs, how they quiver! Every bone has been put out of joint by the dashing of the Cross into that socket! How He weeps! How He sighs! How He sobs! No, more—hark how at last He shrieks in agony, "My God, My God, why have You forsaken Me?" O sun, no wonder you did shut your eye and look no longer upon a deed so cruel! O rocks! No wonder that you did melt and rend your hearts with sympathy, when your Creator died! Never man suffered as this Man suffered. Even death itself relented and many of those who had been in their graves arose and came into the city.

This however, is but the outward. Believe me, Brethren, the inward was far worse. What our Savior suffered in His body was nothing compared to what He endured in His soul. You cannot guess, and I cannot help you to guess, what He endured within. Suppose for one moment—to repeat a sentence I have often used—suppose a man who has passed into Hell—suppose his eternal torment could all be brought into one hour, and then suppose it could be multiplied by the number of the saved, which is a number past all human enumeration. Can you now think what a vast aggregate of misery there would have been in the sufferings of all God's people, if they had been punished through all eternity?

And recollect that Christ had to suffer an equivalent for all the Hells of all His redeemed. I can never express that thought better than by using those oft-repeated words—it seemed as if Hell was put into His cup, He seized it, and, "At one tremendous draught of love, He drank damnation dry." So that there was nothing left of all the pangs and miseries of Hell for His people ever to endure. I say not that He suffered the same, but He did endure an equivalent for all this and gave God the satisfaction for all the sins of all His people—and consequently gave Him an equivalent for all their punishment. Now can you dream, can you guess the great redemption of our Lord Jesus Christ?

IV. I shall be very brief upon the next head. The fourth way of measuring the Savior's agonies is this—we must compute them by THE GLORIOUS DELIVERANCE WHICH HE HAS EFFECTED.

Rise up, Believer, stand up in your place and this day testify to the greatness of what the Lord has done for you! Let me tell it for you! I will tell your experience and mine in one breath. Once my soul was laden with sin. I had revolted against God and grievously transgressed. The terrors of the Law got hold upon me. The pangs of conviction seized me. I saw myself guilty. I looked to Heaven and I saw an angry God sworn to punish me. I looked beneath me and I saw a yawning Hell ready to devour me. I sought by good works to satisfy my conscience. But all in vain. I endeavored, by attending to the ceremonies of religion to, appease the pangs that I felt within—but all without effect.

My soul was exceeding sorrowful almost unto death. I could have said with the ancient mourner, "My soul chooses strangling and death rather than life." This was the great question that always perplexed me—"I have sinned. God must punish me. How can He be just if He does not? Then, since He is just, what is to become of me?" At last my eyes turned to that sweet Word which says, "The blood of Jesus Christ His Son cleans from all sin." I took that text to my chamber. I sat there and meditated. I saw one hanging on a Cross. It was my Lord Jesus. There was the crown of thorns and there the emblems of unequalled and peerless misery.

I looked upon Him and my thoughts recalled that Word which says, "This is a faithful saying, and worthy of all acceptation that Christ Jesus came into the world to save sinners." Then said I within myself, "Did this Man die for sinners? I am a sinner. Then He died for me. Those He died for He will save. He died for sinners. I am a sinner. He died for me. He will save me." My soul relied upon that Truth. I looked to Him—and as I "viewed the flowing of His soul-redeeming blood," my spirit rejoiced, for I could say—

"Nothing in my hands I bring,
Simply to His Cross I cling.
Naked I look to Him for dress,
Helpless, I come to Him for grace!
Black, I to this fountain fly—
Wash me, Savior, or I die!"

And now, Believer, you shall tell the rest. The moment that you believed, your burden rolled from your shoulder and you became light as air. Instead of darkness you had light. For the garments of heaviness you had the robes of praise. Who shall tell of your joy since then? You have sung on earth hymns of Heaven and in your peaceful soul you have anticipated the eternal Sabbath of the redeemed. Because you have believed you have entered into rest. Yes, tell it to the whole world over—they that believe, by Jesus' death are justified from all things from which they could not be freed by the works of the Law. Tell it in Heaven—none can lay anything to the charge of God's elect. Tell it upon earth—God's redeemed are free from sin in Jehovah's sight. Tell it even in Hell—God's elect can never go there—Christ has died for His elect and who is he that shall condemn them?

I have hurried over that, to come to the last point, which is the sweetest of all. Jesus Christ, we are told in our text, came into the world, "to give His life a ransom for many." The greatness of Christ's redemption may be measured by the EXTENT OF THE DESIGN OF IT. He gave His life "a ransom for many." I must now return to that controverted point again. We are often told (I mean those of us who are commonly nicknamed by the title of Calvinists—and we are not very much ashamed of that). We think that Calvin, after all, knew more about the Gospel than almost any uninspired man who has ever lived. We are often told that we limit the atonement of Christ because we say that Christ has not made a satisfaction for all men, or all men would be saved.

Now, our reply to this is, that, on the other hand, our opponents limit it—we do not. The Arminians say Christ died for all men. Ask them what they mean by it. Did Christ die so as to secure the salvation of all men? They say, "No, certainly not." We ask them the next question—Did Christ die so as to secure the salvation of any man in particular? They answer, "No." They are obliged to admit this if they are consistent. They say "No, Christ has died that any man may be saved if"—and then follow certain conditions of salvation. We say, then, we will just go back to the old statement—Christ did not die so as beyond a doubt to secure the salvation of anybody, did he? You must say, "No." You are obliged to say so, for you believe that even after a man has been pardoned, he may yet fall from grace and perish.

Now, who is it that limits the death of Christ? Why, you. You say that Christ did not die so as to infallibly secure the salvation of anybody. We beg your pardon, when you say we limit Christ's death. We say, "No, my dear Sir, it is you that do it. We say Christ so died that He infallibly secured the salvation of a multitude that no man can number, who through Christ's death not only may be saved but are saved, must be saved and cannot by any possibility run the hazard of being anything but saved. You are welcome to your atonement. You may keep it. We will never renounce ours for the sake of it."

Now, Beloved, when you hear anyone laughing or jeering at a limited atonement, you may tell him this—general atonement is like a great wide bridge with only half an arch. It does not go across the stream. It only professes to go half way—it does not secure the salvation of anybody. Now, I had rather put my foot upon a bridge as narrow as Hungerford, which went all the way across, than on a bridge that was as wide as the world, if it did not go all the way across the stream. I am told it is my duty to say that all men have been redeemed, and I am told that there is a Scriptural warrant for it—"Who gave himself a ransom for all, to be testified in due time."

Now, that looks like a very great argument, indeed, on the other side of the question. For instance, look here—"The whole world is gone after Him." Did all the world go after Christ? "Then went all Judea and were baptized of him in Jordan." Was all Judea, or all Jerusalem baptized in Jordan? "You are of God, little children," and "the whole world lies in the wicked one." Does "the whole world" there mean everybody? If so, how was it, then, that there were some who were "of God"? The words "world" and "all" are used in some seven or eight senses in Scripture. And it is very rarely that "all" means all persons taken individually. The words are generally used to signify that Christ has redeemed some of all sorts—some Jews, some Gentiles, some rich, some poor—and has not restricted His redemption to either Jew or Gentile.

Leaving controversy, however, I will now answer a question. Tell me then, Sir, who did Christ die for? Will you answer me a question or two and I will tell you whether He died for you. Do you want a Savior? Do you feel that you need a Savior? Are you this morning conscious of sin? Has the Holy Spirit taught you that you are lost? Then Christ died for you and you will be saved. Are you this morning conscious that you have no hope in the world but Christ? Do you feel that you of yourself cannot offer an atonement that can satisfy God's justice? Have you given up all confidence in yourselves? And can you say upon your bended knees "Lord, save, or I perish"? Christ died for you.

If you are saying this morning, "I am as good as I ought to be. I can get to Heaven by my own good works," then, remember, the Scripture says of Jesus, "I came not to call the righteous, but sinners to repentance." So long as you are in that state I have no atonement to preach to you. But if this morning you feel guilty, wretched, conscious of your guilt and are ready to take Christ to be your only Savior, I can not only say to you that you may be saved, but what is better still, that you will be saved.

When you are stripped of everything but hope in Christ. When you are prepared to come empty handed and take Christ to be your All and to be yourself nothing at all–then you may look up to Christ and you may say, "You dear, You bleeding Lamb of God! Your griefs were endured for me. By Your stripes I am healed and by Your sufferings I am pardoned." And then see what peace of mind you will have–for if Christ has died for you, you cannot be lost. God will not punish twice for one thing.

If God punished Christ for your sin, He will never punish you. "Payment, God's justice cannot twice demand, first, at the bleeding Surety's hand, and then again at mine." We can today, if we believe in Christ, march to the very Throne of God, stand there, and if it is said, "Are you guilty?" We can say, "Yes, guilty." But if the question is put, "What have you to say why you should not be punished for your guilt?" We can answer, "Great God, Your justice and Your love are both our guarantees that You will not punish us for sin. For did You not punish Christ for sin for us? How can You, then, be just–how can You be God at all, if You punish Christ the Substitute, and then punish man himself afterwards?"

Your only question is, "Did Christ die for me?" And the only answer we can give is–"This is a faithful saying, and worthy of all acceptation, that Christ came into the world to save sinners." Can you write your name down among the sinners? Not among the complimentary sinners, but among those that feel it, bemoan it, lament it, seek mercy on account of it? Are you a sinner? That felt, that known, that professed–you are now invited to believe that Jesus Christ died for you, because you are a sinner–and you are bidden to cast yourself upon this great immovable Rock and find eternal security in the Lord Jesus Christ.

IV

Irresistable Grace

EFFECTUAL CALLING

MARCH 30, 1856, AT NEW PARK STREET CHAPEL, SOUTHWARK

"When Jesus came to the place, he looked up, and saw him, and said unto him, Zaccheus, make haste and come down; for today I must abide at your house."
Luke 19:5

Notwithstanding our firm belief that you are, for the most part, well instructed in the doctrines of the everlasting Gospel, we are continually reminded in our conversation with young converts how absolutely necessary it is to repeat our former lessons and repeatedly assert and prove over and over again those doctrines which lie at the basis of our holy religion. Our friends, therefore, who have many years ago been taught the great doctrine of effectual calling, will believe that while I preach very simply this morning, the sermon is intended for those who are young in the fear of the Lord, that they may better understand this great starting point of God in the heart, the effectual calling of men by the Holy Spirit.

    I shall use the case of Zaccheus as a great illustration of the doctrine of effectual calling. You remember the story. Zaccheus had a curiosity to see the wonderful man, Jesus Christ, who was turning the world upside down and causing an immense excitement in the minds of men. We sometimes find fault with curiosity and say it is sinful to come to the house of God from that motive. I am not quite sure that we should hazard such an assertion. The motive is not sinful, though certainly it is not virtuous—yet it has often been proved that curiosity is one of the best allies of grace. Zaccheus, moved by this motive, desired to see Christ—but there were two obstacles in the way—first, there was such a crowd of people that he could not get near the Savior. Second, he was so exceedingly short in stature that there was no hope of his reaching over people's heads to catch a glimpse of Him.

What did he do? He did as the boys were doing—for the boys of old times were no doubt just like the boys of the present age—they were perched up in the boughs of the tree to look at Jesus as He passed along. Elderly man though he is, Zaccheus jumps up and there he sits among the children. The boys are too much afraid of that stern old Publican, whom their fathers dreaded, to push him down or cause him any inconvenience. Look at him there. With what anxiety he is peeping down to see which is Christ—for the Savior had no pompous distinction. No one is walking before Him with a silver mace. He did not hold a golden crozier in His hand—He had no pontifical dress. In fact, He was just dressed like those around Him. He had a coat like that of a common peasant, made of one piece from top to bottom. Zaccheus could scarcely distinguish Him. However, before he has caught a sight of Christ, Christ has fixed His eye upon him and standing under the tree, He looks up and says, "Zaccheus, make haste and come down; for today I must abide at your house." Down comes Zaccheus. Christ goes to his house. Zaccheus becomes Christ's follower and enters into the kingdom of Heaven.

Now, first, effectual calling is a very gracious Truth of God. You may guess this from the fact that Zaccheus was a character whom we should suppose the last to be saved. He belonged to a bad city—Jericho—a city which had been cursed and no one would suspect that anyone would come out of Jericho to be saved. It was near Jericho that the man fell among thieves—we trust Zaccheus had no hand in it—but there are some who, while they are Publicans, can be thieves, also. We might as well expect converts from St. Giles's, or the lowest parts of London, from the worst and vilest dens of infamy, as from Jericho in those days.

Ah, my Brethren, it matters not where you come from—you may come from one of the dirtiest streets, one of the worst back slums in London—if effectual grace calls you, it is an effectual call, which knows no distinction of place. Zaccheus also was of an exceedingly bad trade and probably cheated the people in order to enrich himself. Indeed, when But, my Brethren, grace knows no distinction. It is no respecter of persons. God calls whom He wills and He called this worst of Publicans, in the worst of cities, from the worst of trades. Besides, Zaccheus was one who was the least likely to be saved because he was rich. It is true, rich and poor are welcome—no one has the least excuse for despair because of his condition—yet it is a fact that "not many great men" after the flesh, "not many mighty" are called, but "God has chosen the poor of this world—rich in faith."

But even here grace knows no distinction. The rich Zaccheus is called from the tree. Down he comes and he is saved. I have thought it one of the greatest instances of God's condescension that He can look down on man. But I will tell you there was a greater condescension than that when Christ looked up to see Zaccheus. For God to look down on His creatures—that is mercy—but for Christ so to humble Himself that He has to look up to one of His own creatures—that becomes mercy, indeed!

Ah, many of you have climbed up the tree of your own good works and perched yourselves in the branches of your holy actions and are trusting in the free will of the poor creature, or resting in some worldly maxim. Nevertheless, Christ looks up even to proud sinners and calls them down. "Come down," says He, "today I must abide at your house." Had Zaccheus been a humble-minded man, sitting by the wayside, or at the feet of Christ, we should then have admired Christ's mercy. But here he is lifted up and Christ looks up to him and bids him come down.

Next it was a personal call. There were boys in the tree as well as Zaccheus but there was no mistake about the person who was called. It was, "Zaccheus, make haste and come down." There are other calls mentioned in Scripture. It is said especially, "Many are called, but few are chosen." Now that is not the effectual call which is intended by the Apostle when he said, "Whom He called, them He also justified." That is a general call which many men, yes, all men reject, unless there comes after it the personal, particular call, which makes us Christians. You will bear me witness that it was a personal call that brought you to the Savior. It was some sermon which led you to feel that you were, no doubt, the person intended.

The text, perhaps, was "You, God, see me." And perhaps the minister laid particular stress on the word "me," so that you thought God's eyes were fixed upon you. And before the sermon was concluded you thought you saw God open the books to condemn you and your heart whispered, "Can any hide himself in secret places that I shall not see him? says the Lord." You might have been perched in the window, or stood packed in the aisle—but you had a solemn conviction that the sermon was preached to you and not to other people. God does not call His people in shoals but in units.

"Jesus said unto her, Mary; and she turned and said unto him, Rabboni, which is to say, Master." Jesus sees Peter and John fishing by the lake and He says to them, "Follow Me." He sees Matthew sitting at the table at the receipt of custom and He says unto him, "Arise and follow Me," and Matthew did so. When the Holy Spirit comes home to a man, God's arrow goes into his heart—it does not graze his helmet, or make some little mark upon his armor—it penetrates between the joints of the harness, entering the marrow of the soul. Have you felt, dear Friends, that personal call? Do you remember when a voice said, "Arise, He calls you." Can you look back to when you said, "My Lord, my God"—when you knew the Spirit was striving with you and you said, "Lord, I come to You, for I know that You call me"? I might call the whole of you throughout eternity but if God call one, there will be more effect through His personal call of one than my general call of multitudes.

Thirdly, it is a hastening call. "Zaccheus, make haste." The sinner, when he is called by the ordinary ministry, replies, "Tomorrow." He hears a telling sermon and he says, "I will turn to God by-and-by." The tears roll down his cheek but they are wiped away. Some goodness appears but like the cloud of the morning it is dissipated by the sun of temptation. He says, "I solemnly vow from this time to be a reformed man. After I have once more indulged in my darling sin I will renounce my lusts and decide for God." Ah, that is only a minister's call and is good for nothing. Hell, they say, is paved with good intentions. These good intentions are begotten by general calls.

The road to perdition is laid all over with branches of the trees whereon men are sitting, for they often pull down branches from the trees but they do not come down themselves. The straw laid down before a sick man's door causes the wheels to roll more noiselessly. So there are some who strew their path with promises of repentance and so go more easily and noiselessly down to perdition. But God's call is not a call for tomorrow. "Today if you will hear His voice, harden not your hearts: as in the provocation, when your fathers tempted Me." God's grace always comes with dispatch—and if you are drawn by God, you will run after God and not be talking about delays. Tomorrow—it is not written in the almanac of time.

Tomorrow—it is in Satan's calendar and nowhere else. Tomorrow—it is a rock whitened by the bones of mariners who have been wrecked upon it. Tomorrow is the wrecker's light gleaming on the shore, luring poor ships to destruction. Tomorrow—it is the idiot's cup which he lies at the foot of the rainbow, but which none has ever found. Tomorrow—it is the floating island of Loch Lomond,[38] which none has ever seen. Tomorrow—it is a dream. Tomorrow—it is a delusion. Tomorrow, yes, tomorrow you may lift up your eyes in Hell, being in torment. Yonder clock says "today." Your pulse whispers "today." I hear my heart speak as it beats and it says, "today." Everything cries "today." And the Holy Spirit is in union with these things and says, "Today if you will hear His voice, harden not your hearts." Sinners, are you inclined now to seek the Savior? Are you breathing a prayer now? Are you saying, "Now or never! I must be saved now"? If you are, then I hope it is an effectual call, for Christ, when He gives an effectual call, says, "Zaccheus, make haste."

Next, it is a humbling call. "Zaccheus, make haste and come down." Many a time has a minister called men to repentance with a call which has made them proud, exalted them in their own esteem and led them to say, "I can turn to God when I like. I can do so without the influence of the Holy Spirit." They have been called to go up and not to come down. God always humbles a sinner. Can I not remember when God told me to come down? One of the first steps I had to take was to go right down from my good works. And oh, what a fall was that! Then I stood upon my own self-sufficiency and Christ said, "Come down! I have pulled you down from your good works and now I

---

[38] Lake in Scotland; largest lake in Great Britain by surface area

will pull you down from your self-sufficiency."

Well, I had another fall and I felt sure I had gained the bottom, but Christ said "Come down!" And He made me come down till I fell on some point at which I felt I was not savable. "Down, Sir! come down, yet." And down I came until I had to let go of every branch of the tree of my hopes in despair. Then I said, "I can do nothing. I am ruined." The waters were wrapped round my head and I was shut out from the light of day and thought myself a stranger from the commonwealth of Israel.

"Come down lower yet, Sir! You have too much pride to be saved." Then I was brought down to see my corruption, my wickedness, my filthiness. "Come down," says God, when He means to save. Now, proud Sinners, it is of no use for you to be proud, to stick yourselves up in the trees—Christ will have you down. Oh, you that dwell with the eagle on the craggy rock, you shall come down from your elevation—you shall fall by grace, or you shall fall with a vengeance one day. He "has cast down the mighty from their seat and has exalted the humble and meek."

Next, it is an affectionate call. "Today I must abide at your house." You can easily conceive how the faces of the multitude change! They thought Christ to be the holiest and best of men and were ready to make Him a king. But He says, "Today I must abide at your house." There was one poor Jew who had been inside Zaccheus' house—he had "been on the carpet," as they say in country villages when they are taken before the justice and he recollected what sort of a house it was. He remembered how he was taken in there and his conceptions of it were something like what a fly would have of a spider's den after he had once escaped.

There was another who had been restrained of nearly all his property—the idea he had of walking in there was like walking into a den of lions. "What?" said they, "Is this holy man going into such a den as that, where we poor wretches have been robbed and ill-treated? It was bad enough for Christ to speak to him up in the tree, but the idea of going into his house!" They all murmured at His going to be "a guest with a man who was a sinner." Well, I know what some of His disciples thought—they thought it very imprudent—it might injure His character and He might offend the people. They thought He might have gone to see this man at night, like Nicodemus, and give him an audience when nobody saw Him! To acknowledge such a man publicly was the most imprudent act He could commit.

Why did Christ do as He did? Because He would give Zaccheus an affectionate call. "I will not come and stand at your threshold, or look in at your window, but I will come into your house—the same house where the cries of widows have come into your ears and you have disregarded them. I will come into your parlor, where the weeping of the orphan has never moved your compassion. I will come there, where you, like a ravenous lion have devoured your prey. I will come there, where you have blackened your house and made it infamous. I will come into the place where cries have risen to high Heaven, wrung from the lips of those whom you have oppressed.

"I will come into your house and give you a blessing." Oh, what affection there was in that! Poor Sinner, my Master is a very affectionate Master. He will come into your house. What kind of a house have you got? A house that you have made miserable with your drunkenness—a house you have defiled with your impurity—a house you have defiled with your cursing and swearing—a house where you are carrying on an illegal trade that you would be glad to get rid of? Christ says, "I will come into your house." And I know some houses now that once were dens of sin where Christ comes every morning. Husband and wife, who once only could quarrel and fight, bend their knees together in prayer. Christ comes there at dinnertime, when the workman comes home for his meals. Some of my hearers can scarce come for an hour to their meals but they must have word of prayer and reading of the Scriptures.

Christ comes to them. Where the walls were plastered up with the lascivious songs and idle pictures, there is a Christian almanac in one place. There is a Bible on the chest of drawers—and though it is only one room they live in—if an angel should come in and God should say, 'What have you seen in that house?" He would say, "I have seen good furniture, for there is a Bible there—here and there a religious book—the filthy pictures are pulled down and burned. There are no cards in the man's cupboard now. Christ has come into his house." Oh, what a blessing that we have our household God as well as the Romans! Our God is a household God. He comes to live with His people!

He loves the tents of Jacob.

Now, poor rag-muffin Sinner, you who live in the filthiest den in London, if such an one be here, Jesus says to you, "Zaccheus, make haste and come down; for today I must abide at your house."

Again, it was not only an affectionate call, but it was an abiding call. Today I must abide at your house." A common call is like this, "Today I shall walk in at your house at one door and out at the other." The common call which is given by the Gospel to all men is a call which operates upon them for a time and then it is all over—but the saving call is an abiding call. When Christ speaks, He does not say, "Make haste, Zaccheus and come down, for I am just coming to look in." No. He says, "I must abide at your house. I am coming to sit down to eat and drink with you. I am coming to have a meal with you. Today I must abide at your house."

"Ah," says one, "you cannot tell how many times I have been impressed, Sir. I have often had a series of solemn convictions and I thought I really was saved—but it all died away—like a dream. When one awakes, all has vanished that he dreamed. So was it with me." Ah, but poor Soul, do not despair. Do you feel the strivings of Almighty Grace within your heart bidding you repent today? If you do, it will be an abiding call. If it is Jesus at work in your soul, He will come and tarry in your heart and consecrate you for His own forever. He says, "I will come and dwell with you and that forever. I will come and say—

"*Here I will make My settled rest,*
No more will go and come;
No more a stranger or a guest,
But Master of this home."

"Oh," you say, "that is what I want. I want an abiding call, something that will last. I do not want a religion that will wash out, but a fast-color religion." Well, that is the kind of call Christ gives. His ministers cannot give it—but when Christ speaks, He speaks with power and says, "Zaccheus, make haste and come down; for today I must abide at your house."

There is one thing, however, I cannot forget and that is that it was a necessary call. Just read it over again. "Zaccheus, make haste and come down; for today I must abide at your house." It was not a thing that He might do, or might not do—it was a necessary call. The salvation of a sinner is as much a matter of necessity with God as the fulfillment of His Covenant that the rain shall no more drown the world. The salvation of every blood-bought child of God is a necessary thing for three reasons:

It is necessary because it is God's purpose. It is necessary because it is Christ's purchase and it is necessary because it is God's promise. It is necessary that the child of God should be saved. Some divines think it is very wrong to lay a stress on the word "must," especially in that passage where it is said, "He must go through Samaria." "Why," they say, "He must needs go through Samaria because there was no other way He could go and therefore He was forced to go that way." Yes, Gentlemen, we reply, no doubt. But then there might have been another way. Providence made it so that He must go through Samaria and that Samaria should lie in the route He had chosen.

"He must needs go through Samaria." Providence directed man to build Samaria directly in the road and grace constrained the Savior to move in that direction. It was not, "Come down, Zaccheus, because I may abide at your house," but "I must." The Savior felt a strong necessity. Just as much a necessity as there is that man should die. As strong a necessity as there is that the sun should give us light by day and the moon by night—just so much a necessity is there that every blood-bought child of God shall be saved.

"Today I must abide at your house." And oh, when the Lord comes to this—that He must—then He will. What a thing it is with the poor sinner, then, at other times we ask, "Shall I let Him in at all? There is a stranger at the door. He is knocking now—He has knocked before—shall I let Him in?" But this time it is, "I must abide at your house." There was no knocking at the door, but smash went the door into atoms! And in He walked—I must, I shall, I will—I care not for your protecting your vileness, your unbelief. I must, I will—I must abide at your house."

"Ah," says one, "I do not believe God would ever make me to believe as you believe, or become a Christian at all." Ah, but if He shall but say, "Today I must abide at your house," there will be no resistance in you. There are some of you who would scorn the very idea of being a canting Methodist—"What, Sir? Do you suppose I would ever turn into one of your religious people?" No, my Friend, I don't suppose it—I know it for a certainty. If God says "I must," there is no standing against it. Let Him say "must," and it must be.

I will just tell you an anecdote proving this. "A father was about sending his son to college, but as he knew the influence to which he would be exposed, he was not without a deep and anxious solicitude for the spiritual and eternal welfare of his favorite child. Fearing lest the principles of Christian faith, which he had endeavored to instill into his mind would be rudely assailed, but trusting in the efficacy of that Word which is quick and powerful, he purchased, unknown to his son, an elegant copy of the Bible and deposited it at the bottom of his trunk.

The young man entered upon his college career. The restraints of a pious education were soon broken off and he proceeded from speculation to doubts and from doubts to a denial of the reality of religion. After having become in his own estimation, wiser than his father, he discovered one day, while rummaging his trunk, with great surprise and indignation, the sacred deposit. He took it out and while deliberating on the manner in which he should treat it, he determined that he would use it as waste paper, on which to wipe his razor while shaving. Accordingly, every time he went to shave, he tore out a leaf or two of the holy book and thus used it till nearly half the volume was destroyed.

But while he was committing this outrage upon the sacred book, a text now and then met his eye and was carried like a barbed arrow to his heart. At length, he heard a sermon, which discovered to him his own character and his exposure to the wrath of God. It riveted upon his mind the impression which he had received from the last torn leaf of the blessed, yet insulted volume. Had worlds been at his disposal, he would freely have given them all, could they have availed, in enabling him to undo what he had done. At length he found forgiveness at the foot of the Cross. The torn leaves of that sacred volume brought healing to his soul—for they led him to repose on the mercy of God, which is sufficient for the chief of sinners.

I tell you there is not a reprobate walking the streets and defiling the air with his blasphemies. There is not a creature abandoned so as to be well-nigh as bad as Satan himself—if he is a child of life—who is not within the reach of mercy. And if God says, "Today I must abide at your house," He then assuredly will.

Do you feel, my dear Hearer, just now, something, in your mind which seems to say you have held out against the Gospel a long while, but today you can hold out no longer? Do you feel that a strong hand has got hold of you and do you hear a voice saying, "Sinner, I must abide at your house. You have often scorned Me, you have often laughed at Me, you have often spit in the face of mercy, often blasphemed Me, but Sinner, I must abide at your house. You banged the door yesterday in the missionary's face. You burned the tract, you laughed at the minister, you have cursed God's house, you have violated the Sabbath—but, Sinner, I must abide at your house and I will"?

"What? Lord," you say, "abide at my house! Why it is covered all over with iniquity. Abide in my house! Why there is not a chair or a table but would cry out against me. Abide in my house! Why the joists and beams and flooring would all rise up and tell You that I am not worthy to kiss the hem of Your garment. What? Lord, abide at my house!" "Yes," says He, "I must. There is a strong necessity, My powerful love constrains Me and whether you will let Me or not, I am determined to make you willing and you shall let Me in."

Does not this surprise you, poor Trembler—you who thought that mercy's day was gone and that the bell of your destruction had tolled your death-knell? Oh, does not this surprise you, that Christ not only asks you to come to Him, but invites Himself to your table, and what is more, when you would put Him away, kindly says, I must—I will come in"? Only think of Christ going after a sinner, crying after a sinner, begging a sinner to let Him save him—and that is just what Jesus does to His chosen ones.

The sinner runs away from Him, but free grace pursues him and says, "Sinner, come to Christ." And if our hearts are shut up, Christ puts His hand in at the door and if we do not rise, but repulse Him coldly, He says, "I must, I will come in." He weeps over us till His tears win us. He cries after us till His cries prevail—and at last in His own well-determined hour He enters into our heart and there He dwells. "I must abide at your house," said Jesus.

And now, lastly, this call was an effectual one, for we see the fruits it brought forth. Open was Zaccheus' door, spread was his table, generous was his heart, washed were his hands, unburdened was his conscience, joyful was his soul. "Here, Lord," says he, "the half of my goods I give to the poor. I dare say I have robbed them of half my property—and now I restore it. And if I have taken anything from anyone by false accusation, I will restore it to him fourfold." Away goes another portion of his property. Ah, Zaccheus, you will go to bed tonight a great deal poorer than when you got up this morning—but infinitely richer, too!

Poor, very poor, in this world's goods, compared with what you were when you first did climb that sycamore tree. But richer—infinitely richer—in heavenly treasure. Sinner, we shall know whether God calls you by this—if He calls, it will be an effectual call—not a call which you hear and then forget—but one which produces good works. If God has called you this morning, down will go that drunken cup, up will go your prayers. If God has called you this morning, there will not be one shutter down today in your shop, but all and you will have a notice stuck up, "This house is closed on the Sabbath-Day and will not again on that day, be opened."

Tomorrow there will be such-and-such worldly amusement—but if God has called you, you will not go. And if you have robbed anybody (and who knows but I may have a thief here), if God calls you, there will be a restoration of what you have stolen—you will give up all that you have—so that you will follow God with all your heart. We do not believe a man to be converted unless he does renounce the error of his ways—unless, practically, he is brought to know that Christ Himself is Master of his conscience and His Law is his delight.

"Zaccheus, make haste and come down, I must abide at your house." And he made haste and came down and Jesus received him joyfully. "And Zaccheus stood and said unto the Lord, Behold, Lord, the half of my goods I give to the poor; and if I have taken anything from any man by false accusation, I restore him fourfold. And Jesus said unto him, This day is salvation come to this house, forasmuch as he also is a son of Abraham. For the Son of Man is come to seek and to save that which was lost."

Now, one or two lessons. A lesson to the proud. Come down, proud heart, come down! Mercy runs in valleys, but it goes not to the mountaintop. Come down, come down, lofty spirit! The lofty city—He lays it low even to the ground and then He builds it up. Again, a lesson to the poor despairing soul—I am glad to see you in God's house this morning—it is a good sign. I care not what you came for. You heard there was a strange kind of man that preached here, perhaps. Never mind about that. You are all quite as strange as he is. It is necessary that there should be strange men to gather in other strange men.

Now, I have a mass of people here. And if I might use a figure, I should compare you to a great heap of ashes, mingled with which are a few steel filings. Now, my sermon, if it is attended with Divine Grace, will be a sort of magnet—it will not attract any of the ashes—they will keep just where they are—but it will draw out the steel filings. I have got a Zaccheus there. There is a Mary up there. A John down there, a Sarah, or a William, or a Thomas there—God's chosen ones—they are steel filings in the congregation of ashes and my Gospel, the Gospel of the blessed God, like a great magnet, draws them out of the heap.

There they come, there they come. Why? Because there was a magnetic power between the Gospel and their hearts. Ah, poor Sinner, come to Jesus, believe His love, trust His mercy. If you have a desire to come, if you are forcing your way through the ashes to get to Christ, then it is because Christ is calling you. Oh, all of you who know yourselves to be sinners—every man, woman and child of you—yes, you little children (for God has given me some of you to be my wages), do you feel yourselves sinners?

Then believe on Jesus and be saved. You have come here from curiosity, many of you. Oh, that you might be met with and saved. I am distressed for you lest you should sink into Hell. Oh, listen to Christ while He speaks to you. Christ says, "Come down." This morning go home and humble yourselves in the sight of God. Go and confess your iniquities that you have sinned against Him. Go home and tell Him that you are a wretch, undone without His sovereign grace. Then look to Him, for rest assured He has first looked to you. You say, "Sir, oh, I am willing enough to be saved, but I am afraid He is not willing."

Stop! Stop! No more of that! Do you know that is part blasphemy? Not quite all. If you were not ignorant, I would tell you that it was full blasphemy.

You cannot look to Christ before He has looked to you. If you are willing to be saved, He gave you that will. Believe on the Lord Jesus Christ and be baptized and you shall be saved. I trust the Holy Spirit is calling you.

Young man up there, young man in the window, make haste! Come down! Old man, sitting in these pews, come down! Merchant in yonder aisle, make haste. Matron and youth, not knowing Christ, oh, may He look at you! Old grandmother, hear the gracious call. And you, young lad, Christ may be looking at you—I trust He is—and saying to you, "Make haste and come down, for today I must abide at your house."

V

Perseverance of the Saints

FINAL PERSEVERANCE

APRIL 20, 1856, AT NEW PARK STREET CHAPEL, SOUTHWARK

"For it is impossible for those who were once enlightened and have tasted of the heavenly gift, and were made partakers of the Holy Ghost, and have tasted the good word of God, and the powers of the world to come, if they shall fall away, to renew them again unto repentance, seeing they crucify to themselves the Son of God afresh, and put him to an open shame."
Hebrews 6:4-6

THERE are some spots in Europe which have been the scenes of frequent warfare, as for instance, the kingdom of Belgium which might be called the battlefield of Europe. War has raged over the whole of Europe, but in some unhappy spots, battle after battle has been fought. So there is scarce a passage of Scripture which has not been disputed between the enemies of the Truth of God and the upholders of it—but this passage with one or two others has been the special subject of attack. This is one of the texts which have been trod under the feet of controversy and there are opinions upon it as adverse as the poles. Some assert that it means one thing and some declare that it means another. We think that some of them approach somewhat near the truth—but others of them desperately err from the mind of the Spirit.

We come to this passage ourselves with the intention to read it with the simplicity of a child and whatever we find therein to state it. And if it may not seem to agree with something we have up to now held, we are prepared to cast away every doctrine of our own rather than one passage of Scripture. Looking at the scope of the whole passage, it appears to us that the Apostle wished to push the disciples on. There is a tendency in the human mind to stop short of the heavenly mark. As soon as ever we have attained to the first principles of religion, have passed through Baptism and understand the resurrection of the dead, there is a tendency in us to sit still—to say, "I have passed from death unto life. Here I may take my stand and rest."

The Christian life was intended not to be a sitting still, but a race, a perpetual motion. The Apostle, therefore, endeavors to urge the disciples forward and make then run with diligence the heavenly race, looking unto Jesus. He tells them that it is not enough to have on a certain day passed through a glorious change—to have experienced at a certain time a wonderful operation of the Spirit. Rather, he teaches them it is absolutely necessary that they should have the Spirit all their lives—that they should, as long as they live, be progressing in the Truth of God. In order to make them persevere, if possible, he shows them that if they do not, they must, most certainly be lost—for there is no other salvation but that which God has already bestowed on them and if that does not keep them—carry them forward and present them spotless before God—there cannot be any other. It is impossible, he says, if you are once enlightened and then fall away, that you should ever be renewed again unto repentance.

We shall, this morning, answer one or two questions. The first question will be, Who are the people here spoken of? Are they true Christians, or not? Secondly, What is meant by "falling away"? And thirdly, What is intended, when it is asserted, that it is impossible to renew them to repentance?

First, then, we answer the question, WHO ARE THE PEOPLE HERE SPOKEN OF? If you read Dr. Gill,[39] Dr. Owen[40] and almost all the eminent Calvinistic writers they all of them assert that these persons are not Christians. They say that enough is said here to represent a man who is a Christian externally

---

[39] John Gill, an eighteenth-century English Baptist pastor, biblical scholar, and Calvinist theologian

[40] John Owen, a seventeenth-century English Congregational pastor, Calvinist theologian, and academic administrator at the University of Oxford

but not enough to give the portrait of a true Believer. Now, it strikes me they would not have said this if they had not had some doctrine to uphold—for a child reading this passage would say that the persons intended by it must be Christians. If the Holy Spirit intended to describe Christians, I do not see that He could have used more explicit terms than there are here. How can a man be said to be enlightened, to taste of the heavenly gift and to be made partaker of the Holy Spirit, without being a child of God? With all deference to these learned doctors, and I admire and love them all, I humbly conceive that they allowed their judgments to be a little warped when they said that.

And I think I shall be able to show that none but true Believers are here described. First, they are spoken of as having been once enlightened. This refers to the enlightening influence of God's Spirit, poured into the soul at the time of conviction—when man is enlightened with regard to his spiritual state. When he is made to see how evil and bitter a thing it is to sin against God, made to feel how utterly powerless he is to rise from the grave of his corruption—and is further enlightened to see, that "by the deeds of the Law shall no flesh living be justified," and to behold Christ on the Cross, as the sinner's only hope.

The first work of grace is to enlighten the soul. By nature we are entirely dark. The Spirit, like a lamp, sheds light into the dark heart, revealing its corruption, displaying its sad state of destitution and, in due time, revealing also Jesus Christ, so that in His light we may see light. I cannot consider a man truly enlightened unless he is a child of God. Does not the term indicate a person taught of God? It is not the whole of Christian experience—but is it not a part?

Having enlightened us, as the text says, the next thing that God grants to us is a taste of the heavenly gift, by which we understand the heavenly gift of salvation, including the pardon of sin, justification by the imputed righteousness of Jesus Christ, regeneration by the Holy Spirit and all those gifts and graces in which the earlier dawn of spiritual life convey salvation. All true Believers have tasted of the heavenly gift. It is not enough for a man to be enlightened—the light may glare upon his eyeballs—and yet he may die—he must taste as well as see that the Lord is good. It is not enough to see that I am corrupt—I must taste that Christ is able to remove my corruption. It is not enough for me to know that He is the only Savior—I must taste of His flesh and of His blood and have a vital union with Him.

We most certainly think that when a man has been enlightened and has had an experience of grace, he is a Christian. Whatever those great divines might hold, we cannot think that the Holy Spirit would describe an unregenerate man as having been enlightened and as having tasted of the heavenly gift. No, my Brethren, if I have tasted of the heavenly gift, then that heavenly gift is mine. If I have had ever so short an experience of my Savior's love, I am one of His. If He has brought me into the green pastures and made me taste of the still waters and the tender grass, I need not fear as to whether I am really a child of God.

Then the Apostle gives a further description, a higher state of grace—sanctification by participation of the Holy Spirit. It is a peculiar privilege to Believers, after their first tasting of the heavenly gift, to be made partakers of the Holy Spirit. He is an indwelling Spirit. He dwells in the hearts, souls and minds of men. He makes this mortal flesh His home—He makes our soul His palace and there He rests. We do assert (and we think on the authority of Scripture), that no man can be a partaker of the Holy Spirit and yet be unregenerate. Where the Holy Spirit dwells there must be life and if I have participation with the Holy Spirit and fellowship with Him, then I may rest assured that my salvation has been purchased by the blood of the Savior. You need not fear, Beloved—if you have the Holy Spirit, you have that which ensures your salvation. If you, by an inward communion, can participate in His Spirit and if by a perpetual indwelling the Holy Spirit rests in you, you are not only a Christian, but you have arrived at some maturity in and by grace. You have gone beyond mere enlightenment—you have passed from the bare taste—you have attained to a positive feast and a partaking of the Holy Spirit.

Lest there should be any mistake, however, about the persons being children of God, the Apostle goes to a further stage of grace. They "have tasted the good Word of God." Now I will venture to say there are some good Christian people here who have tasted the heavenly gift, who have never "tasted the good Word of God." I mean by that, that they are really converted, have tasted the heavenly gift, but have not grown so strong in grace as to know the sweetness, the richness and the fatness of the very Word that saved them. They have been saved by the Word—but they have not come yet to realize, love and feed upon the Word as many others have.

It is one thing for God to work a work of grace in the soul—it is quite another thing for God to show us that work. It is one thing for the Word to work in us—it is another thing for us really and habitually to relish, taste and rejoice in that Word. Some of my hearers are true Christians but they have not got to that stage wherein they can love election and suck it down as a sweet morsel. They have not got wherein they can take the great doctrines of grace and feed upon them. But these people had. They had tasted the good Word of God as well as received the good gift—they had attained to such a state that they had loved the Word, had tasted and feasted upon it. It was the man of their right hand. They had counted it sweeter than honey, yes, sweeter than the droppings of the honeycomb. They had "tasted the good Word of God." I say again, if these people are not Believers—who are?

And they had gone further still. They had attained the summit of piety. They had received "the powers of the world to come." Not miraculous gifts which are denied us in these days but all those powers with which the Holy Spirit endows a Christian. And what are they? Why, there is the power of faith, which commands even the heavens themselves to rain and they rain, or stop the bottles of Heaven, that they rain not. There is the power of prayer, which puts a ladder between earth and Heaven and bids angels walk up and down, to convey our wants to God and bring down blessings from above. There is the power with which God girds His servant when he speaks by inspiration, which enables him to instruct others and lead them to Jesus. And whatever other power there may be—the power of holding communion with God, or the power of patiently waiting for the Son of Man—they were possessed by these individuals.

They were not simply children, but they were MEN—they were not merely alive but they were entitled with power. They were men whose muscles were firmly set, whose bones were strong. They had become giants in grace and had received not only the light, but the power also of the world to come. These, we say, whatever the meaning of the text must have been, were beyond a doubt none other than true and real Christians.

II. And now we answer the second question, WHAT IS MEANT BY FALLING AWAY? We must remind our friends that there is a vast distinction between falling away and falling. It is nowhere said in Scripture that if a man fall he cannot be renewed. On the contrary, "the righteous falls seven times, but he rises up again." And however many times the child of God does fall, the Lord still holds the righteous. Yes, when our bones are broken He binds up our bones again and sets us once more upon a rock. He says, "Return, you backsliding children of men, for I am married unto you," and if the Christian does backslide ever so far, still Almighty mercy cries, "Return, return, return and seek an injured Father's heart." He still calls His children back again.

Falling is not falling away. Let me explain the difference. A man who falls may behave just like a man who falls away and yet there is a great distinction between the two. I can use no better illustration than the distinction between fainting and dying. There lies a young creature—she can scarcely breathe—she cannot, herself, lift up her hand and if lifted up by anyone else, it falls. She is cold and stiff, she is faint, but not dead. There is another one, just as cold and stiff as she is, but there is this difference—she is dead. The Christian may faint and may fall down in a faint, too. And some may pick him up and say he is dead—but he is not. If he falls, God will lift him up again, but if he falls away, God Himself cannot save him. For it is impossible, if the righteous fall away, "to renew them again unto repentance."

Moreover, to fall away is not to commit sin under a temporary surprise and temptation. Abraham goes to Egypt. He is afraid that his wife will be taken away from him and he says, "She is my sister." That was a sin under a temporary surprise—a sin, of which, by-and-by he repented and God forgave him. Now that is falling—but it is not falling away. Even Noah might commit a sin which has degraded his memory even till now and shall disgrace it to the latest time—but, doubtless, Noah repented and was saved by Sovereign Grace. Noah fell, but Noah did not fall away. A Christian may go astray once and speedily return again—and though it is a sad, woeful and evil thing to be surprised into a sin—yet there is a great difference between this and the sin which would be occasioned by a total falling away from grace.

Nor can a man who commits a sin which is not exactly a surprise, be said to fall away. I believe that some Christian men–(God forbid that we should say much of it!–let us cover the nakedness of our brother with a cloak)–but I do believe that there are some Christians, who, for a period of time, have wandered into sin and yet have not positively fallen away. There is that black case of David–a case which has puzzled thousands. Certainly for some months David lived without making a public confession of his sin, but, doubtless, he had achings of heart, for grace had not ceased its work. There was a spark among the ashes that Nathan stirred up which showed that David was not dead, or else the match which the Prophet applied would not have caught light so readily. And so, Beloved, you may have wandered into sin for a time and gone far from God–and yet you are not the character here described, concerning whom it is said that it is impossible you should be saved. Wanderer though you are, you are your Father's son still, and mercy cries, "Repent, repent! Return unto your first husband, for then it was better with you than it is now. Return, O Wanderer, return."

Again, falling away is not even a giving up of profession. Some will say, "Now there is So-and-So, he used to make a profession of Christianity and now he denies it–and what is worse, he dares to curse and swear and says that he never knew Christ at all. Surely he must be fallen away." My Friend, he has fallen, fallen fearfully and fallen woefully–but I remember a case in Scripture of a man who denied his Lord and Master before His own face! You remember his name–he is an old friend of yours–our friend Simon Peter! He denied Him with oaths and curses and said, "I say unto you that I know not the man." And yet Jesus looked on Simon. He had fallen, but he had not fallen away–for, only two or three days after that, there was Peter at the tomb of his Master running there to meet his Lord, to be one of the first to find Him risen!

Beloved, you may even have denied Christ by open profession and yet if you repent there is mercy for you. Christ has not cast you away, you shall repent yet. You have not fallen away. If you had, I might not preach to you–for it is impossible for those who have fallen away to be renewed again unto repentance.

But someone says, "What is falling away?" Well, there never has been a case of it yet and therefore I cannot describe it from observation. But I will tell you what I suppose it is. To fall away would be for the Holy Spirit entirely to go out of a man—for His grace entirely to cease—not to lie dormant, but to cease to be—for God, who has begun a good work, to leave off doing it entirely—to take His hand completely and entirely away and say, "there, Man! I have halfsaved you, now I will damn you." That is what falling away is.

It is not to sin temporarily. A child may sin against his father and still be alive. Falling away is like cutting the child's head off clean. Not falling merely, for then our Father could pick us up—but being dashed down a precipice where we are lost forever. Falling away would involve God's grace changing its living nature, God's immutability becoming variable, God's faithfulness becoming changeable and God Himself being undefied—for all these things falling away would necessitate.

III. But if a child of God could fall away and grace could cease in a man's heart—now comes the third question—Paul says, IT IS IMPOSSIBLE FOR HIM TO BE RENEWED. What did the Apostle mean? One eminent commentator says he meant that it would be very hard. It would be very hard, indeed, for a man who fell away, to be saved. But we reply, "My dear Friend, it does not say anything about its being very hard—it says it is impossible and we like to read our Bible just as a child would read it." It says it is impossible and we say that it would be utterly impossible, if such a case as is supposed were to happen—impossible for man and also impossible for God—for God has purposed that He never will grant a second salvation to save those whom the first salvation has failed to deliver.

Methinks, however, I hear someone say, "It seems to me that it is possible for some such to fall away," because it says, 'It is impossible, if they shall fall away, to renew them again into repentance.' " Well, my Friend, I will grant you your theory for a moment. You are a good Christian this morning. Let us apply it to yourself and see how you will like it. You have believed in Christ and committed your soul to God and you think that in some unlucky hour you may fall entirely away. Mark you, if you come to me and tell me that you have fallen away, how would you like me to say to you, "My Friend, you are as much damned as the devil in Hell! For it is impossible to renew you to repentance"?

"Oh, no, Sir," you would say, "I will repent again and join the Church." That is just the Arminian[41] theory all over—but it is not in God's Scripture. If you once fall away you are as damned as any man who suffers in the gulf forever. And yet we have heard a man talk about people being converted three, four, and five times, and regenerated over and over again. I remember a good man (I suppose he was) pointing to a man who was walking along the street and saying, "That man has been born again three times, to my certain knowledge," (I could mention the name of the individual but I refrain from doing so) "and believe he will fall again," said he. "He is so much addicted to drinking that I do not believe the grace of God will do anything for him, unless he becomes a teetotaler."

Now, such men cannot read the Bible, because in case their members do positively fall away, here it is stated as a positive fact that it is impossible to renew them again unto repentance. But I ask my Arminian friend, does he not believe that as long as there is life there is hope? "Yes," he says—

"While the lamp holds out to burn,

The vilest sinner may return."

Well, that is not very consistent—to say this—and in the very next breath tell us that there are some people who fall away and consequently fall into such a condition that they cannot be saved. I want to know how you make these two things fit each other? I want you to make these two doctrines agree and until some enterprising individual will bring the north pole and set it on the top of the south, I cannot tell how you will accomplish it. The fact is you are quite right in saying, "While there is life there is hope"—but you are wrong in saying that any individual ever did fall into such a condition that it was impossible for him to be saved.

We come now to do two things—first to prove the doctrine, that if a Christian

---

[41] The belief that God's sovereignty and man's free will are compatible; the soteriological (study of salvation) rival to Calvinism

falls away, he cannot be saved. And, secondly, to improve the doctrine, or to show its use.

Now I am going to prove the doctrine that if a Christian FALL AWAY—not fall—for you understand how I have explained that—but if a Christian ceases to be a child of God and if grace dies out in his heart—he is then beyond the possibility of salvation and it is impossible for him ever to be renewed. Let me show you why. First, it is utterly impossible, if you consider the work which has already broken down. When men have built bridges across streams, if they have been built of the strongest material and in the most excellent manner and yet the foundation has been found so bad that none will stand, what do they say? Why, "We have already tried the best which engineering or architecture has taught us, the best has already failed. We know nothing that can exceed what has been tried. And we do, therefore, feel that there remains no possibility of ever bridging that stream, or ever running a line of railroad across this bog or this morass, for we have already tried what is acknowledged to be the best scheme."

As the Apostle says, "These people have been once enlightened. They have had once the influence of the Holy Spirit revealing to them their sin—what now remains to be tried? They have been once convicted—is there anything superior to conviction? Does the Bible promise that the poor sinner shall have anything over and above the conviction of his sin to make him sensible of it? Is there anything more powerful than the sword of the Spirit? If that has not pierced the man's heart—is there anything else which will do it? Here is a man who has been under the hammer of God's Law but that has not broken his heart—can you find anything stronger? The lamp of God's Spirit has already lit up the caverns of his soul—if that is not sufficient, where will you borrow another?

Ask the sun—has he a lamp more bright than the illumination of the Spirit? Ask the stars—have they a light more brilliant than the light of the Holy Spirit? Creation answers No. If that fails, then there is nothing else. These people, moreover, had tasted the heavenly gift—and though they had been pardoned and justified, yet pardon through Christ and justification were not enough (on this supposition) to save them. How else can they be saved? God has cast them away. After He has failed in saving them by these, what else can deliver them? Already they have tasted of the heavenly gift—is there a greater mercy for them? Is there a brighter dress than the robe of Christ's righteousness? Is there a more efficacious bath than that "fountain filled with blood"? No. All the earth echoes, "No." If the one has failed, what else does there remain?

These persons, too, have been partakers of the Holy Spirit—if that fails what more can we give them? If, my Hearer, the Holy Spirit dwells in your soul and that Holy Spirit does not sanctify you and keep you to the end, what else can be tried? Ask the blasphemer whether he knows a being, or dares to suppose a being superior to the Holy Spirit! Is there a being greater than Omnipotence? Is there a might greater than that which dwells in the Believer's new-born heart? And if already the Holy Spirit has failed, O, Heaven, tell us where we can find anything that can excel His might?

If that is ineffectual, what next is to be tried? These people, who had "tasted the good Word of Life," had loved the doctrines of grace. Those doctrines had entered into their souls and they had fed upon them. What new doctrines shall be preached to them? Prophet of ages! Where will you find another system of Divinity? Who shall we have? Shall we raise up Moses from the tomb? Shall we fetch up all the ancient seers and bid them prophesy? If, then, there is only one doctrine that is true and if these people have fallen away after receiving that, how can they be saved?

Again, these people, according to the text, have had "the powers of the world to come." They have had power to conquer sin—power in faith, power in prayer, power of communion. With what greater power shall they be endowed? This has already failed—what next can be done? O you angels! Answer, what next? What other means remain? What else can avail, if already the great things of salvation have been defeated? What else shall now be attempted? He had been once saved—but yet it is supposed that he is lost. How, then, can he now be saved? Is there a supplementary salvation? Is there something that shall overtop Christ and be a Christ where Jesus is defeated?

And then the Apostle says that the greatness of their sin which they would incur, if they did fall away, would put them beyond the bounds of mercy. Christ died and by His death He made an atonement for His own murderers.

He made an atonement for those sins which crucified Him once, but do we read that Christ will ever die for those who crucify Him twice? But the Apostle tells us that if Believers do fall away, they will "crucify the Son of God afresh and put Him to an open shame." Where, then, would be an atonement for that? He has died for me. What? Though the sins of all the world were on my shoulders, still they only crucified Him once and that one crucifixion has taken all those sins away. But if I crucified Him again, where would I find pardon? Could heavens, could earth, could Christ Himself with His heart full of love, point me to another Christ—show to me a second Calvary—give me a second Gethsemane? Ah, no! The very guilt itself would put us beyond the pale of hope, if we were to fall away!

Again Beloved, think what it would necessitate to save such a man. Christ has died for him once, yet he has fallen away and is lost. The Spirit has regenerated him once and that regenerating work has been of no use. God has given him a new heart (I am only speaking, of course, on the supposition of the Apostle)—He has put His Law in that heart—yet He has departed from him—contrary to the promise that He should not. He has made him "like a shining light," but he did not "shine more and more unto the perfect day," he shone only unto blackness. What next? There must be a second incarnation, a second Calvary, a second Holy Spirit, a second regeneration, a second justification, although the first was finished and complete—in fact, I know not what. It would necessitate the upsetting of the whole kingdom of nature and grace and it would, indeed, be a world turned upside down, if after the gracious Savior failed, He were to attempt the work again.

If you read the 7th verses, you will see that the Apostle calls nature in to his assistance. He says, "The earth which drinks in the rain that comes often upon it and brings forth herbs meet for them by whom it is dressed, receives blessing from God: But that which bears thorns and briars is rejected and is nigh unto cursing; whose end it is to be burned." Look! There is a field. The rain comes on it and it brings forth good fruit. Well, then, there is God's blessing on it. But there is, according to your supposition, another field on which the same rain descends, which the same dew moistens. It has been plowed and harrowed as well as the other and the farmer has exercised all his craft upon it and yet it is not fertile.

Well, if the rain of Heaven did not fertilize it, what next? Already all the arts of agriculture have been tried, every implement has been worn out on its surface and yet it has been of no avail. What next? There remains nothing but that it shall be burned and cursed—given up like the desert of Sahara and resigned to destruction. So, my Hearer, could it be possible that grace could work in you and then not affect your salvation? That the influence of Divine Grace could come down, like rain from Heaven and yet return unto God void? There could not be any hope for you, for you would be "nigh unto cursing," and your end would be "to be burned."

There is one idea which has occurred to us. It has struck us as a singular thing that our Friends should hold that men can be converted, made into new creatures, then fall away and be converted again. I am an old creature by nature. God creates me into a new thing. He makes me a new creature. I cannot go back into an old creature for I cannot be uncreated. But yet, supposing that new creatureship of mine is not good enough to carry me to Heaven. What is to come after that? Must there be something above a new creature—a new, new creature? Really, my Friends, we have got into the country of Dreamland—but we were forced to follow our opponents into that region of absurdity for we do not know how else to deal with them.

And one thought more. There is nothing in Scripture which teaches us that there is any salvation, save the one salvation of Jesus Christ—nothing that tells us of any other power, super-excellent and surpassing the power of the Holy Spirit. These things have already been tried on the man and yet, according to the supposition, they have failed, for he has fallen away. Now God has never revealed a supplementary salvation for men on whom one salvation has had no effect. And until we are pointed to one Scripture which declares this, we will still maintain that the doctrine of the text is this—that if grace is ineffectual, if grace does not keep a man, then there is nothing left but that he must be damned. And what is that but to say, only going a little round about, that grace will do it? So that these words instead of militating against the Calvinistic doctrine of final perseverance, form one of the firmest proofs of it that could be afforded.

And now, lastly, we come to clarify this doctrine. If Christians can fall away and cease to be Christians, they cannot be renewed again to repentance. "But," says one, "You say they cannot fall away. What is the use of putting this 'if' in, like a bugbear to frighten children, or like a ghost that can have no existence?" My learned Friend, "Who are you that replies against God?" If God has put it in, He has put it in for wise reasons and for excellent purposes. Let me show you why.

First, O Christian, it is put in to keep you from falling away. God preserves His children from falling away. But He keeps them by the use of means—and one of these is the terrors of the Law—showing them what would happen if they were to fall away. There is a deep precipice—what is the best way to keep anyone from going down there? Why to tell him that if he did he would inevitably be dashed to pieces. In some old castle there is a deep cellar where there is a vast amount of fixed air and gas which would kill anybody who went down. What does the guide say?

"If you go down you will never come up alive." Who thinks of going down? The very fact of the guide telling us what the consequences would be, keeps us from it. Our Friend puts away from us a cup of arsenic, he does not want us to drink it, but he says, "If you drink it, it will kill you." Does he suppose for a moment that we should drink it? No. He tells us the consequence and he is sure we will not do it. So God says, "My child, if you fall over this precipice you will be dashed to pieces." What does the child do? He says, "Father, keep me. Hold me up and I shall be safe." It leads the Believer to greater dependence on God, to a holy fear and caution, because he knows that if he were to fall away he could not be renewed and he stands far away from that great gulf, because he knows that if he were to fall into it there would be no salvation for him.

It is calculated to excite fear and this holy fear keeps the Christian from falling. If I thought as the Arminian thinks, that I might fall away and then return again, I should pretty often fall away. For sinful flesh and blood would think it very nice to fall away and be a sinner—go and see the play at the theater, or get drunk—and then come back to the Church and be received again as a dear Brother who had fallen away for a little while. No doubt the minister would say, "Our Brother Charles is a little unstable at times." A little unstable?! He does not know anything about grace—for grace engenders a holy caution, because we feel that if we were not preserved by Divine power we should perish.

We tell our friend to put oil in his lamp, that it may continue to burn! Does that imply that it will be allowed to go out? No, God will give him oil to pour into the lamp continually. Like John Bunyan's[42] figure—there was a fire and he saw a man pouring water upon it. "Now," says the Preacher, "don't you see that fire would go out, that water is calculated to put it out and if it does, it will never be lighted again?" But God does not permit that! For there is a man behind the wall who is pouring oil on the fire—and we have cause for gratitude in the fact that if the oil were not put in by a heavenly hand, we should inevitably be driven to destruction. Take care, then Christian, for this is a caution.

It is to excite our gratitude. Suppose you say to your little boy, "Don't you know, Tommy, if I were not to give you your dinner and your supper you would die? There is nobody else to give Tommy dinner and supper." What then? The child does not think that you are not going to give him his dinner and supper—he knows you will—and he is grateful to you for them. The chemist tells us that if there were no oxygen mixed with the air, animals would die. Do you suppose that there will be no oxygen and therefore we shall die? No, he only teaches you the great wisdom of God, in having mixed the gases in their proper proportions.

Says one of the old astronomers, "There is great wisdom in God, that He has put the sun exactly at a right distance—not so far away that we should be frozen to death and not so near that we should be scorched." He says, "If the sun were a million miles nearer to us we should be scorched to death." Does the man suppose that the sun will be a million miles nearer, and, therefore, we shall be scorched to death? He says, "If the sun were a million miles farther off we should be frozen to death." Does he mean that the sun will be a million miles farther off, and therefore we shall be frozen to death? Not at all. Yet it

---

[42] Seventeenth-century English Puritan preacher and writer; author of *The Pilgrim's Progress*

is quite a rational way of speaking to show us how grateful we should be to God. So says the Apostle. Christian—if you should fall away, you could never be renewed unto repentance—then, by His grace, He keeps you—

"*See a stone that hangs in air, see a spark in ocean live:*
Kept alive with death so near, I to God the glory give."

There is a cup of sin which would damn your soul, O Christian. Oh, what grace is that which holds your arm and will not let you drink it? There you are, at this hour, like the bird-catcher of St. Kilda[43]—you are being drawn to Heaven by a single rope—if that hand which holds you let you go, if that rope which grasps you breaks—you are dashed on the rocks of damnation. Lift up your heart to God, then, and bless Him that His arm is not wearied and is never shortened that it cannot save. Lord Kenmure,[44] when he was dying, said to Rutherford, "Man! My name is written on Christ's hand and I see it! That is bold talk, Man, but I see it!" Then, if that is the case, His hand must be severed from His body before my name can be taken from Him. And if it is engraved on His heart, His heart must be rent out before they can rend my name out.

Hold on, then and trust, Believer! You have an anchor of the soul both sure and steadfast, which enters within the veil—the winds are bellowing, the tempests howling—should the cable slip, or your anchor break, you are lost. See those rocks on which myriads are driving?—You are wrecked there if grace leaves you. See those depths in which the skeletons of sailors sleep?—You are there if that anchor fails you. It would be impossible to moor you again, if once that anchor broke, for there are no other anchors. There can be no other salvation—if that one fails you, it is impossible that you ever should be saved. Therefore thank God that you have an Anchor that cannot fail and then loudly sing—

"*How can I sink with such a prop,*
As my eternal God

---

[43] A Scottish island chain

[44] William Gordon, 6th Viscount of Kenmure, leader of the Lowlands nobles in the early eighteenth century

FINAL PERSEVERANCE

Who bears the earth's huge pillars up,
And spreads the heavens abroad?
How can I die, when Jesus lives
Who rose and left the dead?
Pardon and grace my soul receives
From my exalted Head."

THE FINAL PERSEVERANCE OF THE SAINTS

JUNE 24, 1877, AT THE METROPOLITAN TABERNACLE, NEWINGTON

"The righteous also shall hold on his way."
Job 17:9

THE man who is righteous before God has a way of his own. It is not the way of the flesh, nor the way of the world. It is a way marked out for him by the Divine command in which he walks by faith. It is the King's highway of holiness—the unclean shall not pass over it—only the ransomed of the Lord shall walk there and these shall find it a path of separation from the world. Once entered upon the way of life, the pilgrim must persevere in it or perish, for thus says the Lord, "If any man draw back, My soul shall have no pleasure in him." Perseverance in the path of faith and holiness is a necessity of the Christian, for only, "He that endures to the end, the same shall be saved." It is in vain to spring up quickly like the seed that was sown upon the rock and then, by-and-by, to wither when the sun is up. That would but prove that such a plant has no root in itself.

But "the trees of the Lord are full of sap" and they abide and continue and bring forth fruit, even in old age, to show that the Lord is upright. There is a great difference between nominal Christianity and real Christianity and this is generally seen in the failure of the one and the continuance of the other. Now, the declaration of the text is that the truly righteous man shall hold on his way—he shall not go back, he shall not leap the hedges and wander to the right hand or the left—he shall not lie down in idleness, neither shall he faint and cease to go upon his journey. He "shall hold on his way." It will frequently be very difficult for him to do so, but he will have such resolution, such power of inward Grace given him, that he will "hold on his way" with stern determination, as though he held on by his teeth, resolving never to let go.

Perhaps he may not always travel with equal speed. It is not said that he shall hold on his pace, but he shall hold on his way. There are times when we run and are not weary and at other times, when we walk, we are thankful that we do not faint. Yes, and there are periods when we are glad to go on all fours and creep upward with pain. But still we prove that "the righteous shall hold on his way." Under all difficulties the face of the man whom God has justified is steadfastly set towards Jerusalem—nor will he turn aside till his eyes shall see the King in His beauty. This is a great wonder! It is a marvel that any man should be a Christian at all, and a greater wonder that he should continue so!

Consider the weakness of the flesh, the strength of inward corruption, the fury of Satanic temptations, the seductions of wealth and the pride of life, the world and the fashions thereof—all these things are against us and yet behold, "greater is He that is for us than all they that are against us!" Defying sin, Satan, death and Hell, the righteous holds on his way. I take our text as accurately setting forth the doctrine of the Final Perseverance of the Saints. "The righteous shall hold on his way."

Years ago, when there was an earnest and even bitter controversy between Calvinists and Arminians,[45] it was the habit of each side to caricature the other. Very much of the argument was not directed against the real sentiment of the opposite party, but against what had been imputed to them. They made a man of straw and then they burned him, which is a pretty easy thing to do. But I trust we have left these things behind. The glorious Truth of the Final Perseverance of the Saints has survived controversy and, in some form or

---

[45] The belief that God's sovereignty and man's free will are compatible; the soteriological (study of salvation) rival to Calvinism

other, is the cherished belief of the children of God. Take care, however, to be clear as to what it is. The Scripture does not teach that a man will reach his journey's end without continuing to travel along the road. It is not true that one act of faith is all—that nothing is needed of daily faith, prayer and watchfulness. Our doctrine is the very opposite, namely, that the righteous shall hold on his way! Or, in other words, shall continue in faith, in repentance, in prayer and under the influence of the Grace of God.

We do not believe in salvation by a physical force which treats a man as a dead log and carries him, whether he wills dale till he reaches his journey's end. We never thought, nor even dreamed, that merely because a man supposes that he once entered on this way he may, therefore, conclude that he is certain of salvation, even if he leaves the way immediately. No, but we say that he who truly receives the Holy Spirit, so that he believes in the Lord Jesus Christ, shall not go back, but persevere in the way of faith.

It is written, "He that believes and is baptized shall be saved," and this he cannot be if he were left to go back and delight in sin as he did before! And, therefore, he shall be kept by the power of God through faith unto salvation. Though the Believer, to his grief, will commit many a sin, still, the tenor of his life will be holiness to the Lord and he will hold on in the way of obedience. We detest the doctrine that a man who has once believed in Jesus will be saved even if he altogether forsakes the path of obedience. We deny that such a turning aside is possible to the true Believer and, therefore, the idea imputed to us is clearly an invention of the adversary. No, Beloved, a man, if he is, indeed, a Believer in Christ, will not live after the will of the flesh!

When he does fall into sin, it will be his grief and misery—and he will never rest till he is cleansed from guilt. But I will say this of the Believer, that if he could live as he would like to live, he would live a perfect life. If you ask him if, after believing, he may live as he wishes, he will reply, "Would God I could live as I wish, for I desire to live altogether without sin! I would be perfect, even as my Father in Heaven is perfect." The doctrine is not the licentious idea that a Believer may live in sin, but that he cannot and will not do so! This is the doctrine and we, first, will prove it. Secondly, in the Puritanical sense of the word, we will briefly improve it by drawing two spiritual lessons from it.

LET US PROVE THE DOCTRINE. Please follow me with your Bibles open. You, dear Friends, have, most of you, received as a matter of faith the Doctrines of Grace and, therefore, to you the doctrine of Final Perseverance cannot require any proving, because it follows from all the other doctrines. We believe that God has an elect people whom He has chosen unto eternal life and that Truth of God necessarily involves the perseverance in Grace. We believe in special redemption and this secures the salvation and consequent perseverance of the redeemed.

We believe in effectual calling, which is bound up with justification—a justification which ensures glorification. The Doctrines of Grace are like a chain—if you believe in one of them you must believe the next, for each one involves the rest—therefore I say that you who accept any of the doctrines of Grace must receive this, also, as involved in them. But I am about to try to prove this to those who do not believe the Doctrines of Grace. I would not argue in a circle and prove one thing which you doubt by another thing which you doubt, but, "to the Law and to the Testimony," to the actual Words of Scripture we shall refer the matter.

Before we advance to the argument, it will be well to remark that those who reject the doctrine frequently tell us that there are many cautions in the Word of God against apostatizing and that those cautions can have no meaning if it is true that the righteous shall hold on his way. But what if those cautions are the means, in the hand of God, of keeping His people from wandering? What if they are used to excite a holy fear in the minds of His children and so become the means of preventing the evil which they denounce? I would also remind you that in the Epistle to the Hebrews, which contains the most solemn warnings against apostasy, the Apostle always takes care to add words which show that he did not believe that those whom he warned would actually apostatize.

Turn to Hebrews 6:9. He has been telling these Hebrews that if those who had been once enlightened should fall away, it would be impossible to renew them again into repentance and he adds, "But, Beloved, we are persuaded better things of you, and things that accompany salvation, though we thus speak." In the 10th chapter he gives an equally earnest warning, declaring that those who should do despite to the Spirit of Grace are worthy of worse punishment than those who despised Moses' Law, but he closes the chapter with these words, "Now the just shall live by faith; but if any man draws back, My soul shall have no pleasure in him. But we are not of them who draw back unto perdition; but of them that believe to the saving of the soul." Thus he shows what the consequences of apostasy would be, but he is convinced that they will not choose to incur such a fearful doom.

Again, objectors sometimes mention instances of apostasy which are mentioned in the Word of God, but on looking into them it will be discovered that these are cases of persons who did but profess to know Christ, but were not really possessors of the Divine Life. John, in His first Epistle, 2:19, fully describes these apostates–"They went out from us, but they were not of us; for if they had been of us, they would no doubt have continued with us; but they went out, that they might be made manifest that they were not all of us." The same is true of that memorable passage in John, where our Savior speaks of branches of the vine which are cut off and cast into the fire–these are described as branches in Christ that bear no fruit! Are those real Christians? How can they be so if they bear no fruit? "By their fruits you shall know them." The branch which bears fruit is purged, but it is never cut off! Those which bear no fruit are not figures of true Christians, but they fitly represent mere professors. Our Lord, in Matthew 7:22, tells us concerning many who will say in that day "Lord, Lord," that He will reply, "I never knew you." Not, "I have forgotten you," but, "I never knew you"–they were never really His disciples.

But now to the argument itself. First, we argue the Perseverance of the Saints most distinctly from the nature of the life which is imparted at regeneration. What does Peter say concerning this life? In 1 Peter 1:23 he speaks of the people of God as "being born again, not of corruptible seed, but of incorruptible, by the Word of God, which lives and abides forever." The new life which is planted in us, when we are born again, is not like the fruit of our first birth, for that is subject to mortality. No, it is a Divine principle which cannot die nor be corrupt and, if it is so, then he who possesses it must live forever! He must, indeed, be evermore with the Spirit of God—regeneration has made him so!

In 1 John 3:9 we have the same thought in another form. "Whoever is born of God does not commit sin, for His seed remains in him and he cannot sin because he is born of God." That is to say, the bent of the Christian's life is not towards sin. It would not be a fair description of his life that he lives in sin—on the contrary, he fights and contends against sin because he has an inner principle which cannot sin. The new life sins not—it is born of God and cannot transgress—and though the old nature wars against it, yet does the new life so prevail in the Christian that he is kept from living in sin. Our Savior, in His simple teaching of the Gospel to the Samaritan woman, said to her (John 4:13), "Whoever drinks of this water shall thirst again; but whoever drinks of the water that I shall give him shall never thirst; but the water that I shall give him shall be in him a well of water springing up into everlasting life."

Now, if our Savior taught this to a sinful and ignorant woman at His first interview with her, I take it that this doctrine is not to be reserved for the inner circle of full-grown saints, but to be preached among the common people and to be held up as a most blessed privilege! If you receive the Grace which Jesus imparts to your souls, it shall be like the good part which Mary chose—it shall not be taken away from you! It shall abide in you, not as the water in a cistern, but as a living fountain springing up unto everlasting life.

We all know that the life given in the new birth is intimately connected with faith. Now, faith is, in itself, a conquering principle. In the First Epistle of John, which is a great treasury of argument (1 John 5:4) we are told, "Whatever is born of God overcomes the world. And this is the victory that overcomes the world—our faith. Who is he that overcomes the world, but he that believes that Jesus is the Son of God?" See, then, that which is born of God in us, namely, the new life, is a conquering principle—there is no hint given that it can ever be defeated! And faith, which is its outward sign, is, also, in itself, triumphant forevermore! Therefore, because God has implanted such a wondrous life in us in bringing us out of darkness into His marvelous light, He has begotten us, again, unto a lively hope by the resurrection of Jesus Christ from the dead.

And because the eternal and ever-blessed Spirit has come to dwell in us, we conclude that the Divine Life within us shall never die. "The righteous shall hold on his way."

The second argument to which I shall call your attention shall be drawn from our Lord's own express declarations. Here we shall look to the Gospel of John, again, and in that blessed third of John, where our Lord was explaining the Gospel in the simplest possible style to Nicodemus, we find Him laying great stress upon the fact that the life received by faith in Himself is eternal. Look at that precious verse, the fourteenth—"As Moses lifted up the serpent in the wilderness, even so must the Son of Man be lifted up; that whoever believes in Him should not perish, but have eternal life." Do men, therefore, believe in Him and yet perish? Do they believe in Him and receive a spiritual life which comes to an end? It cannot be, for, "God gave His only begotten Son that whoever believes in Him should not perish." But he would perish if he did not persevere to the end and, therefore, he must persevere to the end!

The Believer has eternal life—how then can he die so as to cease to be a Believer? If he does not abide in Christ, he evidently does not have eternal life—therefore he shall abide in Christ, even to the end. "For God so loved the world, that He gave His only begotten Son, that whoever believes in Him should not perish, but have everlasting life." To this, some reply that a man may have everlasting life and lose it. To which we answer, the words cannot mean that! Such a statement is a self-evident contradiction! If the life is lost, the man is dead! How, then, did he have everlasting life? It is clear that he had a life which lasted only for a while—he certainly did not have everlasting life, for if he had it, he must live forever! "He that believes on the Son has everlasting life" (John 3:36).

The saints in Heaven have eternal life and no one expects them to perish! Their life is eternal—and eternal life is eternal life—whether the person possessing it dwells on earth or in Heaven! I need not read all the passages in which the same Truth of God is taught but further on, in John 6:47, our Lord told the Jews, "Verily, verily, I say unto you, he that believes on Me has everlasting life." Not temporary life, but, "everlasting life." And in the 51st verse He said, "I am the living bread which came down from Heaven. If any man eats of this bread, he shall live forever." Then comes that famous declaration of the Lord Jesus Christ, which, if there were no other at all, would be quite sufficient to prove our point—John 10:28—"And I give unto My sheep eternal life, and they shall never perish, neither shall anyone" (the word, "man," is not in the original) "pluck them out of my hand. My Father, which gave them to Me, is greater than all, and no one is able to pluck them out of My Father's hand."

What can He mean but this, that He has grasped His people and that He means to hold them securely in His mighty hand?—

"Where is the power can reach us there,
Or what can pluck us from there?"

Over and above the hand of Jesus which was pierced comes the hand of the Omnipotent Father as a sort of second grasp. "My Father, which gave them to Me, is greater than all, and no one is able to pluck them out of My Father's hand." Surely this must show that the saints are secure from anything and everything which would destroy them and, consequently, safe from total apostasy. Another passage speaks to the same effect—it is to be found in Matthew 24:24, where the Lord Jesus has been speaking of the false prophets that should deceive many. "There shall arise false christs and false prophets, and they shall show great signs and wonders, insomuch that, if it were possible, to deceive the very elect."

This shows that it is impossible for the elect to be deceived by them. Of Christ's sheep it is said, "A stranger will they not follow, for they know not the voice of strangers," but by Divine instinct they know the voice of the Good Shepherd and they follow Him. Thus has our Savior declared, as plainly as words possibly can express, that those who are His people possess eternal life within themselves and shall not perish but shall enter into everlasting happiness. "The righteous shall hold on his way."

A very blessed argument for the safety of the Believer is found in our Lord's intercession. You need not turn to the passage, for you know it well, which shows the connection between the living intercession of Christ and the perseverance of His people—"Therefore, also, He is able to save them to the uttermost that come unto God by Him, seeing He ever lives to make intercession for them" (Heb. 7:25). Our Lord Jesus is not dead! He has risen! He has gone up into Glory and now, before the eternal Throne, He pleads the merit of His perfect work! And as He pleads there for all His people whose names are written on His heart—as the names of Israel were written on the jeweled breastplate of the high priest—His intercession saves His people even to the uttermost!

If you would like an illustration of it you must turn to the case of Peter which is recorded in Luke 22:31 where our Lord said, "Simon, Simon, behold, Satan has desired to have you, that he may sift you as wheat; but I have prayed for you that your faith fail not; and when you are restored, strengthen your brethren." The intercession of Christ does not save His people from being tried, or tempted, or tossed up and down like wheat in a sieve. It does not save them, even, from a measure of sin and sorrow. But it does save them from total apostasy. Peter was kept and though he denied his Master, yet it was an exception to the great rule of his life. By Grace he did hold on his way, because not only then, but many a time beside, though he sinned, he had an Advocate with the Father—Jesus Christ the Righteous!

If you desire to know how Jesus pleads, read at your leisure at home that wonderful 17th of John—the Lord's prayer. What a prayer it is! "While I was with them in the world, I kept them in Your name; those that You gave Me I have kept and none of them is lost, but the son of perdition; that the Scripture might be fulfilled." Judas was lost, but he was only given to Christ as an Apostle and not as one of His sheep. He had a temporary faith and maintained a temporary profession—he never had eternal life or he would have lived on. Those groans and cries of the Savior which accompanied His pleas in Gethsemane were heard in Heaven and answered. "Holy Father, keep through Your own name those whom You have given Me." The Lord keeps them by His Word and Spirit—and will keep them!

If the prayer of Christ in Gethsemane were answered, how much more that which now goes up from the eternal Throne itself!—

"With cries and tears He offered up
His humble suit below.
But with authority He asks,

Enthroned in Glory, now.
For all that come to God by Him,
Salvation He demands.
Points to their names upon His breast,
And spreads His wounded hands."

Ah, if my Lord Jesus pleads for me, I cannot be afraid of earth or Hell! That living, intercessory Voice has power to keep the saints and so has the living Lord Himself, for He has said–"Because I live you shall live also" (John 14:19).

Now for a fourth argument. We gather sure confidence of the perseverance of the saints from the Character and work of Christ. I will say little about that, for I trust my Lord is so well known to you that He needs no word of commendation from me to you. But if you know Him, you will say what the Apostle does in 2 Timothy 1:12– "I know whom I have believed, and am persuaded that He is able to keep that which I have committed unto Him against that day." He did not say, "I know in whom I have believed," as most people quote it, but, "I know whom I have believed." He knew Jesus! He knew His heart and His faithfulness! He knew His Atonement and its power! He knew His intercession and its might and he committed his soul to Jesus by an act of faith–and he felt secure.

My Lord is so excellent in all things that I need give you but one glimpse of His Character and you will see what He was when He dwelt here among men. At the commencement of John 13 we read, "Having loved His own which were in the world, He loved them unto the end." If He had not loved His disciples to the end when here, we might conclude that He was changeable now as then–but if He loved His chosen to the end while yet in His humiliation below–it brings us the sweet and blessed confidence that now that He is in Heaven He will love to the end all those who confide in Him. Fifthly, we infer the perseverance of the saints from the tenor of the Covenant of Grace.

Would you like to read it for yourselves? If so, turn to the Old Testament, Jeremiah 32, and there you will find the Covenant of Grace set forth at some length. We shall only be able to read the 40th verse: "And I will make an Everlasting Covenant with them, that I will not turn away from them, to do them good; but I put My fear in their hearts, that they shall not depart from

Me." He will not depart from them and they shall not depart from Him—what can be a greater assurance of their perseverance even to the end?

Now that this is the Covenant of Grace under which we live is clear from the Epistle to the Hebrews, for the Apostle, in the 8th chapter, quotes that passage to this very end. The question runs thus—"Behold, the days come, says the Lord, when I will make a new Covenant with the house of Israel and with the house of Judah; not according to the Covenant that I made with their fathers in the day when I took them by the hand to lead them out of the land of Egypt because they continued not in My Covenant, and I regarded them not, says the Lord. For this is the Covenant that I will make with the house of Israel after those days, says the Lord; I will put My Laws into their mind, and write them in their hearts; and I will be to them a God, and they shall be to Me a people."

The old Covenant had an "if" in it, and so it suffered shipwreck. It was—"If you will be obedient, then you shall be blessed" and, therefore, there came a failure on man's part and the whole Covenant ended in disaster. It was the Covenant of Works and under it we were in bondage until we were delivered from it and introduced to the Covenant of Grace, which has no "if" in it, but runs upon the strain of promise. It is, "I will," and, "you shall," all the way through. "I will be your God and you shall be My people." Glory be to God, this Covenant will never pass away, for see how the Lord declares its enduring character in the book of Isaiah (54:10)—"For the mountains shall depart, and the hills be removed; but My kindness shall not depart from you, neither shall the Covenant of My peace be removed, says the Lord that has mercy on you."

And again in Isaiah 55:3: "I will make an Everlasting Covenant with you, even the sure mercies of David." The idea of falling utterly away from Grace is a relic of the old legal spirit. It is a going away from Grace to come under Law, again, and I charge you who have once been emancipated slaves and have had the fetters of legal bondage struck from off your hands, never consent to wear those bonds again! Christ has saved you, if, indeed, you are believers in Him. He has not saved you for a week, or a month, or a quarter, or a year, or 20 years, but He has given you eternal life and you shall never perish—neither shall any pluck you out of His hands. Rejoice in this blessed Covenant of

Grace!

The sixth most forcible argument is drawn from the faithfulness of God. Look at Romans 11:29. What does the Apostle say there, speaking by the Holy Spirit? "For the gifts and calling of God are irrevocable," which means that He does not give life and pardon to a man and call him by Grace and afterwards repent of what He has done and withdraw the good things which He has bestowed. "God is not a man, that He should lie; neither the son of man, that He should repent." When He puts forth His hands to save, He does not withdraw them till the work is accomplished. His Word is, "I am the Lord, I change not; therefore you sons of Jacob are not consumed" (Mal. 3:6). "The Strength of Israel will not lie nor repent" (1 Sam. 15:29).

The Apostle would have us ground our confidence of perseverance upon the confirmation which Divine faithfulness is sure to bestow upon us. He says in 1 Corinthians 1:8, "Who shall, also, confirm you unto the end, that you may be blameless in the day of our Lord Jesus Christ. God is faithful, by whom you were called unto the fellowship of His Son Jesus Christ our Lord." And again he speaks to the same effect in 1 Thessalonians 5:24, "Faithful is He that calls you, who, also, will do it." It was of old the will of God to save the people whom He gave to Jesus and from this He has never turned, for our Lord said, "And this is the Father's will which has sent Me, that of all which He has given Me I should lose nothing, but should raise it up again at the last day" (John 6:39). Thus you see from these passages, and there are numbers of others, that God's faithfulness secures the preservation of His people and, "the righteous shall hold on his way."

The seventh and last argument shall be drawn from what has already been done in us. I shall do little more than quote the Scriptures and leave them to sink into your minds. A blessed passage is that in Jeremiah 31:3 – "The Lord has appeared of old unto me, saying, yes, I have loved you with an everlasting love; therefore with lovingkindness have I drawn you." If He did not mean that His love should be everlasting, He would never have drawn us at all! But because that love is everlasting, therefore with loving kindness has He drawn us. The Apostle argues this in a very elaborate manner in Romans 5:9, 10 – "Much more then, being now justified by His blood, we shall be saved from wrath through Him. For if, when we were enemies, we were reconciled to God by the death of His Son, much more, being reconciled, we shall be saved by His life." I cannot stop to show how every word of this passage is emphatic, but it is—if God reconciled us when we were enemies, He certainly will save us, now we are His friends. And if our Lord Jesus has reconciled us by His death, much more will He save us by His life, so that we may be certain He will not leave nor forsake those whom He has called. Do you need me to bring to your minds that golden chapter, the 8th of Romans, the noblest of all language that was ever written by human pen? "Whom He did foreknow, He, also, did predestinate to be conformed to the image of His Son. Moreover, whom He did predestinate, them He, also, called; and whom He called, them He, also, justified; and whom He justified, them He, also, glorified."

There is no break in the chain between Justification and Glory! And no supposable breakage can occur, for the Apostle puts that out of all possibility, by saying, "Who shall lay anything to the charge of God's elect? It is God that justifies. Who is he that condemns? It is Christ that died, yes, rather, that is risen again, who is even at the right hand of God, who, also, makes intercession for us. Who shall separate us from the love of Christ?" Then he heaps on all the things that might be supposed to separate, and says, "For I am persuaded, that neither death, nor life, nor angels, nor principalities, nor powers, nor things present, nor things to come, nor height, nor depth, nor any other creature shall be able to separate us from the love of God, which is in Christ Jesus our Lord."

In the same manner the Apostle writes in Philippians 1:6—"Being confident of this very thing, that He who has begun a good work in you will perform it until the day of Jesus Christ." I cannot stay to mention the many other Scriptures in which what has been done is made an argument that the work shall be completed, but it is after the manner of the Lord to go through with whatever He undertakes. "He will give Grace and glory," and perfect that which concerns us. One marvelous privilege which has been bestowed upon us is of peculiar significance—we are one with Christ by close, vital, spiritual union. We are taught of the Spirit that we enjoy a marriage union with Christ Jesus our Lord—shall that union be dissolved?

We are married to Him! Has He ever given a bill of divorce? There has never been a case where the heavenly Bridegroom divorced from His heart a chosen soul to whom He has been united in the bonds of Grace! Listen to these words from the prophecy of Hosea 2:19, 20 – "And I will betroth you unto Me forever; yes, I will betroth you unto Me in righteousness, and in judgment, and in loving kindness, and in mercies. I will even betroth you unto Me in faithfulness; and you shall know the Lord." This marvelous union is set forth by the figure of the head and the body – we are members of the body of Christ. Do the members of His body rot away? Is Christ amputated? Is He fitted with new limbs as old ones are lost?

No, being members of this body, we shall not be divided from Him. "He that is joined unto the Lord," says the Apostle, "is one spirit," and if we are made one spirit with Christ, that mysterious union does not allow for the supposition, even, of a separation! The Lord has worked another great work upon us, for He has sealed us by the Holy Spirit. The possession of the Holy Spirit is the Divine seal which sooner or later is set upon all the chosen. There are many passages in which that seal is spoken of and is described as being an earnest, an earnest of the inheritance. But how can it be an earnest if after receiving it, we do not attain the purchased possession? Think over the words of the Apostle in 2 Corinthians 1:21, 22 – "Now He who establishes us with you in Christ and has anointed us is God, who also has sealed us and given us the Spirit in our hearts as a guarantee."

To the same effect the Holy Spirit speaks in Ephesians 1:13, 14 – "In whom you, also, trusted, after that you heard the Word of Truth, the Gospel of your salvation, in whom, also, after that you believed, you were sealed with that Holy Spirit of promise, which is the earnest of our inheritance until the redemption of the purchased possession, unto the praise of His glory." Beloved, we feel certain that if the Spirit of God dwells in us, He that raised up Jesus Christ from the dead will keep our souls and will, also, quicken our mortal bodies and present us complete before the Glory of His face at the last.

Therefore we sum up the argument with the confident expression of the Apostle when he said (2 Tim. 4:18), "The Lord shall deliver me from every evil work and will preserve me unto His heavenly kingdom. To Him be glory forever and ever. Amen."

II. Now, how shall we IMPROVE THE DOCTRINE OF THE FINAL PERSEVERANCE OF THE SAINTS PRACTICALLY? The first improvement is for encouragement to the man who is on the road to Heaven. "The righteous shall hold on his way." If I had to take a very long journey, say from London to John o' Groats,[46] with my poor tottering limbs to carry me, and such a weight to carry, too, I might begin to despair and, indeed, the very first day's walking would knock me out. But if I had a Divine assurance unmistakably saying, "You will hold on your way and you will get to your journey's end," I feel that I would brace myself up to achieve the task.

One might hardly undertake a difficult journey if he did not believe that he would finish it. But the sweet assurance that we shall reach our home makes us pluck up courage. The weather is wet, rainy, blusterous—but we must keep on, for the end is sure. The road is very rough and runs up hill and down dale. We pant for breath and our limbs are aching—but as we shall get to our journey's end, we push on. We are ready to creep into some cottage and lie down to die of weariness, saying, "I shall never accomplish my task." But the confidence which we have received sets us on our feet and off we go again! To the right-hearted man the assurance of success is the best stimulus for labor.

If it is so, that I shall overcome the world, that I shall conquer sin, that I shall not be an apostate, that I shall not give up my faith, that I shall not fling away my shield, that I shall come home a conqueror—then will I play the man and fight like hero! This is one of the reasons why British troops have so often won the fight, because the drummer boys did not know how to beat a retreat and the rank and file did not believe in the possibility of defeat! They were beaten oftentimes by the French, so the French tell us, but they would not believe it and, therefore, would not run away! They felt like winning and so they stood like solid rocks amidst the dread artillery of the foe till victory was declared on their side.

Brothers and Sisters, we shall do the same if we realize that we are preserved in Christ Jesus—kept by the power of God through faith unto salvation! Every

---

[46] A village in northern Scotland

true Believer shall be a conqueror and, therefore, the reason for warring a good warfare. There is laid up for us in Heaven a crown of life that fades not. The crown is laid up for us and not for chance comers. The crown reserved for me is such that no one else can wear it! And if it is so, then will I battle and strive to the end, till the last enemy is overcome and death, itself, is dead.

Another improvement is this—what an encouragement this is to sinners who desire salvation. It should lead them to come and receive it with grateful delight. Those who deny this doctrine offer sinners a poor two penny-halfpenny salvation not worth having—and it is no marvel that they turn away from it. As the Pope gave England to the Spanish king—if he could get it—so do they proffer Christ's salvation if a man will deserve it by his own faithfulness. According to some, eternal life is given to you, but then it may not be eternal! You may fall from it. It may last only for a time.

When I was but a child I used to trouble myself because I saw some of my young companions who were a little older than myself, when they became apprentices and came to London, become vicious. I have heard their mother's laments and seen their tears. I have heard their fathers expressing bitterest sorrow over the boys whom I knew in my class to be quite as good as ever I had been—and it used to strike me with horror that perhaps I might sin as they had done! They became Sabbath-breakers—in one case there was a theft from the till to go into Sunday pleasuring. I dreaded the very thought!

I desired to maintain an unsullied character and when I heard that if I gave my heart to Christ, He would keep me, that was the very thing which won me! It seemed to be a celestial life assurance for my character, that if I would really trust Christ with myself, He would save me from the errors of youth, preserve me amid the temptations of manhood and keep me to the end. I was charmed with the thought that if I was made righteous by believing in Christ Jesus I should hold on my way by the power of the Holy Spirit.

That which charmed me in my boyhood is even more attractive to me in middle life! I am happy to preach to you a sure and everlasting salvation! I feel that I have something to bring before you, this morning, which is worthy of every sinner's eager acceptance. I have neither an, "if," nor a, "but," with which to dilute the pure Gospel of my message! Here it is—"He that believes and is baptized shall be saved." I dropped a piece of ice upon the floor yesterday and I said to one who was in the room, "Is not that a diamond?" "Ah," he said, "you would not leave it on the floor, I guarantee you, if it were a diamond of that size."

Now I have a diamond here—eternal life, everlasting life! I pray you will be in haste to take it up at once, to be saved now, to be saved in living, to be saved in dying, to be saved in rising again, forever and ever, by the eternal power and infinite love of God! Is not this worth having? Grasp at it, poor Soul! You may have it if you but believe in Jesus Christ, or, in other words, trust your soul with Him. Deposit your eternal destiny in this Divine bank—then you can say—"I know whom I have believed and I am persuaded that He is able to keep that which I have committed to Him against that day." The Lord bless you, for Christ's sake. Amen.

VI

The Doctrines of Grace in the Christian Life

SOVEREIGN GRACE AND MAN'S RESPONSIBILITY

AUGUST 1, 1858, AT THE MUSIC HALL, ROYAL SURREY GARDENS

"But Isaiah is very bold, and says, I was found of them that sought me not; I was made manifest unto them that asked not after me. But to Israel he says, All day long I have stretched forth my hands unto a disobedient and gainsaying people."
Romans 10:20-21

DOUBTLESS these words primarily refer to the casting away of the Jews and to the choosing of the Gentiles. The Gentiles were a people who sought not after God, but lived in idolatry. Nevertheless, Jehovah was pleased in these latter times to send the Gospel of His grace to them—while the Jews who had long enjoyed the privileges of the Word of God—on account of their disobedience and rebellion were cast away. I believe, however, that while this is the primary object of the words of our text, yet, as Calvin says, the Truth taught in the text is a type of a universal fact. As God did choose the people who knew Him not, so has He chosen, in the abundance of His grace, to manifest His salvation to men who are out of the way, while, on the other hand, the men who are lost, after having heard the Word, are lost because of their willful sin. For God does all the day long "stretch forth His hands unto a disobedient and gainsaying people."

The system of Truth is not one straight line, but two. No man will ever get a right view of the Gospel until he knows how to look at the two lines at once. I am taught in one book to believe that what I sow, I shall reap. I am taught in another place that, "it is not of him that wills nor of him that runs, but of God that shows mercy." I see in one place God presiding over all in Providence. And yet I see and I cannot help seeing, that man acts as he pleases and that God has, in a great measure, left his actions to his own will. Now, if I were to declare that man was so free to act that there was no Providence of God over his actions, I should be driven very near to Atheism. And if, on the other hand, I declare that God so overrules all things, as that man is not free enough to be responsible, I am driven at once into Antinomianism[47] or fatalism.[48]

That God predestines and that man is responsible, are two things that few can see. They are believed to be inconsistent and contradictory. But they are not. It is the fault of our own weak judgment. Two Truth of God cannot be contradictory to each other. If, then, I find taught in one place that everything is fore-ordained, that is true. And if I find in another place that man is responsible for all his actions, that is true. And it is my folly that leads me to imagine that two Truth of God can ever contradict each other. These two Truths, I do not believe, can ever be welded into one upon any human anvil, but one they shall be in eternity. They are two lines that are so nearly parallel that the mind that shall pursue them farthest will never discover that they converge. But they do converge and they will meet somewhere in eternity, close to the Throne of God, from where all Truth does spring.

Now, this morning I am about to consider the two doctrines. In the 20th verse, we have taught us the doctrines of Sovereign Grace—"But Isaiah is very bold and says, I was found of them that sought me not. I was made manifest unto them that asked not after me." In the next verse, we have the doctrine of man's guilt in rejecting God. "To Israel He says, all day long I have stretched forth My hands unto a disobedient and gainsaying people."

First, then, DIVINE SOVEREIGNTY AS EXEMPLIFIED IN SALVATION. If any man is saved, he is saved by Divine Grace and by Divine Grace alone. And

---

[47] The belief that those saved are not required to follow moral laws; rejects all forms of legalism

[48] The belief in destiny as the driving force for all actions and events

the reason of his salvation is not to be found in him, but in God. We are not saved as the result of anything that we do or that we will. But we will and do as the result of God's good pleasure and the work of His grace in our hearts. No sinner can prevent God, that is, he cannot go before Him, cannot anticipate Him. God is always first in the matter of salvation. He is before our convictions, before our desires, before our fears, before our hopes. All that is good or ever will be good in us is preceded by the grace of God and is the effect of a Divine cause within.

Now in speaking of God's gracious acts of salvation this morning, I notice first, that they are entirely unmerited. You will see that the people here mentioned certainly did not merit God's grace. They found Him, but they never sought Him. He was made manifest to them, but they never asked for Him. There never was a man saved yet who merited it. Ask all the saints of God and they will tell you that their former life was spent in the lusts of the flesh—that in the days of their ignorance they revolted against God and turned back from His ways—that when they were invited to come to Him they despised the invitation and, when warned, cast the warning behind their back.

They will tell you that their being drawn by God was not the result of any merit before conversion, for some of them, so far from having any merit, were the very vilest of the vile. They plunged into the very kennel of sin. They were not ashamed of all the things of which it would be a shame for us to speak. They were ringleaders in crime—very princes in the ranks of the enemy. And yet Sovereign Grace came to them and they were brought to know the Lord.

They will tell you that it was not the result of anything good in their disposition, for although they trust that there is now something excellent implanted in them, yet in the days of their flesh they could see not one quality which was not perverted to the service of Satan. Ask them whether they think they were chosen of God because of their courage, they will tell you, no. If they had courage it was defaced, for they were courageous to do evil. Question them whether they were chosen of God because of their talent, they will tell you, no—they had talent, but they prostituted it to the service of Satan.

Question them whether they were chosen because of the openness and generosity of their disposition. They will tell you that that very openness of temper and that very generosity of disposition led them to plunge deeper into the depths of sin, than they otherwise would have done, for they were "hail fellow, well met," with every evil man and ready to drink and join every jovial party which should come in their way. There was in them no reason whatever why God should have mercy upon them and the wonder to them is that He did not cut them down in the midst of their sins, blot out their names from the Book of Life and sweep them into the gulf where the fire burns that shall devour the wicked.

But some have said that God chooses His people because He foresees that after He chooses them they will do this, that and the other, which shall be meritorious and excellent. Refer again to the people of God and they will tell you that since their conversion they have had much to weep over. Although they can rejoice that God has begun the good work in them, they often tremble lest it should not be God's work at all. They will tell you that if they are abundant in faith yet there are times when they are superabundant in unbelief. If sometimes they are full of works of holiness, yet there are times when they weep many tears to think that those very acts of holiness were stained with sin. The Christian will tell you that he weeps over his very tears. He feels that there is filth even in the best of desires, that he has to pray to God to forgive his prayers, for there is sin in the midst of his supplications and that he has to sprinkle even his best offerings with the atoning blood, for he never can bring an offering without spot or blemish.

You shall appeal to the brightest saint, to the man whose presence in the midst of society is like the presence of an angel and he will tell you that he is still ashamed of himself. "Ah," he will say, "you may praise me, but I cannot praise myself. You speak well of me, you applaud me, but if you knew my heart you would see abundant reason to think of me as a poor sinner saved by grace, who has nothing whereof to glory and must bow his head and confess his iniquities in the sight of God." Grace, then, is entirely unmerited.

Again, the grace of God is sovereign. By that word we mean that God has the absolute right to give that grace where He chooses and to withhold it when He pleases. He is not bound to give it to any man, much less to all men and if He chooses to give it to one man and not to another, His answer is, "Is your eye evil because My eye is good? Can I not do as I will with My own? I will have mercy on whom I will have mercy." Now, I want you to notice the sovereignty of Divine Grace as illustrated in the text: "I was found of them that sought Me not, I was made manifest to them that asked not after Me."

You would imagine that if God gave His grace to any He would wait until He found them earnestly seeking Him. You would imagine that God in the highest heavens would say, "I have mercies, but I will leave men alone and when they feel their need of these mercies and seek Me diligently with their whole heart, day and night, with tears and vows and supplications—then will I bless them—but not before." But Beloved, God says no such thing. It is true He does bless them that cry unto Him but He blesses them before they cry, for their cries are not their own cries, but cries He has put into their lips. Their desires are not of their own growth, but desires which He has cast like good seed into the soil of their hearts. God saves the men that do not seek Him.

Oh, wonder of wonders! It is mercy indeed when God saves a seeker, but how much greater mercy when He seeks the lost Himself? Mark the parable of Jesus Christ concerning the lost sheep. It does not run thus: "A certain man had a hundred sheep and one of them did go astray. And he tarried at home and lo, the sheep came back and he received it joyfully and said to his friends, rejoice, for the sheep that I have lost is come back."

No. He went after the sheep—it never would have come after him. It would have wandered farther and farther away. He went after it. Over hills of difficulty, down valleys of despondency he pursued its wandering feet and at last he laid hold of it. He did not drive it before him, he did not lead it, but he carried it himself all the way and when he brought it home he did not say, "the sheep is come back," but, "I have found the sheep which was lost." Men do not seek God first—God seeks them first. And if any of you are seeking Him today it is because He has first sought you.

If you are desiring Him, He desired you first and your good desires and earnest seeking will not be the cause of your salvation, but the effects of previous grace given to you. "Well," says another, "I should have thought that although the Savior might not require an earnest seeking and sighing and groaning and a continuous searching after Him, yet certainly He would have desired and demanded that every man, before He had grace, should ask for it."

That, indeed, Beloved, seems natural, and God will give grace to them that ask for it. But mark, the text says that He was manifested "to them that asked not for Him." That is to say, before we ask, God gives us grace. The only reason why any man ever begins to pray is because God has put previous grace in his heart which leads him to pray. I remember, when I was converted to God, I was an Arminian[49] thoroughly. I thought I had begun the good work myself and I used sometimes to sit down and think, "Well, I sought the Lord four years before I found Him," and I think I began to compliment myself upon the fact that I had perseveringly entreated of Him in the midst of much discouragement.

But one day the thought struck me, "How was it you came to seek God?" and in an instant the answer came from my soul, "Why, because He led me to do it. He must first have shown me my need of Him, or else I should never have sought Him. He must have shown me His preciousness, or I never should have thought Him worth seeking." And at once I saw the doctrines of grace as clear as possible. God must begin.

Nature can never rise above itself. You put water into a reservoir and it will rise as high as that, but no higher, if let alone. Now, it is not in human nature to seek the Lord. Human nature is depraved and therefore there must be the extraordinary pressure of the Holy Spirit put upon the heart to lead us first to ask for mercy. But mark, we do not know anything about that while the Spirit is operating. We find that out afterwards. We ask as much as if we were asking all of ourselves. Our business is to seek the Lord as if there were no Holy Spirit at all. But although we do not know it, there must always be a previous motion of the Spirit in our heart before there will be a motion of our heart towards Him—

"No sinner can be beforehand with You,

---

[49] The belief that God's sovereignty and man's free will are compatible; the soteriological (study of salvation) rival to Calvinism

Your grace is most sovereign, most rich and most free."

Let me give you an illustration. You see that man on his horse surrounded by a body of troopers. How proud he is, how he reins up his horse with conscious dignity. Sir, what have you got there? What are those dispatches you treasure up with so much care? "Oh, Sir, I have that in my hand that will vex the church of God in Damascus. I have dragged the fellows into the synagogue, both men and women. I have scourged them and compelled them to blaspheme. And I have this commission from the high priest to drag them to Jerusalem that I may put them to death."

"Saul! Saul! Have you no love for Christ?" "Love for Him? No. When they stoned Stephen, I took care of the witnesses' clothes and I rejoiced to do it. I wish I had had the crucifying of their Master, for I hate them with perfect hatred and I breathe out threats and slaughter against them." What do you say of this man? If he is saved, will you not grant that it must be some Divine Sovereignty that converts him?

Look at poor Pilate, how much there was that was hopeful in him. He was willing to save the Master, but he feared and trembled. If we had had our choice, we should have said, "Lord, save Pilate, he does not want to kill Christ, he labors to let Him escape. But slay the bloodthirsty Saul, he is the very chief of sinners." "No," says God, "I will do as I will with My own." The heavens open and the brightness of glory descends—brighter than the noonday sun. Stunned with the light, Saul falls to the ground, and a voice is heard addressing him, "Saul, Saul, why do you persecute Me? It is hard for you to kick against the pricks."

He rises up. God appears to him—"Lo, I have made you a chosen vessel to bear My name among the Gentiles." Is not that sovereignty—Sovereign Grace—without any previous seeking? God was found of him that sought not Him. He manifested Himself to one that asked Him not. Some will say that was a miracle. But it is one that is repeated every day in the week. I knew a man once who had not been to the House of God for a long time. And one Sunday morning, having been to market to buy a pair of ducks for his Sunday dinner, he happened to see a House of God opened as he was passing by.

"Well" he thought, "I will hear what these fellows are up to." He went inside. The hymn that was being sung struck his attention. He listened to the sermon, forgot his ducks, discovered his own character, went home and threw himself upon his knees before God and after a short time it pleased God to give him joy and peace in believing. That man had nothing in him to begin with, nothing that could have led you to imagine he ever would be saved. But simply because God would have it so, He struck the effectual blow of grace and the man was brought to Jesus Christ. But we are, each of us who are saved, the very people who are the best illustrations of the matter. To this day, my wonder is that ever the Lord should have chosen me. I cannot understand it. And my only answer to the question is, "Even so, Father, for so it seemed good in Your sight."

I have now, I think, stated the doctrine pretty plainly. Let me only say a few words about it. Some people are very much afraid of this Truth of God. They say, "It is true, I dare say, but still you ought not to preach it before a mixed assembly. It is very well for the comfort of God's people, but it is to be very carefully handled and not to be publicly preached upon." Very well, Sir, I leave you to settle that matter with my Master. He gave me this great Book to preach from and I cannot preach from anything else. If He has put anything in it you think is not fit, go and complain to Him and not to me. I am simply His servant and if His message that I am to tell is objectionable, I cannot help it.

If I send my servant to the door with a message and he delivers it faithfully, he does not deserve to be scolded. Let me have the blame, not the servant. So I say, blame my Master and not me, for I do but proclaim His message. "No," says one, "It is not to be preached." But it is to be preached. Every word of God is given by inspiration and it is profitable for some good end. Does not the Bible say so? Let me tell you, the reason many of our Churches are declining is just because this doctrine has not been preached.

Wherever this doctrine has been upheld, it has always been, "Down with Popery."[50] The first Reformers held this doctrine and preached it. Well said a Church of England divine to some who railed at him, "Look at your own

---

[50] The system and practices of the papal system and Roman Catholicism

Luther. Do you not consider him to be the teacher of the Church of England? What Calvin and the other Reformers taught is to be found in his book upon the freedom of the will." Besides, we can point you to a string of ministers from the beginning even until now. Talk of Apostolic succession! The man who preaches the doctrines of grace has an Apostolic succession, indeed. Can we not trace our pedigree through a whole line of men like Newton[51] and Whitfield[52] and Owen[53] and Bunyan[54], straight on till we come to Calvin, Luther[55] and Zwingli?[56]

And then we can go back from them to Savonarola,[57] to Jerome of Prague,[58] to Hus[59] and then back to Augustine,[60] the mighty preacher of Christianity. And from St. Augustine to Paul is but one step. We need not be ashamed of our pedigree. Although Calvinists are now considered to be heterodox, we are and ever must be orthodox. It is the old doctrine. Go and buy any Puritanical book and see if you can find Arminianism in it. Search all the book stalls over and see if you can find one large folio book of olden times that

---

[51] Sir Isaac Newton, a seventeenth and eighteenth-century English mathematician, physicist, astronomer, theologian, and writer

[52] Eighteenth-century English Anglican cleric and evangelist; one of the founders of Methodism; unlike his Arminian associate, John Wesley, Whitefield was a Calvinist

[53] John Owen, a seventeenth-century English Congregational pastor, Calvinist theologian, and academic administrator at the University of Oxford

[54] Seventeenth-century English Puritan preacher and writer; author of *The Pilgrim's Progress*

[55] Martin Luther, a sixteenth-century German theologian, composer, priest, monk, and leader within the Protestant Reformation; father of the Lutheran Church

[56] Huldrych Zwingli, a sixteenth-century theologian and leader of the Reformation in Switzerland

[57] Girolamo Savonarola, a fifteenth-century Italian Dominican friar and preacher of the Renaissance Florence

[58] A Czech philosopher, theologian, reformer, and professor

[59] Jan Hus, a fourteenth and fifteenth-century Czech theologian, philosopher, and church reformer

[60] Augustine of Hippo, a fourth and fifth-century Roman theologian, doctor of the Church, and philosopher; one of the most important Church fathers and heavily influential on Western Christianity

has anything in it but the doctrine of the Free Grace of God. Let this once be brought to bear upon the minds of men and away go the doctrines of penance and confession—away goes paying for the pardon of your sin.

If grace is free and sovereign in the hand of God, down goes the doctrine of priestcraft! Away go buying and selling indulgences and such like things. They are swept to the four winds of Heaven and the efficacy of good works is dashed in pieces like Dagon before the ark of the Lord. "Well," says one, "I like the doctrine. Still there are very few that preach it and those that do are very high." Very likely. But I care little what anybody calls me. It signifies very little what men call you. Suppose they call you a "hyper"—that does not make you anything wicked, does it? Suppose they call you an Antinomian—that will not make you one. I must confess, however, that there are some men who preach this doctrine who are doing ten thousand times more harm than good because they don't preach the next doctrine I am going to proclaim, which is just as true.

They have this to be the sail, but they have not the other to be the ballast. They can preach one side, but not the other. They can go along with the high doctrine but they will not preach the whole of the Word. Such men caricature the Word of God. And just let me say here, that it is the custom of a certain body of Ultra-Calvinists, to call those of us who teach that it is the duty of man to repent and believe, "Mongrel Calvinists." If you hear any of them say so, give them my most respectful compliments and ask them whether they ever read Calvin's works in their lives.

Not that I care what Calvin said or did not say, but ask them whether they ever read his works. And if they say "No," as they must say, for there are forty-eight large volumes—you can tell them that the man whom they call "a Mongrel Calvinist," though he has not read them all, has read a very good share of them and knows their spirit. And he knows that he preaches substantially what Calvin preached—that every doctrine he preaches may be found in Calvin's Commentaries on some part of Scripture or other.

We are TRUE Calvinists, however. Calvin is nobody to us. Jesus Christ and Him crucified and the old fashioned Bible are our standards. Beloved, let us take God's Word as it stands. If we find high doctrine there, let it be high. If we find low doctrine, let it be low. Let us set up no other standard than the Bible affords.

II. Now then for the second point. "There now," says my ultra friend, "he is going to contradict himself." No, my Friend, I am not. I am only going to contradict you. The second point is MAN'S RESPONSIBILITY. "But to Israel He says, All day long I have stretched forth My hands unto a disobedient and gainsaying people." Now, these people whom God had cast away had been wooed, had been sought, had been entreated to be saved. But they would not and inasmuch as they were not saved it was the effect of their disobedience and their gainsaying. That lies clearly enough in the text.

When God sent the Prophets to Israel and stretched forth His hands, what was it for? What did He wish them to come to Him for? Why, to be saved. "No," says one, "it was for temporal mercies." Not so, my Friend. The verse before is concerning spiritual mercies and so is this one, for they refer to the same thing. Now, was God sincere in His offer? God forgive the man that dares to say He was not. God is undoubtedly sincere in every act He did. He sent His Prophets, He entreated the people of Israel to lay hold on spiritual things, but they would not. And though He stretched out His hands all the day long, yet they were "a disobedient and gainsaying people," and would not have His love. And on their head rests their blood.

Now let me notice the wooing of God and of what sort it is. First, it was the most affectionate wooing in the world. Lost sinners who sit under the sound of the Gospel are not lost for the want of the most affectionate invitation. God says He stretched out His hands. You know what that means. You have seen the child who is disobedient and will not come to his father. The father puts out his hands and says, "Come, my child, come, I am ready to forgive you." The tear is in his eye and his heart moves with compassion and he says, "Come, come."

God says this is what He did—"He stretched out His hands." That is what He has done to some of you. You that are not saved today are without excuse for God stretched out His hands to you and He said, "Come, come." Long have you sat beneath the sound of the ministry and it has been a faithful one I trust, and a weeping one. Your minister has not forgotten to pray for your souls in secret or to weep over you when no eye saw him and he has endeavored to persuade you as an ambassador from God. God is my witness, I have sometimes stood in this pulpit and I could not have pleaded harder for my own life than I have pleaded with you.

In Christ's name I have cried, "Come unto Me all you that are weary and heavy laden and I will give you rest." I have wept over you as the Savior did and used His words on His behalf, "O Jerusalem, Jerusalem, how often would I have gathered your children together as a hen gathers her chickens under her wings and you would not." And you know that your conscience has often been touched. You have often been moved—you could not resist it. God was so kind to you, He invited you so affectionately by the Word. He dealt so gently with you by His Providence, His hands were stretched out and you could hear His voice speaking in your ears, "Come unto Me, come. Come now, let us reason together, though your sins are as scarlet they shall be as wool, though they are red like crimson they shall be whiter than snow."

You have heard Him cry, "Everyone that thirsts, come you to the waters." You have heard Him say with all the affection of a father's heart, "let the wicked forsake his way and the unrighteous man his thoughts and let him turn unto the Lord and He will have mercy upon him and unto our God, for He will abundantly pardon." Oh, God does plead with men that they would be saved and this day He says to every one of you, "Repent and be converted for the remission of your sins. Turn you unto Me. Thus says the Lord of Hosts, consider your ways." And with love Divine He woos you as a father woos his child, putting out His hands and crying, "Come unto Me, come unto Me." "No," says one strong-doctrine man, "God never invites all men to Himself. He invites none but certain characters." Stop, Sir, that is all you know about it. Did you ever read that parable where it is said, "My oxen and my fatlings are killed and all things are ready: come unto the marriage." And they that were bid would not come. And did you never read that they all began to make excuse and that they were punished because they did not accept the invitations?

Now, if the invitation is not to be made to anybody but to the man who will accept it, how can that parable be true? The fact is the oxen and fatlings are killed, the wedding feast is ready and the trumpet sounds, "Everyone that thirsts, come and eat, come and drink." Here are the provisions spread, here is an all-sufficiency, the invitation is free—it is a great invitation without limitation. "Whosoever will let him come and take of the water of life freely." And that invitation is couched in tender words, "Come to Me, My child, come to Me." "All day long I have stretched forth My hands."

And note again, this invitation was very frequent. The words, "all the day long," may be translated "daily." "Daily have I stretched forth My hands." Sinner, God has not called you once to come and then let you alone but every day has He been at you. Every day has conscience spoken to you. Every day has Providence warned you and every Sabbath has the Word of God wooed you. Oh, how much some of you will have to account for at God's great bar! I cannot now read your characters, but I know there are some of you who will have a terrible account at last. All the day long has God been wooing you. From the first dawn of your life, He wooed you through your mother and she used to put your little hands together and teach you to say—

"Gentle Jesus meek and mild,

Look upon a little child,

Pity my simplicity;

Suffer me to come to You."

And in your boyhood, God was still stretching out His hands after you. How your Sunday-School teacher endeavored to bring you to the Savior! How often your youthful heart was affected. But you put all that away and you are still untouched by it. How often did your mother speak to you and your father warn you. And you have forgotten the prayer in that bedroom when you were sick, when your mother kissed your burning forehead, knelt down and prayed to God to spare your life and then added that prayer, "Lord, save my boy's soul!"

And you remember the Bible she gave you when you first went out to apprentice and the prayer she wrote on that yellow front leaf. When she gave it, you did not perhaps know, but you may now—how earnestly she longed after you, that you might be formed anew in Christ Jesus. How she followed you with her prayers and how she entreated with her God for you.

And you have not yet surely forgotten how many Sabbaths you have spent and how many times you have been warned. Why you have had wagon-loads of sermons wasted on you. A hundred and four sermons you have heard every year and some of you, more, and yet you are still just what you were.

But Sinners, sermon-hearing is an awful thing unless it is blessed to our souls. If God has kept on stretching out His hands every day and all the day, it will be a hard thing for you when you shall be justly condemned not only for your breaches of the Law, but for your willful rejection of the Gospel. It is probable that God will keep on stretching out His hands to you until your hairs grow gray, still continually inviting you—and perhaps when you are nearing death He will still say, "Come unto Me, come unto Me."

But if you still persist in hardening your heart, if you still reject Christ, I beseech you let nothing make you imagine that you shall go unpunished. Oh, I do tremble sometimes when I think of that class of ministers who tell sinners that they are not guilty if they do not seek the Savior. How they shall be found innocent at God's Great Day I do not know. It seems to be a fearful thing that they should be lulling poor souls into sleep by telling them it is not their duty to seek Christ and repent. But that they may do as they like about that and that when they perish they will be none the more guilty for having heard the Word. My Master did not say that. Remember how He said, "And you, Capernaum, which are exalted unto Heaven, shall be brought down to Hell: for if the mighty works which have been done in you, had been done in Sodom, it would have remained until this day. But I say unto you. That it shall be more tolerable for the land of Sodom in the day of judgment, than for you."

Jesus did not talk thus when He spoke to Chorazin and Bethsaida—He said, "Woe unto you, Chorazin! Woe unto repented long ago in sackcloth and ashes. But I say unto you, It shall be more tolerable for Tyre and Sidon at the day of judgment, than for you."

It was not the way Paul preached. He did not tell sinners that there was no guilt in despising the Cross. Hear the Apostle's words once more—"For if the Word spoken by angels was steadfast and every transgression and disobedience received a just recompense of reward, how shall we escape, if we neglect so great salvation, which at the first began to be spoken by the Lord and was confirmed unto us by them that heard Him?"

Sinner, at the Great Day of God you must give an account for every warning you have ever had, for every time you have read your Bible, yes, and for every time you have neglected to read it. For every Sunday when the House of God was open and you did neglect to avail yourself of the opportunity of hearing the Word and for every time you did hear it and did not listen.

You who are careless hearers, are tying fire wood for your own burning forever. You that hear and straightaway forget, or hear with levity, are digging for yourselves a pit into which you must be cast. Remember, no one will be responsible for your damnation but yourself at the last Great Day. God will not be responsible for it. "As I live says the Lord" – and that is a great oath – "I have no pleasure in the death of him that dies. But had rather that he should turn unto Me and live." God has done much for you. He sent you His Gospel. You are not born in a heathen land. He has given you the Book of Books. He has given you an enlightened conscience. And if you perish under the sound of the ministry, you perish more fearfully and terribly than if you had perished anywhere else.

This doctrine is as much God's Word as the other. You ask me to reconcile the two. I answer, they do not want any reconcilement. I never tried to reconcile them to myself because I could never see a discrepancy. If you begin to put fifty or sixty quibbles to me, I cannot give any answer. Both are true. No two Truths can be inconsistent with each other and what you have to do is to believe them both. With the first one, the saint has most to do. Let him praise the free and Sovereign Grace of God and bless His name. With the second, the sinner has the most to do. O Sinner, humble yourself under the mighty hand of God! Think how often He has shown His love to you by bidding you come to Himself. Think how often you have spurned His Word and refused His mercy. Think how you have turned a deaf ear to every invitation and have gone your way to rebel against a God of love. Think how often you have violated the commands of Him that loved you.

And now how shall I conclude? My first exhortation shall be to Christian people. My dear Friends, I beseech you do not in any way give yourselves up to any system of faith apart from the Word of God. The Bible and the Bible alone, is the religion of Protestants. I am the successor of the great and venerated Dr. Gill,[61] whose theology is almost universally received among the stronger Calvinistic Churches. But although I venerate his memory and believe his teachings, yet he is not my Rabbi. What you find in God's Word is for you to believe and to receive.

Never be frightened at a doctrine. And above all, never be frightened at a name. Someone said to me the other day that he thought the Truth of God lay somewhere between the two extremes. He meant right, but I think he was wrong. I do not think the Truth of God lies between the two extremes, but in them both. I believe the higher a man goes the better when he is preaching the matter of salvation. The reason why a man is saved is grace, grace, grace. And you may go as high as you like there. But when you come to the question as to why men are damned, then the Arminian is far more right than the Antinomian. I care not for any denomination or party, I am as high as Huntingdon[62] upon the matter of salvation, but question me about damnation and you will get a very different answer. By the grace of God I ask no man's applause. I preach the Bible as I find it. Where we get wrong is where the Calvinist begins to meddle with the question of damnation and interferes with the justice of God—or when the Arminian denies the doctrine of grace.

My second exhortation is—Sinners, I beseech every one of you who are unconverted and ungodly this morning to put away every form and fashion of excuse that the devil would have you make concerning your being unconverted. Remember that all the teaching in the world can never excuse you for being enemies to God by wicked works. When we beseech you to be reconciled to Him, it is because we know you will never be in your proper place until you are reconciled. God has made you. Can it be right that you should disobey

---

[61] John Gill, an eighteenth-century English Baptist pastor, biblical scholar, and Calvinist theologian

[62] William Huntingdon, an eighteenth and nineteenth-century English Antinomian preacher and theologian

Him? God feeds you every day. Can it be right that you should still live in disobedience to Him? Remember, when the heavens shall be on a blaze, when Christ shall come to judge the earth in righteousness and His people with equity, there will not be one excuse that you can make which will be valid at the last Great Day.

If you should attempt to say, "Lord, I have never heard the Word." His answer would be, "You did hear it. You heard it plainly." "But Lord, I had an evil will." "Out of your own mouth will I condemn you. You had that evil will and I condemn you for it. This is the condemnation—that light is come into the world, and men love darkness rather than light, because their deeds are evil." "But Lord" some will say, "I was not predestinated." "What had you to do with that? You did do according to your own will when you did rebel. You would not come unto Me and now I destroy you forever. You have broken My Law—on your own head is the guilt."

If a sinner could say at the Great Day, "Lord I could not be saved anyhow," his torment in Hell would be mitigated by that thought. But this shall be the very edge of the sword and the very burning of the fire—"You knew your duty and you did it not. You trampled on everything that was holy. You neglected the Savior and how shall you escape if you neglect so great salvation?"

Now, with regard to myself—you may some of you go away and say that I was Antinomian in the first part of the sermon and Arminian at the end. I care not. I beg of you to search the Bible for yourselves. To the Law and to the Testimony. If I speak not according to His Word, it is because there is no light in me. I am willing to come to that test. Have nothing to do with me where I have nothing to do with Christ. Where I separate from the Truth of God, cast my words away. But if what I say is God's teaching, I charge you, by Him that sent me, give these things your thoughts and turn unto the Lord with all your hearts.

HUMAN RESPONSIBILITY

MAY 16, 1858, AT THE MUSIC HALL, ROYAL SURREY GARDENS

"If I had not come and spoken to them, they had not had sin: but now they have no cloak for their sin."
John 15:22

THE peculiar sin of the Jews, the sin which aggravated above everything their former iniquities, was their rejection of Jesus Christ as the Messiah. He had been very plainly described in the books of the Prophets and they who waited for Him, such as Simeon and Anna, no sooner beheld Him even in His infant state, than they rejoiced to see Him and understood that God had sent forth His salvation.

But because Jesus Christ did not answer the expectation of that evil generation—because He did not come arrayed in pomp and clothed with power, because He had not the outward garnishing of a prince and the honors of a king, they shut their eyes against Him. He was "a root out of a dry ground," He was "despised and they esteemed Him not." Nor did their sin stop there. Not content with denying his Messiahship, they were exceeding hot against Him intheir anger. They hunted Him all His life, seeking His blood. Nor were they content till their fiendish malice had been fully glutted by sitting down at the foot of the Cross and watching the dying throes and the expiring agonies of their crucified Messiah. Though over the Cross itself the words were written, "Jesus of Nazareth, the King of the Jews," yet they knew not their king, God's everlasting Son. And knowing Him not, they crucified Him, "for had they known Him, they would not have crucified the Lord of Glory."

Now, the sin of the Jews is every day repeated by the Gentiles. That which they did once, many have done every day. Are there not many of you now present this day, listening to my voice, who forget the Messiah? You do not trouble yourself to deny Him. You would not degrade yourselves, in what is called a Christian country, by standing up to blaspheme His name. Perhaps you hold the right doctrine concerning Him and believe Him to be the Son of God as well as the Son of Mary. But still you neglect His claims and give Him no honor and do not accept Him as worthy of your trust. He is not your Redeemer. You are not looking for His second advent, nor are you expecting to be saved through His blood. No, even worse—you are this day crucifying Him—for know you not that as many as put away from them the Gospel of Christ, they crucify the Lord afresh and open wide His wounds?

As often as you hear the Word preached and reject it, as often as you are warned and stifle the voice of your conscience, as often as you are made to tremble and yet say, "Go your way for this time, when I have a more convenient season, I will send for you," so often do you in effect grasp the hammer and the nail and once more pierce His hands and make the blood issue from His side. And there are other ways by which you wound Him through His members. As often as you despise His ministers, cast stumbling blocks in the way of His servants, impede His Gospel by your evil example, or by your hard words seek to pervert the seeker from the way of the Truth of God—then you commit that great iniquity which brought the curse upon the Jew and which has doomed him to wander through the earth, until the day of the second advent when He shall come who shall even by the Jew be acknowledged the King of the Jews—for whom both Jew and Gentile are now looking with anxious expectation, even Messiah, the Prince who came once to suffer, but who comes again to reign.

And now I shall endeavor this morning to show the parallel between your case and that of the Jew. Not doing so in set phrase, but yet incidentally, as God shall help me. I will appeal to your conscience and make you feel that in rejecting Christ you commit the same sin and incur the same doom. We shall note, first of all, the excellence of the ministry, since Christ comes in it and speaks to men—"If I had not spoken to them." We shall notice, secondly, the aggravation of sin caused by the rejection of Christ's message—"If I had not spoken to them they had not had sin." Thirdly, the death of all excuses, caused by the preaching of the Word—"Now they have no cloak for their sin." And then, in the last place, we shall briefly, but very solemnly announce the fearfully aggravated doom of those who thus reject the Savior and increase their guilt by despising Him.

In the first place, this morning it is ours to say and to say truly, too, that in THE PREACHING OF THIS GOSPEL THERE IS TO MAN'S CONSCIENCE THE COMING OF OUR LORD JESUS CHRIST AND THE SPEAKING OF THE SAVIOR THROUGH US. When Israel of old despised Moses and murmured against him, Moses meekly said, "You have not murmured against us, but you have murmured against the Lord God of Israel." And truly the minister may, with Scripture warrant, say the same—he that despises us, despises not us, but Him that sent us. He who rejects the message rejects not what we say, but rejects the message of the everlasting God.

The minister is but a man. He has no priestly power, but is a man called out of the rest of mankind and endowed with the Holy Spirit to speak to his fellow men. And when he preaches the Truth of God with power sent down from Heaven, God owns him by calling him His ambassador and puts him in the high and responsible position of a watchman on the walls of Zion. And God bids all men take heed that a faithful message, faithfully delivered, when despised and trampled on, amounts to rebellion against Him and to sin and iniquity against the Most High.

As for what I may say, as a man, it is but little that I should say it. But if I speak as the Lord's ambassador, take heed that you slight not the message. It is the Word of God sent down from Heaven which we preach with the power of the Holy Spirit, earnestly beseeching you to believe it. And remember, it is at the peril of your own souls that you put it from you, for it is not we that speak, but the Spirit of the Lord our God who speaks in us. With what a solemnity does this invest the Gospel ministry!

O you sons of men, the ministry is not the speaking of men, but the speaking of God through men. As many as are the real, called, and sent servants of

God, are not the authors of their message. But they first hear it from their Master and they speak it to the people and they see ever before their eyes these solemn words—"Take heed unto yourself and unto the doctrine. Continue in them—for in doing this you shall both save yourself and them that hear you."

And they hear behind them this awful threat—"If you warn them not they shall perish, but their blood will I require at your hand." Oh, that you might see written in letters of fire before you this day the words of the Prophet—"O earth, earth, earth, hear the Word of the Lord." For as far as our ministry is true and untainted by error, it is God's Word and it has the same right and claim to your belief as if God Himself should speak it from the top of Sinai, instead of speaking it through the humble ministry of the Word of God.

And now let us pause over this doctrine and let us ask ourselves this solemn question. Have we not all of us grossly sinned against God in the neglect that we have often put upon the means of grace? How often have you stayed away from the House of God when God Himself was speaking there? What would have been the doom of Israel if, when summoned on that sacred day to hear the Word of God from the top of the mountain, they had perversely rambled into the wilderness, rather than attend to hear it?

And yet that is what you have done. You have sought your own pleasure and listened to the siren song of temptation. You have shut your ear against the voice of the Most High. And when He has Himself been speaking in His own House, you have turned aside unto crooked ways and have not regarded the voice of the Lord your God. And when you have come up to the House of God, how often has there been the careless eye, the inattentive ear! You have heard as though you heard not. Your ear has been penetrated, but the hidden man of the heart has been deaf and you have been like the deaf adder. Charm we never so wisely, you would not listen nor regard us.

God Himself has spoken, too, at times in your conscience so that you have heard it. You have stood in the aisle and your knees have knocked together. You have sat in your pew and while some mighty Boanerges has thundered out the Word you have heard it said, as with an angel's voice, "Prepare to meet your God—consider your way—set your house in order, for you shall die and not live." And yet you have gone out of God's House and have forgotten what manner of men you were.

You have quenched the Spirit, you have done despite to the Spirit of Grace. You have put far from you the struggles of your conscience. You have throttled those infant prayers that were beginning to cry in your heart. You have drowned those new-born desires that were just springing up. You have put away from you everything that was good and sacred. You have turned again to your own ways and have once more wandered on the mountains of sin and in the valley of iniquity. Ah, my Friends, just think, then, for a moment, that in all this you have despised God.

I am certain if the Holy Spirit would but apply this one solemn truth to your consciences this morning, this Hall of Music would be turned into a house of mourning and this place would become a Bochim, a place of weeping and lamentation. Oh, to have despised God! To have trampled under foot the Son of Man, to have passed by His Cross, to have rejected the wooings of His love and the warnings of His grace! How solemn! Did you ever think of this before? You have thought it was but despising man—will you now think of it as despising Christ? For Christ has spoken to you.

Ah, God is my witness that oftentimes Christ has wept with these eyes and spoken to you with these lips. I have sought nothing but the winning of your souls. Sometimes with rough words have I endeavored to drive you to the Cross and at other times with weeping accents have I sought to weep you to my Redeemer. And I am sure I did not speak myself then, but Jesus spoke through me. And inasmuch as you did hear and weep and then went away and did forget, remember that Christ spoke to you.

It was He who said, "Look unto Me and be you saved, all the ends of the earth." It was He who said, "Come unto Me, all you that labor and are heavy laden." It was He who warned you that if you neglected this great salvation you must perish. And in having put away the warning and rejected the invitation you have not despised us, but you have despised our Master. And woe unto you, except you repent, for 'tis a fearful thing to have despised the voice of Him that speaks from Heaven.

II. And now we must notice the second point, namely, that THE REJECTION OF THE GOSPEL AGGRAVATES MEN'S SIN. Now, do not let me be misunderstood. I have heard of persons who, having gone to the House of God, have been filled with a sense of sin and at last they have been driven almost to despair, for Satan has tempted them to forsake the House of God. For says he, "The more you go, the more you increase your condemnation." Now I believe that this is an error. We do not increase our condemnation by going to the House of God. We are far more likely to increase it by staying away. For in staying away from the House of God there is a double rejection of Christ.

You reject Him even with the outward mind, as well as with the inward spirit. You neglect even the lying at the pool of Bethesda—you are worse than the man who lay at the pool, but could not get in. You will not lie there and therefore, neglecting the hearing of the Word of God, you do indeed incur a fearful doom. But if you go up to the House of God sincerely seeking a blessing—if you do not get comfort—if you do not find grace in the means, still, if you go there devoutly seeking it, your condemnation is not increased.

Your sin is not aggravated merely by the hearing of the Gospel, but by the willful and wicked rejection of it when it is heard. The man who listens to the sound of the Gospel and after having heard it, turns upon his heel with a laugh, or who, after hearing time after time and being visibly affected, allows the cares and the pleasures of this wicked life to come in and choke the seed—such a man does in a fearful measure increase his guilt.

And now we will just notice why, in a two-fold measure, he does this. Because, in the first place he gets a new sin that he never had before and beside that, he aggravates all his other sins. Bring me here a Hottentot,[63] or a man from Kamschatka[64]—a wild savage who has never listened to the Word. That man may have every sin in the catalogue of guilt except one. But that one I am sure he has not. He has not the sin of rejecting the Gospel when it is preached to him. But you, when you hear the Gospel, have an opportunity for committing a fresh sin. And if you have rejected it, you have added a fresh iniquity to all those others that hang about your neck.

I have often been rebuked by certain men who have erred from the Truth

---

[63] Racial term that refers to the Khoikhoi, the non-Bantu indigenous people of South Africa

[64] Native American tribes of the Pacific Coast

of God, for preaching the doctrine that it is a sin in men, if they reject the Gospel of Christ. I care not for every scornful title—I am certain that I have the warrant of God's Word in so preaching and I do not believe that any man can be faithful to men's souls and clear of their blood unless he bears his frequent and solemn testimony upon this vital subject.

"When He, the Spirit of Truth, is come, He will reprove the world of sin and of righteousness and of judgment—of sin, because they believe not in Me." "And this is the condemnation, that light is come into the world and men loved darkness rather than light." "He that believes not is condemned already, because he has not believed in the name of the only begotten Son of God." "If I had not done among them the works which none other man did, they had not had sin—but now have they both seen and hated both Me and My Father."

"Woe unto you, Chorazin! Woe unto you, Bethsaida! For if the mighty works had been done in Tyre and Sidon, which have been done in you, they had a great while ago repented, sitting in sackcloth and ashes. But I say unto you, it shall be more tolerable for Tyre and Sidon at the Judgment, than for you." "If I had not come and spoken unto them, they had not had sin: but now they have no cloak for their sin." "Therefore we ought to give the more earnest heed to the things which we have heard, lest at any time we should let them slip. For if the word spoken by angels was steadfast and every transgression and disobedience received a just recompense of reward, how shall we escape if we neglect so great salvation?"

"He that despised Moses' law died without mercy under two or three witnesses; of how much sorer punishment, suppose you, shall he be thought worthy, who has trodden under foot the Son of God and has counted the blood of the Covenant, wherewith he was sanctified, an unholy thing and has done despite unto the Spirit of grace? For we know Him that has said, Vengeance belongs unto Me, I will recompense, says the Lord. And again, the Lord shall judge His people. It is a fearful thing to fall into the hands of the living God."

I have been quoting, you see, some Scripture passages and if they do not mean that unbelief is a sin and the sin, which, above all others, damns men's souls, they do not mean anything at all, but they are just a dead letter in the

Word of God. Now, adultery, murder, theft and lying—all these are damning and deadly sins—but repentance can cleanse all these, through the blood of Christ. But to reject Christ destroys a man hopelessly. The murderer, the thief, the drunkard may yet enter the kingdom of Heaven, if, repenting of his sins, he will lay hold on the Cross of Christ. But with these sins a man is inevitably lost if he believes not on the Lord Jesus Christ.

And now, my Hearers, will you consider for one moment what an awful sin this is, which you add to all your other sins? Everything lies in the heart of this sin—the rejecting of Christ. There is murder in this. For if the man on the scaffold rejects a pardon, does he not murder himself? There is pride in this. For you reject Christ because your proud hearts have turned you aside. There is rebellion in this. For we rebel against God when we reject Christ. There is high treason in this. For you reject a king. You put far from you Him who is crowned king of the earth and you incur therefore the weightiest of all guilt.

Oh, to think that the Lord Jesus should come from Heaven—to think for a moment that He should hang upon the tree—that there He should die in agonies extreme and that from that Cross He should this day look down upon you and should say, "Come unto Me, you weary and you heavy laden"—that you should still turn away from Him—it is the unkindest stab of all. What more brutish, what more devilish, than to turn away from Him who gave His life for you? Oh that you were wise, that you understood this, that you would consider your latter end!

But again, we do not only add a new sin to the catalogs of guilt but we aggravate all the rest. You cannot sin so cheaply as other people, you who have had the Gospel. When the unenlightened and ignorant sin, their conscience does not prick them. And there is not that guilt in the sin of the ignorant that there is in the sin of the enlightened. Did you steal before? That was bad enough. But hear the Gospel and continue a thief and you are a thief, indeed. Did you lie before you heard the Gospel? The liar shall have his portion in the lake. But lie after hearing the Gospel, and it seems as if the fire of Tophet should be fanned up to a seven-fold fury. He who sins ignorantly has some little excuse. But he who sins against light and knowledge sins presumptuously.

Under the Law there was no atonement for this—presumptuous sins were out of the pole of legal atonement. But blessed be God, Christ has atoned for even these and he that believes shall be saved, despite even his guilt. Oh, I beseech you, remember that the sin of unbelief blackens every other sin. It is like Jeroboam. It is said of him he sinned and made Israel to sin. So unbelief sins itself and leads to every other sin. Unbelief is the file by which you sharpen the axe—the coulter and the sword which you use in rebellion against the Most High. Your sins become more exceeding sinful the more you disbelieve in Christ, the more you know of Him and the longer you reject Him. This is God's Truth. But a Truth that is to be spoken with reluctance and with many groans in our spirits.

Oh to have such a message to deliver to you, to you I say, for if there is a people under Heaven to whom my text applies, it is you. If there is one race of men in the world who have more to account for than others, it is yourselves. There are doubtless others who are on an equality with you, who sit under a faithful and earnest ministry. But as God shall judge between you and me at the Great Day to the utmost of my power I have been faithful to your souls. I have never in this pulpit sought by hard words, by technical language, to magnify my own wisdom.

I have spoken to you plainly. And not a word, to the best of my knowledge, has escaped these lips which every one of you could not understand. You have had a simple Gospel. I have not stood here and preached coldly to you. I could say as I came up yon stairs, "The burden of the Lord was upon me." For my heart has come here heavy and my soul has been hot within me. And when I have preached feebly, my words may have been uncouth and my language far from proper, but my heart never has been wanting. This whole soul has spoken to you. And if I could have ransacked Heaven and earth to find language that might have won you to the Savior, I would have done so.

I have not shunned to reprove you, I have never minced matters. I have spoken to this age of its iniquities and to you of your sins. I have not softened down the Bible to suit the carnal tastes of men. I have said damn, where God said damn—I have not sweetened it into "condemn." I have not minced matters, nor endeavored to veil or conceal the Truth of God, but as to every man's conscience in the sight of God, have I endeavored to commend the Gospel earnestly and with power and with a plain, outspoken, earnest and honest ministry.

I have not kept back the glorious doctrines of grace, although by preaching them the enemies of the Cross have called me an Antinomian.[65] Nor have I been afraid to preach man's solemn responsibility, although another tribe have slandered me as an Arminian.[66] And in saying this, I say it not in a way of glorying. I say it for your rebuke – if you have rejected the Gospel – for you shall have sinned far above that of any other men in casting away Christ. a double measure of the fury of the wrath of God shall fall on you. Sin, then, is aggravated by the rejection of Christ.

III. And now, in the third place, THE PREACHING OF THE GOSPEL OF CHRIST TAKES AWAY ALL EXCUSE FROM THOSE WHO HEAR IT AND REJECT IT. "Now have they no cloak for their sin." A cloak is a very poor covering for sin. When there is an all-seeing eye to look through it in the great day of the tempest of God's wrath, a cloak will be a very poor shelter. But man is always fond of a cloak in the day of cold and rain. We see men gathering their cloaks about them and if they have no shelter and no refuge, still they feel a little comforted by their garment. And so it is with you. You will gather together, if you can, an excuse for your sin and when conscience pricks you, you will seek to heal the wound with an excuse.

And even in the Day of Judgment, although a cloak will be a sorry covering, yet it will be better than nothing at all. "But now you have no cloak for your sin." The traveler is left in the rain without his covering, exposed to the tempest without that garment which once did shelter him. "Now you have no cloak for your sin" – discovered, detected and unmasked, you are left inexcusable, without a cloak for your iniquity. And now let me just notice how the preaching of the Gospel, when it is faithfully performed, takes away all cloaks for sin.

---

[65] The belief that those saved are not required to follow moral laws; rejects all forms of legalism

[66] The belief that God's sovereignty and man's free will are compatible; the soteriological (study of salvation) rival to Calvinism

In the first place, one man might get up and say, "I did not know I was doing wrong when I committed such and such an iniquity." Now, that you cannot say. God has by His Law told you solemnly what is wrong. There stand the Ten Commandments. And there stands the comment of our Master where He has enlarged upon the Commandment and told us that the old Law "you shall not commit adultery" forbade also all sins of the lascivious look and the evil eye. If the Sepoy[67] commits iniquity, there is a cloak for it. I doubt not that his conscience tells him that he does wrong, but his sacred books teach that he is doing right and therefore he has that cloak.

If the Mohammedan[68] commits lust, I doubt not his conscience does prick him, but his sacred books give him liberty. But you profess to believe your Bibles and have them in your houses and have the preachers of them in all your streets. And therefore when you sin, you sin with the proclamation of the Law upon the very wall before your eyes—you do willfully violate a well-known Law which has come from Heaven and come to you.

Again—you might say, "When I sinned, I did not know how great would be the punishment." Of this also, by the Gospel, you are left without excuse. Did not Jesus Christ tell you and does He not tell you every day, that those who will not have Him shall be cast into outer darkness, where there shall be weeping and gnashing of teeth? Has He not said, "These shall go away into everlasting punishment, but the righteous into life eternal"? Does He not Himself declare that the wicked shall be burned up with unquenchable fire?

Has He not told you of a place where their worm dies not and where their fire is not quenched? And the ministers of the Gospel have not shunned to tell you this, too. You have sinned, though you knew you would be lost by it. You have taken the poisonous draught, not thinking that it was harmless—you knew that every drop in the cup was scalding with damnation and yet you have taken the cup and drained it to its dregs. You have destroyed your own souls with your eyes open. You have gone like a fool to the stocks, like an ox to the slaughter and like a lamb you have licked the knife of the butcher. In

---

[67] An Indian soldier serving under British or European rule

[68] Muslim

this, then, you are left without excuse.

But some of you may say, "Ah, I heard the Gospel, it is true, and I knew that I was doing wrong, but I did not know what I must do to be saved." Is there one among you who can urge such an excuse as this? Methinks you will not have the impudence to do so. "Believe and live," is preached every day in your hearing. Many of you these ten, twenty, thirty, forty, or fifty years have been hearing the Gospel and you dare not say, "I did not know what the Gospel was."

From your earliest childhood many of you have listened to it. The name of Jesus was mingled with the hush of lullaby. You drank in a holy Gospel with your mother's milk and yet despite all that, you have never sought Christ. "Knowledge is power," men say. Alas! Knowledge, when not used, is wrath, WRATH, WRATH to the uttermost, against the man who knows and yet does that which he knows to be wrong.

Methinks I can hear another say, "Well, I heard the Gospel preached, but I never had a good example set me." Some of you may say that and it would be partially true. But there are others of you, concerning whom I may say that this would be a lying excuse. Ah, Man. You have been very fond of speaking of the inconsistencies of Christians. You have said, "They do not live as they ought." And alas, there is too much truth in what you have said. But there was one Christian whom you knew and whose character you were compelled to admire. Do you not remember her? It was the mother who brought you forth.

That has always been the one difficulty with you up to this day. You could have rejected the Gospel very easily, but your mother's example stood before you and you could not overcome that. Do you not remember among the first early darkling of your recollection how you opened your little eyes in the morning and you saw a mother's loving face looking down upon you and you caught her with a tear in her eye and you heard her say, "God bless the child, may he call the Redeemer blessed!" You remember how your father did often chide you—she did seldom chide—she often spoke in tones of love. Recollect that little upper room where she took you aside and putting her arms round your neck, dedicated you to God and prayed that the Lord would save you in your childhood?

Remember the letter she gave you and your book in which she wrote your name when you left the parental roof to go abroad and the sorrow with which she wrote to you when she heard you had begun to plunge in gaiety and mix with the ungodly? Remember that sorrowful look with which she did wring your hand the last time you left her? Remember how she said to you, "You will bring my hairs with sorrow to the grave, if you walk in the ways of iniquity"?

Well, you knew that what she said was not cant. There was reality in that. You could laugh at the minister, you could say it was his business, but at her you could not scoff. She was a Christian, there was no mistake about it. How often did she put up with your angry temper and bear with your rough manners, for she was a sweet spirit, almost too good for earth–can you remember that? You were not there when she was dying, you could not arrive in time. But she said to her friend as she was dying, "There is only one thing that I want, then I could die happy–oh, that I could see my children walking in the Truth of God." Now, I apprehend such an example leaves you without a cloak for your wickedness and if you commit iniquity after that, how fearful must be the weight of your woe!

But others of you can say that you had no such mother. Your first school was the street and the first example you ever had was that of a swearing father. Remember, my Friend, there is one perfect example–Christ and Him you have heard of, though you have not seen Him. Jesus Christ, the Man of Nazareth, was a perfect Man. In Him was there no sin, neither was there guile in His mouth. And if you have never seen anything like Christian worth anywhere else, yet you can see it in Christ. And in venturing such an excuse as this, remember you have ventured upon a lie, for the example of Christ, the works of Christ, as well as the Words of Christ, leave you without excuse for your sin.

Ah, and I think I hear one more excuse offered and that is this: "Well, I certainly had many advantages, but they were never sent home to my conscience so that I felt them." Now, there are very few of you here who can say that. Some of you will say, "Yes, I heard the minister, but he never made an impression upon me." Ah, young men and young women and all of you this morning, I must be a witness against you in the Day of Judgment that this is untrue. For, but now, your consciences were touched. Did I not see some soft tears of repentance—I trust they were such—flowing but just now? No, you have not always been unmoved by the Gospel. You have grown old now and it takes a deal to stir you, but it was not always so.

There was a time in your youth when you were very susceptible of impressing. Remember the sins of your youth will cause your bones to rot, if you have still persevered in rejecting the Gospel. Your old heart has grown hard—still you are without excuse. You did feel once, yes, and even now you cannot help feeling. I know there are some of you that can scarcely keep your seats at the thought of your iniquities. And you have almost vowed, some of you, that this day you will seek God and the first thing you will do will be to climb to your chamber and shut the door and seek the Lord.

Ah, but I remember a story of one who remarked to a minister, what an amazing thing it was to see so many people weeping. "No," said the minister, "I will tell you something more amazing still—that so many will forget all they wept about when they get outside the door." And you will do this. Still, when you have done it, you will remember that you have not been without the strivings of God's Spirit. You will remember that God has, this morning, as it were, put a hurdle across your road, dug a ditch in your way and put up a hand-post and said, "Take warning! Beware, beware, beware! You are rushing madly into the ways of iniquity!"

And I have come before you this morning and in God's name I have said, "Stop, stop, stop, thus says the Lord, consider your ways, why will you die? Turn you, turn you, why will you die O house of Israel?" And, now, if you will put this from you, it must be even so. If you will put out these sparks, if you will quench this first burning torch, it must be so! On your own head be your blood—at your own door lay your iniquities.

IV. But now I have one thing more to do. And it is awful work. For I have, as it were, to PUT ON THE BLACK CAP AND PRONOUNCE THE SENTENCE OF CONDEMNATION. For those who live and die rejecting Christ there is a most fearful doom. They shall perish with utter destruction. There are degrees of punishment. But the highest degree is given to the man who rejects Christ.

You have noticed that passage, I dare say, that the liar and the whoremonger and drunkards shall have their portion—whom do you suppose with?—with unbelievers—as if Hell were made first of all for unbelievers—as if the pit were dug not for whoremongers and swearers and drunkards, but for men who despise Christ, because that is the A-1 sin, the cardinal vice and men are condemned for that.

Other iniquities come following after them, but this one goes before them to judgment. Imagine for a moment that time has passed and that the Day of Judgment is come. We are all gathered together, both quick and dead. The trumpet blast waxes exceeding loud and long. We are all attentive, expecting something marvelous. The exchange stands still in its business—the shop is deserted by the tradesman. The crowded streets are filled. All men stand still. They feel that the last great business day is come and that now they must settle their accounts forever.

A solemn stillness fills the air—no sound is heard. All, all is noiseless. Presently a great white cloud with solemn state sails through the sky and then—hark! the twofold clamor of the startled earth. On that cloud there sits one like unto the Son of Man. Every eye looks and at last there is heard a unanimous shout—"It is He! It is He!" And after that you hear on the one hand, shouts of "Hallelujah, Hallelujah, Hallelujah, Welcome, Welcome, Welcome Son of God."

But mixed with that there is a deep bass, composed of the weeping and the wailing of the men and women who have persecuted Him and who have rejected Him. Listen! I think I can dissect the sonnet, I think I can hear the words as they come separately, each one of them, tolling like a death knell. What say they? They say, "Rocks hide us, mountains fall upon us, hide us from the face of Him that sits upon the throne." And shall you be among the number of those who say to the rocks "Hide us"?

My impenitent Hearer! Suppose for a moment that you have gone out of this world and that you have died impenitent and that you are among those who are weeping and wailing and gnashing their teeth. Oh, what will then be your terror! Blanched cheeks and knocking knees are nothing compared to your horror of heart, when you shall be drunk, but not with wine. And when you shall reel to and fro with the intoxication of amazement and shall fall down and roll in the dust for horror and dismay.

For there He comes and there He is, with fierce, fire-darting eyes. And now the time is come for the great division. The voice is heard, "Gather My people from the four winds of Heaven, My elect in whom My soul delights." They are gathered at the right hand and there they are. And now says He, "Gather up the tares and bind them in bundles to burn." And you are gathered and on the left hand there you are, gathered into the bundle. All that is wanted is the lighting of the pile. Where shall be the torch that shall kindle them? The tares are to be burned—where is the flame?

The flame comes out of His mouth and it is composed of words like these—"Depart, you cursed into everlasting fire, in Hell, prepared for the devil and his angels." Do you linger? "Depart!" Do you seek a blessing? "You are cursed." I curse you with a curse. Do you seek to escape? It is everlasting fire. Do you stop and plead? No, "I called and you refused. I stretched out My hands and you regarded Me not, therefore I will mock at your calamity, I will laugh when your fear comes." "Depart, again, I say, depart forever!"

And you are gone. And what is your reflection? Why, it is this—"Oh, would to God that I never had been born! Oh, that I had never heard the Gospel preached, that I might never have had the sin of rejecting it!" This will be the gnawing of the worm in your conscience—"I knew better but I did not do better. As I sowed the wind, it is right I should reap the whirlwind. I was checked, but I would not be stopped. I was wooed, but I would not be invited. Now I see that I have murdered myself. Oh, thought above all thoughts most deadly! I am lost, lost, lost! And this is the horror of horrors—I have caused myself to be lost. I have put from me the Gospel of Christ. I have destroyed myself."

Shall this be so with you, my Hearer? Shall this be so with you? I pray it may not! O may the Holy Spirit now constrain you to come to Jesus, for I know that you art too vile to yield, unless He compels you. But I hope for you. Methinks I hear you say, "What must I do to be saved?" Let me tell you the way of salvation and then farewell. If you would be saved, "Believe on the Lord Jesus Christ and you shall be saved." For the Scripture says, "He that believes and is immersed shall be saved. He that believes not shall be damned!" There Jesus hangs, dying on His Cross! Look to Him and live—

"Venture on Him, venture wholly,
Let no other trust intrude;
None but Jesus
Can do helpless sinners good."

Be you wicked, filthy, depraved, degraded—you are still invited to Christ. The devil's castaways Christ takes in—the offscouring, the dross, the scum, the chaff, the sewage of this world—are now invited to Christ. Come to Him now and obtain mercy. But if you harden your hearts—

"The Lord in anger dressed
Shall lift His hand and swear,
'You that despised My promised rest,
Shall have no portion there.'"

THE DOCTRINES OF GRACE DO NOT LEAD TO SIN

AUGUST 19, 1883, AT EXETER HALL, STRAND

"For sin shall not have dominion over you: for you are not under the law, but under grace. What then? Shall we sin, because we are not under the law, but under grace? God forbid."
Romans 6:14-15

LAST Sabbath morning I tried to show that the substance and essence of the true Gospel is the Doctrine of God's Grace—that, in fact, if you take away the Grace of God from the Gospel you have extracted from it its very life-blood and there is nothing left worth preaching, worth believing, or worth contending for. Grace is the soul of the Gospel—without it the Gospel is dead. Grace is the music of the Gospel—without it the Gospel is silent as to all comfort. I also endeavored to set forth the Doctrine of Grace in brief terms, teaching that God deals with sinful men upon the footing of pure mercy—finding them guilty and condemned, He gives free pardons, altogether irrespective of past character, or of any good works which may be foreseen. Moved only by pity, He devises a plan for their rescue from sin and its consequences—a plan in which Grace is the leading feature.

Out of free favor He has provided, in the death of His dear Son, an atonement by means of which His mercy can be justly bestowed. He accepts all those who place their trust in this Atonement, selecting faith as the way of salvation, that it may be all of Grace. In this He acts, from a motive found within Himself, and not because of any reason found in the sinner's conduct—past, present, or future. I tried to show that this Grace of God flows towards the sinner from of old and begins its operations upon him when there is nothing good in him—it works in him that which is good and acceptable—and continues so to work in him till the deed of Grace is complete and the Believer is received up into the glory for which he is made meet.

Grace commences to save and it perseveres till all is done. From first to last, from the "A" to the "Z" of the heavenly alphabet, everything in salvation is of Grace and Grace alone! All is of free favor, nothing of merit. "By Grace are you saved through faith; and that not of yourselves; it is the gift of God." "So then it is not of him that wills, nor of him that runs, but of God that shows mercy." No sooner is this doctrine set forth in a clear light than men begin to quibble with it. It is the target for all carnal logic to shoot at. Unrenewed minds never liked it and they never will—it is too humbling to human pride, making light of the nobility of human nature. That men are to be saved by Divine charity; that they must, as condemned criminals, receive pardon by the exercise of the royal prerogative or else perish in their sins is a teaching which they cannot endure!

God alone is exalted in the sovereignty of His mercy—the sinner can do no better than meekly touch the silver scepter and accept undeserved favor just because God wills to give it! This is not pleasant to the great minds of our philosophers and the broad phylacteries of our moralists and, therefore, they turn aside and fight against the empire of Grace. Straightway the unrenewed man seeks out artillery with which to fight against the Gospel of the Grace of God! And one of the biggest guns he has ever brought to the front is the declaration that the Doctrines of the Grace of God must lead to licentiousness! If great sinners are freely saved, then men will more readily become great sinners—and if, when God's Grace regenerates a man, it abides with him, then men will infer that they may live as they like and yet be saved.

This is the constantly repeated objection which I have heard till it wearies me with its vain and false noise. I am almost ashamed to have to refute so rotten an argument! They dare to assert that men will take license to be guilty because God is gracious! And they do not hesitate to say that if men are not to be saved by their works, they will come to the conclusion that their conduct is a matter of indifference and that they may as well sin that Grace may abound! This morning I want to talk a little about this notion, for in part it is a great mistake and in part it is a great lie. In part it is a mistake because it arises from misconception. And in part it is a lie because men know better, or might know better if they pleased.

I begin by admitting that the charge does appear somewhat probable. It does seem very likely that if we are to go up and down the country and say, "The very chief of sinners may be forgiven through believing in Jesus Christ, for God is displaying mercy to the very vilest of the vile," then sin will seem to be a cheap thing. If we are everywhere to cry, "Come, you sinners, come and welcome, and receive free and immediate pardon through the Sovereign Grace of God," it does seem probable that some may basely reply, "Let us sin without ceasing, for we can easily obtain forgiveness." But that which looks to be probable is not, therefore, certain! On the contrary, the improbable and the unexpected full often come to pass. In questions of moral influence, nothing is more deceptive than theory. The ways of the human mind are not to be laid down with a pencil and compasses—man is a singular being.

Even that which is logical is not always inevitable, for men's minds are not governed by the rules of the schools. I believe that the inference which would lead men to sin because Grace reigns is not logical, but the very reverse—and I venture to assert that, as a matter of fact, ungodly men do not, as a rule, plead the Grace of God as an excuse for their sin! As a rule they are too indifferent to care about reasons at all! And if they do offer an excuse, it is usually more flimsy and superficial. There may be a few men of perverse minds who have used this argument, but there is no accounting for the freaks of the fallen understanding. I shrewdly suspect that in any cases in which such reasoning has been put forward, it was a mere pretense and by no means a plea which satisfied the sinner's own conscience.

If men do excuse themselves, it is generally in some veiled manner, for the most of them would be utterly ashamed to state the argument in plain terms. I question whether the devil himself would be found reasoning thus—"God is merciful, therefore let us be more sinful." It is so diabolical an inference that I do not like to charge my fellow men with it, though our moralist opposers do not hesitate thus to degrade themselves! Surely, no intelligent being can really persuade itself that the goodness of God is a reason for offending Him more than ever! Moral insanity produces strange reasoning, but it is my solemn conviction that very rarely do men practically consider the Grace of God to be a motive for sin. That which seems so probable at the first blush is not so when we come to consider it.

I have admitted that a few human beings have turned the Grace of God into lasciviousness, but I trust no one will ever argue against any doctrine on account of the perverse use made of it by the baser sort. Cannot every Truth of God be perverted? Is there a single doctrine of Scripture which graceless hands have not twisted into mischief? Is there not an almost infinite ingenuity in wicked men for making evil out of good? If we are to condemn a Truth because of the misbehavior of individuals who profess to believe it, we would be found condemning our Lord, Himself, for what Judas did – and our holy faith would die at the hands of apostates and hypocrites!

Let us act like rational men. We do not find fault with ropes because poor insane creatures have hanged themselves with them! Nor do we ask that the wares of Sheffield may be destroyed because edged tools are the murderer's instruments.[69] It may appear probable that the Doctrine of Free Grace will be made into a license for sin, but a better acquaintance with the curious working of the human mind corrects the notion. Fallen as human nature is, it is still human and, therefore, does not take kindly to certain forms of evil – such, for instance, as inhuman ingratitude. It is hardly human to multiply injuries upon those who return us continued benefits.

The case reminds me of the story of half-a-dozen boys who had severe fathers, accustomed to flogging them within an inch of their lives. Another boy was with them who was tenderly beloved by his parents and known to be so. These young gentlemen met together to hold a council of war about

---

[69] Sheffield, a region in England and prominent center for blade production since the fourteenth century

robbing an orchard. They were, all of them, anxious to get about it except the favored youth who did not agree with the proposal. One of them cried out, "You need not be afraid! If our fathers catch us at this work, we shall be half-killed, but your father won't lay a hand upon you." The little boy answered, "And do you think because my father is kind to me, that therefore I will do wrong and grieve him? I will do nothing of the sort to my dear father! He is so good to me that I cannot vex him."

It would appear that the argument of the many boys was not overpoweringly convincing to their companion—the opposite conclusion was quite as logical and evidently carried weight with it. If God is good to the undeserving, some men will go into sin, but there are others of a nobler order whom the goodness of God leads to repentance. They scorn the beast-like argument that the more loving God is, the more rebellious we may be—and they feel that against the God of Goodness it is an evil thing to rebel. By the way, I cannot help observing that I have known persons object to the evil influence of the Doctrines of Grace who were by no means qualified, by their own morality, to be judges of the subject! Morals must be in a poor way when immoral persons become their guardians!

The doctrine of Justification by Faith is frequently objected to as injurious to morals. A newspaper, some time ago, quoted a verse from one of our popular hymns—

"*Weary, working, plodding one,*
Why toil you so?
Cease your doing; all was done
Long, long ago!
'Till to Jesus' work you cling
By a simple faith,
Doing' is a deadly thing,
Doing' ends in death."

This is styled mischievous teaching! When I read the article, I felt a deep interest in this corrector of Luther[70] and Paul, and I wondered how much he had drunk in order to elevate his mind to such a pitch of theological knowledge! I have found men pleading against the Doctrines of Grace on the ground that they did not promote morality, to whom I could have justly replied, "What has morality to do with you, or you with it?" These sticklers for good works are not often the doers of them! Let legalists look to their own hands and tongues—and leave the Gospel of Grace and its advocates to answer for themselves!

Looking back in history, I see upon its pages a refutation of the oft-repeated calumny. Who dares to suggest that the men who believed in the Grace of God have been sinners above other sinners? With all their faults, those who throw stones at them will be few if they first prove themselves to be their superiors in character, when have they been the patrons of vice, or the defenders of injustice? Pitch upon the point in English history when this doctrine was very strong in the land—who were the men that held these doctrines most firmly? Men like Owen,[71] Charnock,[72] Manton,[73] Howe![74] And I hesitate not to add Oliver Cromwell![75] What kind of men were these? Did they pander to the licentiousness of a court? Did they invent a Book of Sports for Sabbath Diversion? Did they haunt ale-houses and places of revelry?

Every historian will tell you the greatest fault of these men, in the eyes of their enemies, was that they were too precise for the generation in which they lived—so they called them Puritans and condemned them as holding

---

[70] Martin Luther, a sixteenth-century German theologian, composer, priest, monk, and leader within the Protestant Reformation; father of the Lutheran Church

[71] John Owen, a seventeenth-century English Congregational pastor, Calvinist theologian, and academic administrator at the University of Oxford

[72] Stephen Charnock, a seventeenth-century English Puritan clergyman and divine

[73] Thomas Manton, a seventeenth-century Puritan clergyman and clerk to the Westminster Assembly, and chaplain to Oliver Cromwell

[74] Likely George Howe, a nineteenth-century Presbyterian minister, theologian, professor, and writer

[75] Oliver Cromwell, an English general and statesman; led the Parliament of England's armies against King Charles I in the English Civil War

a gloomy theology! Sirs, if there was iniquity in the land in that day, it was to be found with the theological party which preached up salvation by works! The gentlemen with their womanish locks and perfumed hair, whose speech savored of profanity, were the advocates of salvation by works and, all bedabbled with lust, they pleaded for human merit!

But the men who believed in Grace alone were of another style. They were not in the chambers of rioting and wantonness! Where were they? They might be found on their knees crying to God for help in temptation and in persecuting times they might be found in prison, cheerfully suffering the loss of all things for the Truth of God's sake! The Puritans were the godliest men on the face of the earth! Are men so inconsistent as to nickname them for their purity and yet say that their doctrines lead to sin? Nor is this a solitary instance–this instance of Puritanism–all history confirms the rule and when it is said that these doctrines will create sin, I appeal to facts, and leave the oracle to answer as it may. If we are ever to see a pure and godly England, we must have a gospelized England! If we are to put down drunkenness and the social evil, it must be by the proclamation of the Grace of God!

Men must be forgiven by the Grace of God, renewed by the Grace of God, transformed by the Grace of God, sanctified by the Grace of God and preserved by the Grace of God! And when that comes to pass, the golden age will dawn! But while they are merely taught their duty and left to do it of themselves in their own strength, it is labor in vain! You may flog a dead horse a long while before it will stir–you need to put life into it, or else all your flogging will fail. To teach men to walk who have no feet is poor work–and so is instruction in morals before Grace gives a heart to love holiness! The Gospel, alone, supplies men with motive and strength and, therefore, it is to the Gospel that we must look as the real reformer of men!

I shall fight, this morning, with the objection before us as I shall find strength. The Doctrines of Grace, the whole plan of salvation by Grace, is most promotive of holiness. Wherever it comes, it helps us to say, "God forbid," to the question, "Shall we sin, because we are not under the Law, but under Grace?" This I would set out in the clear sunlight. I wish to call your attention to some six or seven points.

First, you will see that the Gospel of the Grace of God promotes real holiness in men by remembering that THE SALVATION WHICH IT BRINGS IS SALVATION FROM THE POWER OF SIN. When we preach salvation to the vilest of men, some suppose we mean by that a mere deliverance from Hell and an entrance into Heaven. It includes all that and results in that, but that is not what we mean! What we mean by salvation is this—deliverance from the love of sin, rescue from the habit of sin, setting free from the desire to sin. Now listen. If it is so, that that gift of deliverance from sin is the gift of Divine Grace, in what way will that gift, or the free distribution of it, produce sin? I fail to see any such danger. On the contrary, I say to the man who proclaims a gracious promise of victory over sin, "Make all speed—go up and down throughout the world and tell the vilest of mankind that God is willing, by His Grace, to set them free from the love of sin and to make new creatures of them."

Suppose the salvation we preach is this—"You that have lived ungodly and wicked lives may enjoy your sins and yet escape the penalty"? That would be mischievous, indeed! But if it is this—"You that live the most ungodly and wicked lives may yet, by believing in the Lord Jesus, be enabled to change those lives so that you shall live unto God instead of serving sin and Satan"?—what harm can come to the most prudish morals? Why, I say spread such a Gospel and let it circulate through every part of our vast empire! Let all men hear it, whether they rule in the House of Lords or suffer in the house of bondage! Tell them everywhere that God freely and of infinite Grace is willing to renew men and women and make them new creatures in Christ Jesus! Can any evil consequences come of the freest proclamation of this news? The worse men are, the more gladly would we see them embracing this Truth of God, for these are they who most need it!

I say to every one of you, whoever you may be, whatever your past condition—God can renew you according to the power of His Grace so that you who are to Him like dead, dry bones, can be made to live by His Spirit! That renewal will be seen in holy thoughts, pure words and righteous acts to the glory of God. In great love He is prepared to work all these things in all who believe. Why should any man be angry at such a statement? What possible harm can come of it? I defy the most cunning adversary to object, upon the ground of morals, to God's giving men new hearts and right spirits even as He pleases!

II. Secondly, let it not be forgotten as a matter of fact that THE PRINCIPLE OF LOVE HAS BEEN FOUND TO POSSESS VERY GREAT POWER OVER MEN. In the infancy of history, nations dream that crime can be put down by severity and they rely upon fierce punishments—but experience corrects the error. Our forefathers dreaded forgery, which is a troublesome fraud that interferes with the confidence which should exist between man and man. To put it down, they made forgery a capital offense. Alas for the murders committed by that law! Yet the constant use of the gallows was never sufficient to stamp out the crime. Many offenses have been created and multiplied by the penalty which was meant to suppress them.

Some offenses have almost ceased when the penalty against them has been lightened. It is a notable fact as to men that if they are forbidden to do a thing, they straightway pine to do it, though they had never thought of doing it before! Law commands obedience, but does not promote it—it often creates disobedience—and an over-weighted penalty has been known to provoke an offense. Law fails, but love wins! Love in any case makes sin infamous. If one should rob another, it would be sufficiently bad. But suppose a man robbed his friend who had helped him often when he was in need? Everyone would say that his crime was most disgraceful. Love brands sin on the forehead with a red-hot iron. If a man should kill an enemy, the offense would be grievous, but if he slew his father, to whom he owes his life, or his mother, on whose breasts he was nursed in infancy, then all would cry out against the monster! In the light of love, sin is seen to be exceedingly sinful.

Nor is this all. Love has a great constraining power towards the highest form of virtue. Deeds to which a man could not be compelled on the ground of law, men have cheerfully done because of love. Would our brave seamen man the lifeboat to obey an Act of Parliament? No, they would indignantly revolt against being forced to risk their lives! But they will do it freely to save their fellow men. Remember that text of the Apostle, "Scarcely for a righteous (or merely just) man will one die: yet perhaps," says he, "for a good (benevolent) man some would even dare to die." Goodness wins the heart and one is ready to die for the kind and generous! Look how men have thrown away their lives for great leaders. That was an immortal saying of the wounded French soldier. When searching for the bullet the surgeon cut deeply and the patient cried out, "A little lower and you will touch the Emperor," meaning that the Emperor's name was written on his heart!

In several notable instances, men have thrown themselves into the jaws of death to save a leader whom they loved. Duty holds the fort, but love casts its body in the way of the deadly bullet! Who would think of sacrificing his life on the ground of law? Love alone counts not life so dear as the service of the Beloved! Love to Jesus creates a heroism of which law knows nothing. All the history of the Church of Christ, when it has been true to its Lord, is a proof of this. Kindness, also, working by the law of love, has often changed the most unworthy and therein proved that it is not a factor of evil. We have often heard the story of the soldier who had been reduced to the lowest rank, flogged and imprisoned—and yet for all that he would get drunk and misbehave himself.

The commanding officer said, one day, "I have tried almost everything with this man and can do nothing with him. I will try one more thing." When he was brought in, the officer addressed him and said, "You seem incorrigible—we have tried everything with you—there seems to be no hope of a change in your wicked conduct. I am determined to see if another plan will have any effect. Though you deserve flogging and long imprisonment, I shall freely forgive you." The man was greatly moved by the unexpected and undeserved pardon—and became a good soldier. The story wears truth on its brow—we all see that it would probably end so! That anecdote is such a good argument that I will give you another.

A drunkard woke up one morning from his drunken sleep with his clothes on him just as he had rolled down the night before. He saw his only child, his daughter, Millie, getting his breakfast. Coming to his senses, he said to her, "Millie, why do you stay with me?" She answered, "Because you are my father, and because I love you." He looked at himself and saw what a sottish, ragged, good-for-nothing creature he was, and he answered her, "Millie, do you really love me?" The child cried, "Yes, father, I do, and I will never leave you because when mother died she said, 'Millie, stick to your father and always pray for him, and one of these days he will give up drinking and be a good father to you' – so I will never leave you."

Is it wonderful when I add that, as the story has it, Millie's father cast away his drink and became a Christian man? It would have been more remarkable if he had not! Millie was trying Free Grace, was she not? According to our moralists she should have said, "Father, you are a horrible wretch! I have stuck to you long enough! I must now leave you, or else I shall be encouraging other fathers to get drunk." Under such proper dealing I fear Millie's father would have continued a drunkard till he drank himself into Hell. But the power of love made a better man of him. Do not these instances prove that undeserved love has a great influence for good?

Hear another story – In the old persecuting times, there lived in Cheapside[76] one who feared God and attended the secret meetings of the saints. And near him there dwelt a poor cobbler whose needs were often relieved by the merchant. But the poor man was a cross-grained being and, most ungratefully, from hope of reward, laid an information against his kind friend on the score of religion. This accusation would have brought the merchant to death by burning if he had not found a means of escape. Returning to his house, the injured man did not change his generous behavior to the malignant cobbler, but, on the contrary, was more liberal than ever! The cobbler was, however, in an ill mood and avoided the good man with all his might, running away at his approach.

One day he was obliged to meet him face to face and the Christian man asked him, gently, "Why do you shun me? I am not your enemy. I know all that you did to injure me, but I never had an angry thought against you. I have helped you and I am willing to do so as long as I live, only let us be friends." Do you marvel that they clasped hands? Would you wonder if, before long,

---

[76] A street in London; the historic and modern financial center of London

the poor man was found at the Lollards' meeting?[77] All such anecdotes rest upon the assured fact that Grace has a strange subduing power and leads men to goodness—drawing them with cords of love and bands of man! The Lord knows that bad as men are, the key of their hearts hangs on the nail of love. He knows that His almighty goodness, though often baffled, will triumph in the end!

I believe my point is proved. To myself it is so. However, we must pass on.

III. There is no fear that the Doctrines of Grace will lead men to sin, because THEIR OPERATIONS ARE CONNECTED WITH A SPECIAL REVELATION OF THE EVIL OF SIN. Iniquity is made to be exceedingly bitter before it is forgiven or when it is forgiven. When God begins to deal with a man with a view of blotting out his sins and making him His child, He usually causes him to see his evil ways in all their heinousness. He makes him look on sin with fixed eyes, till he cries with David, "My sin is ever before me!" In my own case, when under conviction of sin, no cheering object met my mental eye—my soul saw only darkness and a horrible tempest. It seemed as though a horrible spot were painted on my eyeballs!

Guilt, like a grim chamberlain, drew the curtains of my bed, so that I rested not, but in my slumbers anticipated the wrath to come. I felt that I had offended God and that this was the most awful thing a human being could do. I was out of order with my Creator, out of order with the universe—I had damned myself forever—and I wondered that I did not immediately feel the gnawing of the undying worm. Even to this hour a sight of sin causes the most dreadful emotions in my heart. Any man or woman here who has passed through that experience, or anything like it, will always feel a deep horror of sin. A burnt child dreads the fire. "No," says the sinner to his tempter, "you once deceived me and I so smarted in consequence, but I will not again be deluded. I have been delivered, like a brand from the burning, and I cannot go back to the fire."

---

[77] A pre-Protestant movement in England that existed from the mid-fourteenth to the sixteenth century; led by John Wycliffe, an early reformer, opponent of the Catholic Church, and translator of the Bible into English

By the operations of Grace we are made weary of sin; we loathe both it and its imaginary pleasures. We would utterly exterminate it from the soil of our nature. It is a thing accursed, even as Amalek was to Israel. If you, my Friend, do not detest every sinful thing, I fear you are still in the gall of bitterness, for one of the sure fruits of the Spirit is a love of holiness and a loathing of every false way. A deep inward experience forbids the child of God to sin—he has known within himself its judgment and its condemnation and, therefore, it is a thing abhorrent to him. An enmity both fierce and endless exists between the chosen seed and the serpent brood of evil—therefore the fear that Grace will be abused is abundantly safeguarded.

IV. Remember, also, that not only is the forgiven man thus set against sin by the process of conviction, but EVERY MAN WHO TASTES OF THE SAVING GRACE OF GOD IS MADE A NEW CREATURE IN CHRIST JESUS. Now if the Doctrines of Grace in the hands of an ordinary man might be dangerous, yet they would cease to be so in the hands of one who is quickened by the Spirit and created anew in the image of God. The Holy Spirit comes upon the chosen one and transforms him—his ignorance is removed, his affections are changed, his understanding is enlightened, his will is subdued, his desires are refined, his life is changed—in fact, he is as one newborn, to whom all things have become new. This change is compared in Scripture to the resurrection from the dead, to a creation and to a new birth.

This takes place in every man who becomes a partaker of the Free Grace of God. "You must be born again," said Christ to Nicodemus, and gracious men are born again! One said the other day, "If I believed that I was eternally saved, I should live in sin." Perhaps you would—but if you were renewed in heart you would not! "But," says one, "if I believed God loved me from before the foundation of the world and that, therefore, I would be saved, I would take a full swing in sin." Perhaps you and the devil would, but God's regenerate children are not of so base a nature! To them, the abounding Grace of the Father is a bond to righteousness which they never think of breaking—they feel the sweet constraints of sacred gratitude and desire to perfect holiness in the fear of the Lord.

All beings live according to their nature and the regenerated man works out the holy instincts of his renewed mind! Crying after holiness, warring against sin, laboring to be pure in all things, the regenerate man puts forth all his strength towards that which is pure and perfect. A new heart makes all the difference! Given a new nature, all the propensities run in a different way, and the blessings of almighty love no longer involve peril, but suggest the loftiest aspirations!

V. One of the chief securities for the holiness of the pardoned is found in the way of CLEANSING THROUGH ATONEMENT. The blood of Jesus sanctifies as well as pardons. The sinner learns that his free pardon cost the life of his best Friend and, in order to his salvation the Son of God, Himself, agonized even to a bloody sweat and died forsaken of His God. This causes a sacred mourning for sin as he looks upon the Lord whom he pierced. Love to Jesus burns within the pardoned sinner's breast, for the Lord is his Redeemer and, therefore, he feels a burning indignation against the murderous evil of sin. To him all manner of evil is detestable since it is stained with the Savior's blood.

As the penitent sinner hears the cry of, "Eloi, Sabachthani!" he is horrified to think that One so pure and good should be forsaken of Heaven because of the sin which He bore in His people's place. From the death of Jesus the mind draws the conclusion that sin is exceedingly sinful in the sight of the Lord—for if eternal justice would not spare even the well-beloved Jesus when imputed sin was upon Him, how much less will it spare guilty men? It must be an unutterably thing full of poison which could make even the Immaculate Jesus suffer so terribly!

Nothing can be imagined which can have greater power over gracious minds than the vision of a crucified Savior denouncing sin by all His wounds—and by every falling drop of blood. What? Live in the sin which slew Jesus? Find pleasure in that which worked His death? Trifle with that which laid His Glory in the dust? Impossible! Thus you see that the gifts of Free Grace, when handed down by a pierced hand, are never likely to suggest self-indulgence in sin, but the very reverse.

VI. Sixthly, a man who becomes a partaker of Divine Grace and receives the new nature is ever afterwards A PARTAKER OF DAILY HELPS FROM

GOD'S HOLY SPIRIT. God the Holy Spirit deigns to dwell in the bosom of every man whom God has saved by His Grace. Is not that a wonderful means of sanctifying? By what process can men be better kept from sin than by having the Holy Spirit, Himself, dwell as Vice-Regent within their hearts? The Ever-Blessed Spirit leads Believers to be much in prayer—and what a power for holiness is found in the child of Grace speaking to the heavenly Father! The tempted man flies to his chamber, unloads his grief on God, looks to the flowing wounds of his Redeemer and comes down strong to resist temptation.

The Divine Word, also, with its precepts and promises, is a never-failing source of sanctification. Were it not that we, every day, bathe in the sacred fountain of eternal strength, we might soon be weak and irresolute—but fellowship with God renews us in our vigorous warfare with sin. How is it possible that the Doctrines of Grace could suggest sin to men who constantly draw near to God? The renewed man is also, by God's Spirit, frequently quickened in conscience, so that things which, before, did not strike him as sinful, are seen in a clearer light and are, consequently, condemned. I know that certain matters are sinful to me, today, which did not appear so 10 years ago—my judgment has, I trust, been more and more cleared of the blindness of sin.

The natural conscience is callous and hard, but the gracious conscience grows more and more tender till, at last, it becomes as sensitive as a raw wound. He who has most Grace is most conscious of his need of more Grace. The gracious are often afraid to put one foot before another for fear of doing wrong. Have you not felt this holy fear, this sacred caution? It is by this means that the Holy Spirit prevents your ever turning your Christian liberty into licentiousness, or daring to make the Grace of God an argument for folly! Then, in addition to this, the good Spirit leads us into high and hallowed communion with God—and I defy any man to live upon the mount with God and then come down to transgress like men of the world! If you have walked the palace floor of Glory and seen the King in His beauty, till the light of His Countenance has been your Heaven, you cannot be content with the gloom and murkiness of the tents of wickedness!

To lie, to deceive, to feign, as the men of the world do, will no longer become you. You are of another race and your conversation is above them—"Your speech betrays you." If you do, indeed, dwell with God, the perfume of the ivory palaces will be about you and men will know that you have been in other haunts than theirs. If the child of God goes wrong in any degree, he loses, to some extent, the sweetness of his communion and only as he walks carefully with God does he enjoy full fellowship so that this rising or falling in communion becomes a sort of parental discipline in the house of the Lord. We have no court with a judge, but we have home with its fatherhood, its smile and its rod! We lack not for order in the family of love, for our Father deals with us as with sons. Thus, in a thousand ways, all danger of our presuming upon the Grace of God is effectually removed.

VII. THE ENTIRE ELEVATION OF THE MAN WHO IS MADE A PARTAKER OF THE GRACE OF GOD is also a special preservative against sin. I venture to say, though it may be controverted, that the man who believes the glorious Doctrines of Grace is usually a much higher style of man than the person who has no opinion upon the matter. What do most men think about? Bread and butter, house rent and clothes. But the men who consider the Doctrines of the Gospel muse upon the Everlasting Covenant, predestination, immutable love, effectual calling, God in Christ Jesus, the work of the Spirit, justification, sanctification, adoption and such noble themes! Why, it is a refreshment merely to look over the catalog of these grand Truths of God!

Others are as children playing with little sand heaps on the seashore. But the Believer in Free Grace walks among hills and mountains! The themes of thought around him tower upward, Alps on Alps! The man's mental stature rises with his surroundings and he becomes a thoughtful being, communing with sublimities. This is no small matter, for a thing so apt to grovel as the average human intellect! So far as deliverance from mean vices and degrading lusts must in this way be promoted, I say it is no small thing! Thoughtlessness is the prolific mother of sin! It is a hopeful sign when minds begin to roam among lofty Truths of God.

The man who has been taught of God to think, will not so readily sin as the being whose mind is buried beneath his flesh. The man has now obtained a different view of himself from that which led him to trifle away his time with the idea that there was nothing better for him than to be merry while he could. He says, "I am one of God's chosen, ordained to be His son, His heir, joint-heir with Jesus Christ! I am set apart to be a king and priest unto God and as such I cannot be godless, nor live for the common objectives of life." He rises in the objective of his pursuit—he cannot live unto himself, for he is not his own—he is bought with a price. Now he dwells in the Presence of God and life to him is real, earnest and sublime! He cares not to scrape together gold with the muck-rake of the covetous, for he is immortal and must seek eternal gains.

He feels that he is born for Divine purposes and enquires, "Lord, what would You have me to do?" He feels that God has loved him so that his love may flow forth to others. God's choice of any one man has a bearing upon all the rest—He elects a Joseph that a whole family, a whole nation, no, the whole world, may be preserved alive when famine had broken the staff of bread. We are, each one, as a lamp kindled that we may shine in the dark and light up other lamps. New hopes come crowding on the man who is saved by Grace. His immortal spirit enjoys glimpses of the endless. As God has loved him in time, he believes that the same love will bless him in eternity. He knows that his Redeemer lives and that in the latter days he shall behold Him and, therefore, he has no fear of the future.

Even while here below he begins to sing the songs of the angels, for his spirit spies from afar the dawn of the Glory which is yet to be revealed! Thus with joyous heart and light footsteps he goes forward to the unknown future as merrily as to a wedding feast! Is there a sinner here, a guilty sinner, one who has no merit, no claim to mercy whatever? Is there one willing to be saved by God's Free Grace through believing in Jesus Christ? Then let me tell you, Sinner, there is not a word in God's Book against you, not a line or syllable, but everything is in your favor! "This is a faithful saying, and worthy of all acceptation, that Christ Jesus came into the world to save sinners," even the chief! Jesus came into the world to save you! Only trust Him and rest in Him!

I will tell you what ought to fetch you to Christ at once—it is the thought of His amazing love! A profligate son had been a great grief to his father. He had robbed him and disgraced him and, at last, he ended by bringing his gray hairs with sorrow to the grave. He was a horrible wretch of a son—no one could have been more graceless! However, he attended his father's funeral and he stayed to hear the will read. Perhaps it was the chief reason why he was there. He had fully made up his mind that his father would cut him off with a shilling—and he meant to make it very unpleasant for the rest of the family. To his great astonishment, as the will was read, it ran something like this—"As for my son, Richard, though he has fearfully wasted my substance; and though he has often grieved my heart, I would have him know that I consider him to still be my own dear child and, therefore, in token of my undying love, I leave him the same share as the rest of his brothers."

He left the room. He could not stand it. The surprising love of his father had mastered him! He came down to the executor the next morning and said, "You surely did not read correctly?" "Yes I did. there it stands." "Then," he said, "I feel ready to curse myself that I ever grieved my dear old father. Oh, that I could fetch him back again!" Love was born in that base heart by an unexpected display of love. May not your case be similar? Our Lord Jesus Christ is dead, but He has left in His will that the chief of sinners are objects of His choicest mercy! Dying, He prayed, "Father, forgive them." Risen, He pleads for transgressors. Sinners are always on His mind—their salvation is His great objective. His blood is for them, His heart for them, His righteousness for them, His Heaven for them!

Come, O you guilty ones, and receive your legacy! Put out the hand of faith and grasp your portion! Trust Jesus with your souls and He will save you! God bless you. Amen.

www.ingramcontent.com/pod-product-compliance
Lightning Source LLC
Chambersburg PA
CBHW030323100526
44592CB00010B/545